SUNDAY MISCELLANY

SUNDAY MISCELLANY

a selection from 2004 – 2006

edited by CLÍODHNA NÍ ANLUAIN

Sunday Miscellany
First published 2006
by New Island
2 Brookside
Dundrum Road
Dublin 14
www.newisland.ie

ISBN I 905494 I3 0

The quotations from the poetry of Patrick Kavanagh are reprinted from *Collected Poems*, edited
by Antoinette Quinn (Allen Lane, 2004) by kind permission of the Estate of the late
Katherine B. Kavanagh, through the Jonathan Williams Literary Agency.

Excerpt from 'Antartica' by Derek Mahon from *Collected Poems* (1999) by kind permission of
the author and The Gallery Press.

British Library Cataloguing in Publication Data. A CIP catalogue record for this book is available from the British Library.

Front and back cover: Elizabeth Magill, *Like a Bird* (4) 2006, oil on canvas. Courtesy of the
artist and the Kerlin Gallery, Dublin

Printed in the UK by CPD, Ebbw Vale, Wales

New Island received financial assistance from The Arts Council
(An Chomhairle Ealaíon), Dublin, Ireland

10 9 8 7 6 5 4 3 2 I

CONTENTS

August

September

October

November

December

INTRODUCTION

Now in its fourth decade, RTÉ Radio I's *Sunday Miscellany* is one of Ireland's longest-running radio shows. Today the programme continues to captivate audiences with its trademark mix of original spoken essays, reportage, appreciations, memory pieces, poetry, travel writing, personal accounts of events and happenings that capture constantly changing times and the up-to-the-minute thinking of its present-day listeners. *Sunday Miscellany* is essential listening to thousands across Ireland and the world who love crafted speech radio. The programme's pick of 'music and musings' comes through open submission and new writing I specially commission for broadcast. New voices complement more established writers.

This book's selection includes the well-known and loved as well as new Irish and international names. Novelists, poets, senators, actors, lawyers, artists, religious, teachers, journalists, academics, curators, film and travel writers and many others are among them. Indeed, listeners who tune into the radio and more recently also hear the programme on the web tell me that the variety of accents and styles of delivery and the diversity and treatment of subject matter are the great appeals of the programme. They are what *Sunday Miscellany* is all about.

By its nature, the experience of radio is usually immediate and transitory. Nevertheless, I know many people can recall exactly where they were or what they were doing when they heard something on the radio that lingers with them, as I can myself. Their ability to recount so many pieces they hear on *Sunday Miscellany* with such detail long after a broadcast is sure evidence that the programme connects with listeners. It is therefore at once a great opportunity and the challenge of this book to choose a selection of material from the programme that can carry itself in another form as well as reflect the original context of radio in which it appeared in the first place.

This selection from *Sunday Miscellany* broadcasts between mid-2004 and 2006 gives listeners and now readers a new chance to enjoy some of the pieces of the last two years. Having produced over 100 programmes and more than 700 contributions since 2004, I continue to be impressed by the participative nature of dedicated and new listeners who contact the programme to tell me what appeals to them, what pieces literally make them laugh or cry, or indeed enrage or gratify them. The selection I have made answers many requests to experience particular pieces again. May it also whet the appetite of those who have yet to tune into the programme who enjoy the content of this book!

A week never goes by without *Sunday Miscellany* being broadcast. In order to reflect the programme's year-long presence on the air, I decided the book would take the shape of a year in the life of a weekly chronicle of the time and preoccupations of its contributors and listeners. I took a little licence here, as the selection period in fact runs over two broadcast years. This order and the comments of listeners were a great help in the task of selecting what had to be a limited number of pieces from such a rich treasury of original material. The first and final pieces in the book relate to new beginnings and another new year on the turn. In between the year ebbs and flows from one season to another, from one private or public event or engagement to another, as recounted originally on the programme.

Like all radio programmes, *Sunday Miscellany* forms part of a larger radio station schedule. Alongside many other programmes, it has contributed to a variety of themed celebrations and commemorations marked across RTÉ Radio over the last couple of years. These include the centenary of the births of Patrick Kavanagh and Samuel Beckett, Cork City of Culture 2005, Seachtain na Gaeilge, the 90th anniversary of the 1916 Rising and European Day of Broadcasting. Listeners tell me these programmes have been particularly enjoyable and I include a selection from them here.

Icons from popular culture feature in many of the pieces that attract the attention of listeners. These include Darth Vader switching on the Christmas lights in suburbia, dancing to Blondie in McGonagle's night club, a girlish crush on Starsky (or was it Hutch?), watching *Top of the Pops*, contemplating Leonard Cohen at seventy, singing the songs of Johnny Cash and Jim Reeves, catching a private glimpse of Yoko Ono in Paris or recalling impressionable television advertisements from the 1970s to the present.

Our passion for sport is celebrated too. Ireland's Triple Crown win, the joys and disappointments of the All-Ireland championships, the posh game of tennis in a small Irish town, participation in the women's New York City mini marathon, a Dutch ice skating race and revisiting Italia '90 all have their moments. Then there are pieces about ballet dancing, swimming lessons in the bitter cold Irish Sea, ambitions to swim the English Channel and a childhood ritual of climbing Slemish Mountain every St Patrick's Day.

Ordinary moments are made special in pieces relating to such every-day things as getting caught in rush hour traffic, blueberry picking, playing records, doing the laundry, collecting children from school, watching snow fall, catching an island ferry, strumming a guitar or buying a car. Those new to Ireland taking root here figure and the experiences of the Irish finding their feet in other parts of the world are considered too.

The passing and anniversaries of national and international figures, including John McGahern, John Lennon, Pope John Paul II, Tim Kennelly, Betty Friedan, Frank Harte, Mozart and Rosa Parks, are all remembered alongside the personal joy and devastation of the births and deaths of family members and friends.

Contributions relating to figures of the arts and society, contemporary and historical, reflect the diversity of what the programme shares with listeners. These include pieces on Padraig Pearse, Rudolph Nureyev, William Cowper, Jaki Irvine, Agnes Martin, James Barry, Hugh Lane, William Butler Yeats, Hugh Rua O'Neill, Nick Drake, Lennox Robinson, Raymond Carver, Tennessee Williams, Padraic Fiacc, Francis Bacon and William Dargan.

Every project such as this book and the regular RTÉ *Sunday Miscellany* radio programme depends on the work and co-operation of many. I would like to take this opportunity to acknowledge the support of all my colleagues in RTÉ and especially the indispensable work of *Sunday Miscellany*'s broadcasting assistants, Sinéad Renshaw and Elaine Conlon, and producer Liz Sweeney. Malachy Moran of RTÉ has been invaluable also in overseeing the book's publication. Everyone in New Island has been a delight to work with, especially Deirdre Nolan, with whom I worked closely on the editing of the book's content. I would also like to take this opportunity to acknowledge the patience, support and spirit with which Brian Fay and our children, Nora and Eoghan, ensured this book's arrival.

I would like to thank all those who continue to send in material for consideration to the programme as well as those whose work appears here and on whom this book and the radio programme depends. Finally, I would like to thank the thousands of listeners who continue to tune into the programme. As was written before in the first volume of contributions from *Sunday Miscellany* to appear in book form, may I once more wish you good reading and continued good listening.

Clíodhna Ní Anluain
Producer
Sunday Miscellany
RTÉ Radio I
2006

JANUARY

NEW YEAR OMENS

Julie O'Callaghan

If the wind is from the west
on New Year's Eve,
our island will flourish.
And the first foot to enter
our dwelling
on New Year's Day
should be the boot
of a black haired
man or boy.
Let's not forget the cake theory
and how we all need to throw
barm brack at our front doors
to banish hunger and famine.
A time of bells, fires,
the banging of pots
and omens for the coming year.
Some say that dropping a plate on the first day
guarantees a special year.
That's why I will be
eating the cake – not throwing it –
and dropping the plate
for a cracking good year.

COLD

Peter Sirr

The first time I visit the country it's the cold that strikes me: ice on the canals, icicles in the trees, pulsed drama of our breath on the air. It's minus ten, and for the first time in more than twenty years, they are holding the *Elfstedentocht*, the eleven cities tour. Skaters in bright suits, their bodies bent double, flash by on TV sets.

Rain freezes as it hits the streets; I can feel my hair harden. The cold supplies small moments of chaos that I find exhilarating. The main train system breaks down, and I can't go to work. The country sits suspended in silence.

I inhabit the cold more than the country itself, I think.

I have moved to this small town with reluctance, having failed to find anywhere to live in the city after the lease on my flat ran out. I have found a job in the International section of a large Dutch school.

My flat is the upstairs of a house in a quiet terrace; my landlady lives downstairs. I am her first experiment in property letting, and my tenancy seems somehow to trouble her. In one of the rooms there is a set of bookshelves partly filled with books of hers in Dutch, alongside which I have placed my own books. My landlady surveys the scene, her face clouded in anxiety. Then she leaves the room, disappears downstairs and returns bearing a ruler. She bends to the Dutch books, which occupy the lowest shelf, and measures them with the ruler. There are, it seems, fifty centimetres of books. Six months later, on the eve of my departure, she returns with the ruler, measures her books, and finds several centimetres unaccounted for. *Waar zijn mijne boeken?* I realise that my entire residency here has been a barely tolerated act of trespass.

Sometimes she forgets that she has rented her upper floor to me and bolts the front door from inside before leaving by the back door, so that when I return from my teaching I can't get in and have to wile away the hours in the local library until she comes back.

Today, standing in the chilly hall, she suggests a supplement to the rent to allow for the extra heat I will consume in the weeks ahead. The rent is already excessive. I will have to go.

I put my clothes out on the line on the balcony, but when I go to bring them in, the doors have warped, they're stuck solid. I watch my jeans solidify through the window and think of my washing continuing its ghostly, unprofitable tenancy long after I have left. For some reason, this fills me with joy.

This year again they are holding the *Elfstedentocht*. The Icemaster has surveyed the ice and is satisfied. Nothing since 1963, and then two years in a row, the eleven cities of Friesland – Leewarden to Sneek, Ijlst, Sloten, Stavoren, Hindeloopen, Workum, Bolsward, Harlingen, Franeker, Dokkum and back to Leeuwarden again. Things have to be right. The race is a kind of miracle much longed for, and when it happens there is a frenzy of excitement. There are strict regulations. The ice has to be at least fifteen centimetres thick across the whole 200 kilometres. This is only the tenth tour in the twentieth century.

Every winter begins with the question: *Sil it heve?* Will it happen?

The 1963 tour was legendary. January, minus twelve degrees. Of the 9,000 or so amateur skaters, only 69 make it to the finish line. The hospitals along the route are full of wounded skaters. Reiier Paping skates the final 100 kilometres all by himself; it takes well over twenty minutes for the runner-up to finish. It has taken him ten hours and fifty-nine minutes. He has been warmed up with infrared lamps, with the queen mother Juliana repeatedly congratulating him in the tent. *Meneer Paping, I have such admiration for you!*

The fêted folk hero returns to the summerhouse deep in the woods where he lives with his wife because of the housing crisis. The door will barely open. When it does it reveals the pail of water on the floor, the spuds in the pan on the gas stove, the clothes on the back of the chair, all frozen solid.

IT HAPPENED ONE MORNING

Brynn Craffey

They said I was unconscious for an hour — a slender, short-haired, forty-two-year-old woman wearing men's slacks and shoes, an Oxford shirt and a tie, out cold on asphalt still damp from a heavy morning fog off the San Francisco Bay. While the wheels on my mountain bike, its yellow frame brilliant against the dull-grey pavement, slowly spun to a halt, my co-workers formed a growing circle around where I lay sprawled in the street.

I came to, swimming up from a deep dream and believing I was at home in bed. But the murmur of voices all around me didn't fit, one in particular: 'Yeah! I looked up and saw him flying through the air! And he landed. And I expected him to get up, but he didn't ...' As this voice receded, I noticed cold, lumpy hardness beneath me ... Asphalt?! My heart leapt. An image of bicycle handlebars popped into my head, above a fat, knobby bicycle tyre sunk in a roadway rail-groove.

I'd been on my final approach to work, just outside the plant in Berkeley, California, when I'd tried to cross old railroad tracks to skirt a double-parked truck. Slipping on the damp steel, my bicycle tires had dropped into the rail groove. And that was the last thing I remembered.

But the guy flying through the air — couldn't be me! I'd had my first shot of testosterone only a week before and everyone still knew me as a woman — an odd, cross-dressing, strange sort of woman, to be sure, but a woman nonetheless. That I was actually a female-to-male transsexual just beginning transition was still a secret.

Strangers, however, like the driver of the double-parked truck, might look at my clothes and hair and think male ... Oh no! I *must* be lying in the road. My mind raced. Who had heard the driver call me 'he'? With any luck, it'd just be the guards at the gate and they'd think he was confused. I opened my eyes, looked up and saw a circle of people, five or six deep all around me.

I clenched my eyes shut again. Heart racing, fighting pain and nausea, I struggled against the tangle of my bike bag and jacket and managed to get up onto my hands and knees. I actually crawled a few feet toward the road's edge, trying to escape the circle of prying eyes, before I collapsed. No one tried to stop me, not even the plant's 'specially trained first-responders'. It occurred to me then, face down on the roadside, that I might have injured my spine and shouldn't have moved at all. Still, so strong was my embarrassment that co-workers who knew me as a woman had heard the driver call me 'he', I would have kept crawling if I'd been physically able. Instead, I rolled over painfully and stared up at the sky, wishing more than *anything* I could turn back the clock and *walk*, not ride my bicycle over those railroad tracks.

The ambulance arrived minutes later and two paramedics jumped out and knelt beside me. One immediately immobilised my head and neck with his hands while his partner checked my pulse and looked me over for injuries.

'What's your name?' he asked, shining a penlight into my eyes.

'Brynn,' I said.

'What's the date?'

'2nd March, 1994?'

'Who's president?' *They actually ask that?* I wondered as I answered, 'Bill Clinton.'

The two men worked, unfastening my bike bag, removing my jacket, packing sandbags around my head and neck and immobilising my right arm. That's when I heard someone say I'd been unconscious for more than ten minutes. I was pondering the implications of that when the EMT asked his next question. 'Are you on any medication?'

Medication? Testosterone was a medication. I looked up into my co-workers' faces. Would testosterone's side-effects be a concern? I thought ... I'd suffered a concussion – must have to lose consciousness for ten minutes – which can cause the brain to swell. And testosterone, when first injected by a female, leads to water retention. So, could testosterone worsen a concussion?

'*Are you on any medications we need to know about?*' The EMT was growing impatient and the surrounding sea of faces seemed to hang on my reply. If I answered, word would race through the plant and by lunchtime, all the couple thousand employees would know I was a transsexual.

Hardly the way I'd planned to come out.

'I ... I'm ...' Suddenly my stupor cleared enough for me to see a solution. 'Can I just tell you later?' I asked.

The EMT hesitated. Then, 'Sure,' he said. The two men finished strapping me to a body board and loaded me into the ambulance.

If I'd thought about it, I'd always imagined riding in an ambulance would be exciting. The wailing siren, the flashing lights, the drama of being the centre of all that attention. *Well.* My condition didn't warrant a siren, it seemed. A blessing I failed to appreciate at the time, as my head throbbed and my arm and shoulder screamed in pain. Every corner we turned, every bump in the road, every time we accelerated or braked, I struggled not to lose my breakfast. 'I feel sick,' I finally moaned.

'Hey, Joe, ease up,' the EMT spoke through the partition to the driver. Then he turned back to me. 'So, what about those medications?'

In retrospect, I wonder what he expected me to say. Some less-than-legal substance, perhaps? While I was worrying about how to tell this young, straight-looking guy that I was on testosterone. *Was*, in effect, *one of those.* He was probably waiting for me to say 'marijuana'.

No way to soften the blow came to mind in my weakened state, so I finally just blurted it out. 'I'm transsexual and I had my first shot of testosterone a week ago. I don't know if it affects a concussion or not. But ... I thought you should know.'

There was the slightest pause, then, 'That's cool,' he said and wrote something on his clipboard.

The silence lengthened. I felt so *exposed.* Vulnerable. Finally, I could stand it no longer and said, 'So, uh, have you ever seen or dealt with anyone like me before?'

'N-o-ope.' The guy looked over his clipboard at me. 'But that's okay.' His face creased in a smile. 'We're trained to deal with all sorts of things. Don't sweat it.'

I loved him in that moment. I was *so thankful* he wasn't put off! Looking back, it's clear now that as far as I thought I'd come in accepting who I was and being proud, I still had a long way to go. In that moment, I was ready to hug that guy simply because he was willing to treat me like a fellow human being.

Only nausea, and the fact I was strapped down, kept me flat on that stretcher until the ambulance arrived at the emergency room.

JOE

Catherine Foley

We met at every important family occasion in our aunts' sitting room in Helvick. We'd always have Barley's lime cordial as a treat. The men would have Guinness and a glass of whiskey each. My mother would have a port and my aunts drank tea. We'd usually be on our best behaviour, enjoying the visit, listening to the adults recalling old times and waiting for the singsong to start.

We loved being in that room with its two windows which overlooked Helvick Harbour. Those family occasions were always full of stories about long ago and music. We each had our own special song to perform.

My Uncle Joe was often called on first because he loved to sing and because his voice was rich and melodious. He relished singing his favourite songs, especially those by Johnny Cash, Jim Reeves and Roger Whittager. We all loved Whittager's 'The Last Farewell' because it told a story. I especially loved the chorus and its lilting, easy melody which referred to love and the difficulties of expressing it in words. We would all join in, my father and mother, my two aunts – Síle and Gile – and my two sisters, Miriam and Rose Ann.

The opening lines of the song set the scene, and the fact that Joe was a merchant seaman and a fisherman, who had gone to sea as a young man and worked on ocean liners, oil rigs and trawlers all his life, gave the song an added pathos. He had never married. I always felt that the song of lost love was heart-felt when he sang.

After a swallow of Guinness to slack his throat, he'd put down his glass carefully on the coffee table beside him and compose himself. His face would take on a dreamy, serious expression and then he'd lift his head and begin singing in a deep, melodious voice about a ship about to set out on another journey.

The ring of stout around his mouth was a sign that Joe was truly in the moment, and it seemed to add to the piquancy of the words. There was a sadness about Joe that none of us young people ever came close to understanding.

There was a vulnerability and an incongruity about him that made me feel slightly embarrassed sometimes. But his song and his voice would fill the room and we'd all settle to listen, enjoying the music and the moments that remain clear in my memory now, as he conjured up other worlds and times. Out the window in Helvick, we could see the lonely grey sea stretching off down the coastline, towards Hook Head in the distant horizon to the east. The sound of the squawking seagulls as they followed in the wake of an occasional trawler provided a fitting backdrop to Joe's singing.

He usually sang songs about loneliness, drinking and disappointment. The words of Jim Reeves merge now into one collage of melodies. He'd sing these, his shoulders rising in a semi-shrug as if to say he understood very well the loneliness of the song. His voice would catch sometimes as if he'd lived those lines himself and he'd shake his head as if to say, I know this man and he's not alone as he'd sing the song 'Little Old Wine Drinking Me'.

He took his time when he sang, always letting the notes unfold slowly. His voice would rise carefully, effortlessly. Unhurried, he'd pause like any singer if a long breath was required. He'd often close his eyes, but sometimes he'd look into the near distance and sing, putting his heart into the words.

He had thick black eyebrows, wide, clear brown eyes, a rich head of black hair and a strong jaw line. He was handsome in a rough, masculine way. He smoked Major cigarettes and the tops of his fingers were brown from years of holding the stubs in the cup of his hands. He walked with a limp and he had to have one shoe built up by the cobbler to compensate for the leg that had once shrivelled after he'd played too much hurling as a young man. He'd sit in the armchair in his own characteristic way with his shorter leg folded under him, one knee almost touching the floor in a kneeling position.

Years later, when he lay in hospital smiling beautifully and looking so childlike, his eyes like a baby's staring out from a pram, the nurses were always kind to him, always asking to see photographs of him as a young man. They could see the beautiful face and the innocence in his eyes. There had been sadness and pain but I never knew the mysterious cause of it. He died in his late sixties in hospital. We buried him on an icy cold day in January. There were hailstones and the freezing air that day in the graveyard seemed right. All was cleansed and all was wiped away – pure and silver, like he was.

Like the song said, he had gone away to a land full of endless sunshine from a land full of rainy skies and gales; the ship had pulled out. I remembered him singing and the words came back to me as if was there beside me.

NEW BEGINNINGS

Denis Tuohy

There has never been a nobler call for new beginnings than Alfred Lord Tennyson's famous litany:

> *Ring out the old, ring in the new,*
> *Ring, happy bells, across the snow:*
> *The year is going, let him go*
> *Ring out the false, ring in the true.*

But as we read on through the optimistic catalogue, we are forced to realise how sadly relevant to our own time is Tennyson's nineteenth-century dream of new starts in new directions, a dream that is still a long, long way from being fulfilled. Ring out, for instance, the feud of rich and poor, the narrowing lust of gold, the thousand wars of old. Ring in redress for all mankind, the common love of good, the thousand years of peace.

Now, even if it's healthy to keep such fine aspirations in our sights, however hard it may be to achieve them, perhaps the poem adds an unnecessary extra burden by linking them with the turn of the year. Not only must we ring out a depressing record of human failings and ring in a demanding programme of virtues, we are being advised to do so now, without delay, as the wild bells ring out to the wild sky. I'm not sure it's realistic to attempt to change ourselves for the better, even in less radical ways than Tennyson calls for, according to a date in the calendar. Can we really, to use a current cliché, 'draw a line in the sand' at the start of January, dividing old sinfulness from new sanctity?

And in any case, how helpful is it to divide our behaviour into two simple categories — right and wrong, good and bad? Much of what we do, and much of what happens to us, is a mixture of both. Of course there are times when we should indeed wring, not bells, but our hands over things we wish we hadn't done or wish we weren't still doing. But it might also be a good idea to learn to have more respect for our muddled selves, more compassion and yes, more love. Loving others is easier if we are able to love ourselves.

In popular song there is no more defiant expression of self-respect — I think it's fair to call it self-love — than Frank Sinatra's 'My Way'. And it's clearly a message with wide appeal. Let any pub singer launch into it and every tone-deaf punter in the place feels compelled to join in and, God help us, do it their way.

This is someone who is facing 'the final curtain' with few regrets, as we hear at the start of the song, but who surely wouldn't be interested in a new beginning even if there was time left to have one. What's done is done, I am who I am and that's that.

Edith Piaf's great ballad about regret is even more radical: *Je ne regrette rien* ... I regret nothing, nothing at all ... *rien de rien*. Good and bad are the same to me. The past has been paid for, swept away, forgotten, to hell with the past. I've set fire to my memories of sorrow and delight, I have no more need of them. And the song is different from 'My Way' in another sense, too. Although we're not told until the very last line, Piaf doesn't believe *she's* facing the final curtain. Despite all that's happened to her, despite the incinerated memories, a lover's hope wins out over experience. Today a new life begins, with you. *Aujourd'hui ca commence avec toi.*

I think what really matters there is the *aujourd'hui*. Time will tell whether or not things work out with whoever *toi* may be. But today is for living, just as it is. All that we have for sure is *ourselves*, as 'My Way' reminds us, and *now*, not even today, but this moment. So the new beginning that makes most sense, I believe, does not involve making seismic changes in how we live, it's not about looking forward to long-term targets or backward at long-term guilt. It's about taking each new day that comes to us on its own terms, accepting what we have to and achieving what we can.

MEZMERIZE

Joe Kane

i

The shock absorbers were shot.
We were heading for the Fiat dealership
one hundred miles away.
It was a sellers' market as they say,

ten new Puntos in the yard
delivered the previous day.
Take your pick the salesman said,
and off he went.

ii

What do you think?
My daughter said
I like the green one
And the pink one
I like pink she said
So pink it was
We'll have the pink one we said
We don't have pink
It's in the yard we said

We have green and blue
Black and yellow
And I think one red
Walked back to the yard
With the stock list
Yes he said
Green blue
And one yellow
And one red
That's pink we said
Look at the book
Red it says
So we bought red

iii

We have two hands, a left and a right:
where do we hear touch?
We have two eyes, a left and a right:
where do we feel sight?
We have two ears, a left and a right:
where do we touch sound?

iv

In Donegal we look at the sky and say red
in January, when everything from the bay up
is pink. Add a dash of aquamarine shooting
through black. The purple wash of mountains

surrounds us, but it's always pink that comes
from the ground, that takes the sky.
The sun is in the ground in January
and wants to have its say.

I write the winter sky in Donegal and bottle it.
So next time I'm west of Inis Bó Finne
I'll toss it out there with the minkes and hope
The great whale-road takes it, my daughter, to you.

GREYFRIARS BOBBY

Vivien Igoe

Recently I visited Greyfriars Kirkyard in the old town of Edinburgh. Entering from Candlemaker Row, the first memorial I saw was one of granite stone. It stood on its own at the centre of an angular piece of ground between the gateway and the old church. There was a card lying beside it and in a child's hand was written:

> To Bobby from Katie Weatherstone, London.

> Dear Bobby, I read your story and got very sad. I hope you are now happy with your owner in heaven. I miss and love you very much. Love Katie aged 8.

It was the grave of the little Skye terrier known as 'Greyfriars Bobby'.

When John Gray came to Edinburgh in 1853, he got a job as a police constable. His beat included Greyfriars Kirkyard, as body snatching was prevalent at the time. Gray acquired Bobby, then little more than a pup, in 1856 as a watchdog. With his short legs and shaggy coat, he was always at his master's heels. He accompanied him at lunchtime to John Traill's restaurant in Greyfriars Place.

Gray died of tuberculosis in February 1858 and was buried in Greyfriars Kirkyard. Bobby was among the mourners at his funeral. Some days after it, a bedraggled Bobby appeared at lunchtime at the restaurant. Traill recognised the once happy and well cared for dog and gave him a bone. Bobby took it and vanished. The following day, the same event occurred. When Bobby arrived the third day, Traill's curiosity was aroused to the extent that he followed the dog. He discovered that Bobby was making straight for Greyfriars Kirkyard, where he settled to eat his bone by the grave of his master. Apart from his local wanderings, Bobby continued to spend both day and night by his master's grave. In bad weather, he sheltered under the old table-stone grave which adjoined his master's grave.

Among Bobby's friends was Sergeant Scott of the Royal Engineers, who was based at Edinburgh Castle. He taught Bobby to leave for lunch at the same time each day, at one o'clock when the gun was fired from the Half Moon Battery at the Castle.

Bobby became a familiar sight sitting on the grave. *The Scotsman* reported in 1867 that 'the animal has become an object of much interest and many people have gone to see it in its home among the tombs. Mr. Gourlay Steell, the artist, was far advanced with a picture of the faithful sentinel on the grave of his late master ... but while sitting for his portrait in Mr. Steell's studio, Bobby, on hearing the report of the time-gun, his usual call to dinner, got quite excited, and refused to be pacified until supplied with his mid day meal.'

Another report appeared in 1934 in *The Scotsman* from an elderly citizen who wrote that in 1868 or 1869 he remembered seeing Bobby leaving the Kirkyard for his dinner. Crowds of people would gather outside the gates, and 'as the hour drew near there was a hush of expectation. Then bang went the gun in the Castle, and every head turned to the gate. Soon there was a hushed whisper, "Here he comes!" and the grey, shaggy little figure appeared, pattering over the causeway between the two lines of people. Looking to neither one side nor the other, intent only on his own affairs, Bobby hurried round the corner to his right, up the street a few yards and disappeared into Mr. Traill's restaurant for the meal he never failed to get for many years. His dinner finished, with no interval for idle frolics, the devoted dog returned once more to the grave of his master.'

When a new law was passed requiring all dogs to be licensed and collared, the Lord Provost, Sir William Chambers, paid for Bobby's licence. Chambers had a special collar made for him which had a brass band on it engraved: *Greyfriars Bobby from the Lord Provost, 1867, licensed.* This, along with Bobby's dinner dish and other items, can be seen in the Museum of Edinburgh at Canongate on the Royal Mile.

Bobby's vigil by his master's grave lasted fourteen years. He died on 14 January 1872, aged sixteen years. A bronze statue by William Brodie at the corner of Candlemaker Row commemorates him.

The loyalty of the dog to his deceased master may have touched the hearts of mid-nineteenth-century Edinburgh, but it also touched the heart of the little girl who left her own heartfelt message to Bobby in September 2005.

Included on his gravestone are the following lines: *Let his loyalty and devotion be a lesson to us all.*

JAKI IRVINE

Catherine Marshall

A sequence of projections lead us on a journey, both a physical journey through the rooms of the Irish Museum of Modern Art, and a rich, imaginative one through a series of mirrored reflections, embracing the real and the fantastic, the natural and the cultural. It takes us from a random massing of Italian starlings, perhaps gathering for the long flight home, through a landscape, sometimes idyllic, sometimes surreal, to the interior of the bat house at Dublin Zoo and from there to an awkward, tortuous crawl along a disused bridge over the River Liffey to a wonderful acrobatic moment of communion.

We are wandering through *The Silver Bridge*, an installation by Irish artist and filmmaker Jaki Irvine, who was recently elected to Aosdána. The film journey, and our physical progress through it, offers endless narrative possibilities. What is at once challenging and inviting is the artist's deliberate refusal to foreclose on our readings of those narratives. While there is a definite sequence and chronology, the images offer themselves for us to create a narrative structure that is meaningful for us as individuals.

What are we to make of it all, I wonder. The uninhibited freewheeling of the starlings is followed by the back-to-back projections of a bent tree in a wide, expansive field with a lone male figure and a woodland place occupied by companionably grazing deer or, rather more mysteriously, with a cluster of white panelled wooden doors that spring up like sentinels under the trees. The more claustrophobic environment of the bat house of Dublin Zoo provides the scenario for the next paired images. A girl gazes in at these fascinating creatures. A man, the same one I saw earlier, I wonder, passes by. The bats jostle and fight in the clumsy fashion that is their wont and for a moment hang upside down in a surprisingly graceful movement. The girl wanders, next, through the Natural History Museum, evoking a sense of time past that is eerily accentuated by the most languid droop of the eye that I have ever seen. She alone is alive in this tomb of long-preserved animal specimens. What is her relationship to the timeframe suggested here? The final pair of films takes us back outdoors. On a tiny screen a black-clad figure (the girl?) heaves herself laboriously up onto a bridge. I turn from this and am suddenly confronted by a huge projection revealing two similarly black-clad women who clutch each other in an upside down embrace, remarkably like that of the bats, before one of them drops abruptly out of the picture and presumably into the still, green water of the river below.

The only sounds we hear in this mysterious sequence are the ambient sounds of the birds and the distant traffic. No human utterances disturb the dreamlike movement. Questions and ideas crowd into the vacant space they leave. What are the relationships between the people in the different episodes of this work? Is this about man and woman, or woman and woman, or between man and animals? Do the animal relationships fare any better than the human ones?

Whatever the answers we posit to these questions, a fascinating aspect of this artwork is the way in which it draws together differing approaches to creativity and to Modernism. The blank blue screen/sky that is occasionally glimpsed through the starling episode can be read as a homage to the abstract colour-field painting of the 1970s and 80s, a somewhat surprising but nonetheless real source for a filmmaker who, after all, spent formative years at art college. Other passages of film invite thoughts of Samuel Beckett's *Waiting for Godot*, the gothic ennui of Joseph Sheridan Lefanu's Carmella and a robustly modern and surreal visualisation of the episode in Toraíocht Diarmuid agus Gráinne in which a frustrated Fionn Mac Cumhail caused doors to spring out of the landscape in a vain attempt to ensnare the fleeing lovers. Conversations with Jaki Irvine reiterate her desire that the viewer will construct his or her own meaningful narratives from this work, but she does admit that for her it was all about homecoming. She paraphrases Julie Kristeva; before any leave-taking, we must become strangers to ourselves. This remains true even if the final destination is home.

IN SPACE, NO ONE CAN HEAR YOU SMOKE

James Cotter

I was doing what all the hip, beautiful people do these days. I was huddling outside a pub, trying to shelter from the arctic winds and have a smoke at the same time.

It was as glamorous as it sounds.

The doors swung open and I was joined by an old man. At least, I think he was a man. He looked like a cross between a pixie and a walnut – tiny, gnarled and gleeful. He coughed, spat blackly, flashed a toothless grin and lit up a cigarette.

'At this rate, buddy,' he said, 'the only place they'll let us smoke will be in space.'

He was wrong. Of course the government wouldn't let us smoke in space. If we were that far away, they wouldn't be able to tax us. Me, I reckon we'll be banished to underground caves, damned to live a light-less life, bitterly puffing on our heavily taxed death-sticks and working non-stop. While above us, in the clean air, the beautiful, clear-skinned, pink-lunged non-smokers skip merrily through life, living off the labour and taxes of us cigarette-chugging under-grounders.

Of course, there'd be a revolution. And us under-grounders would rush towards the surface to overthrow the oppressors, but by the time we'd climb all those stairs we'd have run out of breath and need to stop for a rest, and maybe a quick fag.

Anyway, chain-smoking walnut-man did have a point. We should really explore space.

We need to get off this planet.

Something's going to go badly wrong with it, soon.

We know that at some point in the distant future, the sun will turn red and expand to a massive size, probably engulfing the earth. Or it'll just explode.

Not that we should worry about it, because before that happens we're bound to be hit by an asteroid.

Or a comet.

Or maybe a meteor.

But by then global warming will mean the oceans are up around Everest and we'll be too busy standing on each other's heads to worry about asteroids.

Of course, that's all assuming we don't just accidentally-on-purpose nuke each other to nothingness.

So wouldn't it be nice, while we're waiting for these catastrophes to fall on our heads, to explore outer space, so we can find somewhere else to live.

'Cause when the world ends, it'd be good if there were a few of us elsewhere to, you know, keep the human race going.

But there's not a lot of exploring going on. It's been thirty years since we last set foot on the moon. The Space Shuttle was old technology when it was built, and that was twenty years ago. Now it's grounded for safety more often than it flies.

So we send robots to other planets instead of people, and like Beagle 2, they often don't work because they're being built on shoe-string budgets. And then people say space travel's a waste of money. That's like giving someone 50 cent to build a car and then complaining that it isn't fuel efficient. Space travel is big and it is expensive. And I'll tell you why, because it's rocket science.

Governments say we can't waste money on something as frivolous as space travel, because there are taxes to be cut and health care to be given and wars to pay for and, and, and, and, we just need the money for more important stuff!

But wasn't it always like that? When we first flung men into space weren't there other, more pressing things to spend the money on? When Armstrong landed on the moon, wasn't America busy fighting a war? That wasn't important, was it?

Exploration is vital – it's what we do, what we've always done; we explore. We go further than our parents, it's in our blood.

Well, if nobody else will do it, I've got a bold suggestion – Ireland should. We could build our launch pad under O'Connell Street. The Spire could tilt over to reveal a gleaming spaceship, just like in the Thunderbirds. It's bound to boost tourism. Anyway, what else are we going to put in O'Connell Street?

I know it's going to be expensive, maybe even as expensive as the Luas. But if we scratched and scraped and skimped on a few bits and pieces, I'm sure we could afford it. All we need do is raise taxes ... or we could just make smoking mandatory.

AMAZING GRACE

Brian Lynch

Every time I hear the hymn 'Amazing Grace', my pulse quickens. Actually, I hear it so often it's a wonder my heart can put up with the excitement. And why does it cause such a reaction? Well, apart from the catchiness of the tune, there are two reasons: I know the history of the priest who wrote the words, John Newton, and the poet who inspired them, William Cowper.

John Newton lived, by any standard, an extraordinary life. Born in 1725, the son of a London shipwright, he was kidnapped at an early age and press-ganged into becoming a sailor. After some years at sea he was again captured and became a slave on an island off the west coast of Africa. The only book he had there was a ragged copy of Euclid's *Geometry*. And the only free time he had was at night. So on the beach he would trace out the theorems in the sand by the light of the tropical moon.

At last Newton escaped and sailed back to England. But his ship was caught in a storm so violent that some of the crew were washed overboard and drowned. Newton, who was at this time a blaspheming atheist, prayed to God for deliverance. The ship was saved and Newton was converted. But he continued to sail the oceans and – oddly for a born-again Christian – to make his living out of trading in slaves. Like most people then, he had nothing against slavery in principle, though, as he said, he did sometimes wonder whether the chains, the whips and the tongue-wedges used to keep the slaves quiet were quite compatible with Christian kindness.

Eventually he left the sea, became a sort of ranting street-preacher in Liverpool and at last, with great difficulty, was ordained a priest of the Church of England, which was then experiencing the revolution of Methodism. The difficulty was caused by the fact that Newton fought with everyone, including John Wesley.

It was at this stage that he met William Cowper, the poet who is the hero of my novel *The Winner of Sorrow*. Cowper was as odd as Newton, but in exactly opposite ways. He was born in 1731 into an aristocratic family – one of his ancestors was the great poet John Donne, and one of his grandfathers had been Lord Lieutenant of Ireland. Cowper was offered a soft job in Parliament, Clerk of the Journals, but he was pathologically shy and the thought of appearing for interview before the House of Lords drove him to attempt suicide – and very nearly to succeed.

After a long period in a mental hospital, the quaintly named College for the Insane, he experienced a religious conversion and moved to the town of Olney in Buckinghamshire, where Newton was the parish priest.

Church-going was a serious business in those days: it was quite common for Newton's sermons to last as long as six hours. He also tried the patience of his parishioners in other ways: when he denounced them for celebrating Christmas as if it was a pagan festival, with lighted candles and, worst of all, with kissing under the mistletoe, they rose up in drunken rebellion, attacked the vicarage with stones and empty bottles and would have burned it to the ground were it not that Newton's wife sent him out in his nightshirt to buy them off with money for more drink. But that was enough for Newton: he packed his bags, departed to London and threw himself into the less troublesome battle for the abolition of slavery.

The relationship between Newton and Cowper was a curious one: the cockney ex-slave trader who could still swear like a sailor, and the trembling aristocrat, afraid of meeting someone who might use the Holy Name in vain.

Newton's method of dealing with his friend's shyness was what we would now call aversion therapy: he bullied him into being a preacher, with disastrous consequences – Cowper soon went mad again. But Newton also cajoled Cowper into helping him to write the once-famous Olney Hymns, one of which is 'Amazing Grace'. It helped, of course, that Cowper was already a great poet in the making. He was to go on to produce some of the best poems in the English language, poems so familiar we have now forgotten who wrote them.

In a marvellous lecture in 2005 in St Patrick's College, Drumcondra, Seamus Heaney showed how much Patrick Kavanagh had been influenced by the poems he had learned off by heart in Iniskeen National School. For example, when Kavanagh describes himself as 'king of banks and stones and every blooming thing', he is echoing these lines by Cowper:

I am monarch of all I survey,
My right there is none to dispute
From the centre all round to the sea,
I am lord of the fowl and the brute.
Oh solitude! Where are the charms
That sages have seen in thy face?
Better dwell in the midst of alarms,
Than reign in this horrible place.

There are other poems which are, or used to be, familiar to generations of schoolchildren. For instance, this beautiful lament for lost times, 'The Poplar Field':

The poplars are felled; farewell to the shade,
And the whispering sound of the cool colonnade ...
Twelve years have elapsed since I first took a view
Of my favourite field, and the bank where they grew;
And now in the grass behold they are laid,
And the tree is my seat that once lent me shade ...
My fugitive years are all hasting away,
And I must ere long lie as lowly as they,
With a turf on my breast, and a stone at my head,
Ere another such grove shall rise in its stead.

And of course there are lines, torn out of context, which have become proverbial or clichéd: 'variety is the spice of life', 'the cup that cheers but not inebriates', and this still startling image:

God moves in a mysterious way
His wonders to perform.
He plants his footsteps in the sea
And rides upon the storm.

'Amazing Grace', too, was written by Cowper — but only the title. As far as we know, Newton wrote the rest of it. And now both of them, the fanatical sea-captain and the suicidal poet, are pretty much neglected, their names remembered, if at all, only by Methodist historians, professors of eighteenth-century literature and novelists with an eye for a good story.

But 'Amazing Grace' lives on. As recently as 1971 it was a Top Twenty hit for Judy Collins. One rather bizarre website, the Hollywood Jesus News, claims that it is the most recorded song of all time. There are certainly more than 2,000 recordings, by artists as diverse as Elvis Presley, George Gershwin, Jimi Hendrix, the Von Trapp Family, and last but not least, our own Frank Patterson. But all the musicians who have done it justice have one thing in common — they've got soul. And if I'm forced to choose the one with the most soul, it's perhaps not surprising that the choice comes down to someone with roots in Gospel music, a black woman, descended from slaves. I mean Mahalia Jackson and, thanks to the amazing grace of radio, we can hear her again.

FEBRUARY

OUR AMERICAN POEMS

Vona Groarke

Awash with sound, we are: Scooby-Doo on the telly,
the microwave's alarmist drone, an ambulance plying
high notes on the pike and the radio's jab at news
of a hotel for frozen stiffs. Still, there's us, reading
to each other from propped-up books while you make
breadcrumbs from artisan loaf and I spread Kraft
on waffles for the kids. Firstly, a dozen lines that fold
a shirt into the creases of a poem. Then, the carriage
from Sweden you want to hitch yourself to.
We sit to coffee, eye up those consumed plums,
Discuss the plausibility of that cup of sour cream.
I read one to you with 'praxis' in it. We look it up.
It means 'custom or habitual practice'. When
I come out of the office with my writing book,
you're there on the couch, about to open yours.

ROSES ARE RED …

Mary Coll

Love is a many splendid thing. It is in the air, it conquers all, it is all you need, it lifts you up where you belong, it is fat free, low carb and, since it registers less than zero on the GI index, it is without doubt the very best thing since the sliced pan. Romance, however, is an entirely different matter, impossible to define and utterly subjective in terms of the manner in which it is experienced by each individual. On celluloid, minus cellulite and using body doubles, romance looks easy, no worse than diving off a skyscraper or confidently steering a runaway bus or taking charge of a captain with seven children. Thus inspired by great cinematic moments, and with our expectations raised to ridiculous levels, we wait impatiently for a man in dress uniform to carry us out of the office to the cheers of our colleagues, or walk home to us from war, barefoot, through snow-covered mountains, or come back to the cave where he's left us with a broken leg, a pencil, a candle and a notebook. Hard to follow that with a bunch of wilting chrysants from the forecourt of the local petrol station, which is why, after only climbing a four-foot garden wall with a small box of Milk Tray under your arm, you're more likely to be greeted with cries of 'Look what you're after doing to your new pants!' than the open arms you might have anticipated. It is also why the professionals advise against amateurs trying to repeat intricate stunts at home.

Here it's sometimes best to clearly spell out romance in order to spare the feelings of everyone involved: 'Roses are red, violets are blue,

I'm expecting the former, plus chocolates from you'. Perhaps not the most romantic verse ever written; however, it's relatively simple for the reader to commit to memory and does not require a PhD in English for the theme and tone to become abundantly clear. Etched carefully across a bathroom mirror in lipstick, on 13 February, for example, the response within twenty-four hours can be overwhelming, if a little predictable, and while some poetry can change lives, despite its brevity, these lines are guaranteed to save them. For a short time at least, they will also ensure that the course of true love continues to run smoothly, that sleeves will remain attached to suits and that the spare room will still be available to visiting friends and relations.

Of course, there are people who are natural-born romantics with a knack for always getting it right, a handful of souls who could convene annually in a two-berth caravan without breaking any by-laws, and who while there would manage to successfully convert that same two-berth caravan into a love shack worthy of a sheikh's harem. For the rest of us, romance is something of an effort — like baking with yeast or exfoliating regularly, we have an idea of what's involved and the best of intentions, but sometimes it's hard work and trying to get it right can often lead to getting it very wrong indeed. Left to spontaneity and our own imagination, one man's romantic bag of chips in a parked car on the seafront is another woman's last date. I have a friend who wept tears of joy over a single Rolo, mailed to her out of the blue one day in a crumpled cigarette box, by a man who could have sent her a crate of diamonds and who didn't even smoke, and another who wept with equal conviction but entirely opposite emotions over a set of absolutely divine lingerie from a poor fellow whose only crime was getting the XL size right.

For my own part, I have bought first editions of obscure women poets for guys who would barely bother to read a signpost, and theatre tickets for men who fall asleep as soon as the lights go down, waking occasionally only to ask if it's 'half time' yet. In return I have received a foot spa, a set of matching egg cups, vouchers for every known treatment and therapy, or the truly heart-warming gift of men's black leather gloves, which were not a subtle reference to any arias from *La Bohème* about tiny hands being frozen, but a practical assessment of both my apparent needs and my skeletal framework. On each occasion I was supposed to have been moved; instead, I moved out.

This is where Valentine's Day truly comes into its own. As subtle as a flying pink fluffy brick and as genuine as Jackie Stallone's smile, it offers one and all the prospect of romantic peace and salvation from the one-stop love shop, irrespective of gender or sexual orientation. Of course you can ignore it and opt out, at your peril, and you can rage all you want about consumerism and emotional manipulation and doing your own thing some other day, which is a little like having Christmas on the August bank holiday weekend ... why bother, who cares and where do you think you'll find a goose? Valentine's Day is there to make the effort of romance effortless. It's idiot proof and gift wrapped and should be gratefully embraced like a lifebelt on the *Titanic*. You don't even have to sign your name to the card, flowers, chocolates or champagne. However, on a note of caution, if all these are accompanied by a flight to Paris, or similar gestures on a truly grand scale, received wisdom suggests a quick skim through the beloved's phone records, text messages and credit card receipts might be advised, but of course not until after the trip, keeping in mind that while romance is all very fine, when push comes to shove diamonds really are a girl's best friend.

YOU DON'T GIVE A CURSOR

Nicola Lindsay

You have gone down in my estimation
Because you just don't give a cursor.
I will be bold and highlight how I feel.
I'm feeling double-spaced
After failing to keep tabs on you
For I'm not quite sure of your alignment.
Just what is on your menu?
I saw you zoom in there and merge
In a deadly embrace. I'm not blind, you know!
It made me flush right
To the very font of my being.
I saw you scanning the options,
Selecting new texts, editing without justification.
I have displayed all the tools in my bar.
Did I not have the right accessories?
I used to be your icon.
Booted up, I tried hard to head your footers,
Inserting where I thought best,
Scrolling around for things to insert you,
Searching through the windows,
Dodging all those damn bullets.
But I was not I.T. superstar.
I tried my best to cut and paste

Over the cracks but, perhaps,
What we had was not worth saving.
I asked for help but your screen's gone blank.
I view the situation with regret.
You just refuse to shift. I'll not return
For there's no point in underlining things.
All I can do now is close down
And, quiet as a mouse, make my exit
While you backspace-delete my memory.

THE STACK OF BARLEY

Michael Harding

The Stack of Barley was a dance I learned in Glangevlin, a gorgeous, delicate European folk dance which required each couple to dance side by side with their heads held very high and their hands linked behind their backs, reminiscent of Flamenco dancers.

My partner was a beautiful girl with pale porcelain skin and hair as black as ravens' feathers, and I glided around the hall with her, the two of us perspiring and laughing, our steps like horses trotting in harmony, and that one dance felt like the biggest achievement of my life.

Years later I met a very old couple who lived in a trailer in Florida and came originally from west Cavan. They were deeply in love and they also knew the dance. They had been in America for sixty years and had recently retired from the anxiety of New York to spend their last days at the seaside. In a trailer in the sun.

She told me that they danced the Stack of Barley on the sidewalk the minute they landed on the shores of the Hudson in 1924. A pair of young swans, glad to be off the high seas.

When the old man got sick, I went to visit him in the hospital. He had a strange brown scar on his chest. He smiled at it and said he got it that first day they arrived, when they danced the Stack of Barley around the sidewalk, a pair of glad eejits, because they had landed in New York. Afterwards he had stretched himself on the grass beside a train station and fallen asleep. She went off to find food and directions to her cousin's bar in Queens, and when she returned to the train station she found himself still stretched on the grass, and sizzling like a rasher.

He never came out of hospital.

I saw them one day bowing their heads when a nurse scolded them for spilling paper cups of coffee on the floor of the corridor. And another day, the old man, a giant cricket of a man, sang *Spancil Hill* in a wispy voice you wouldn't hear behind a paper bag. His dressing gown had Apollo 11 on the back.

She, too, was a tall stick of a woman. All American now, in her custard yellow trouser suit, with thin, straight lips and sparrow eyes darting out through rimless glasses. She leaned forward while he was singing, looked at her shoes, and coyly tapped her two little slippered and varicosed feet in time with his song.

Feet that would never dance the Stack of Barely ever again.

LOVE AND ONIONS

Joe Kearney

True love is not an emotion constructed upon lavish extravaganza but is instead an accumulation of small things, an incremental treasure trove of sincere, simple gesture.

When genuinely offered, such tokens will bring tears to both the eye of the giver and the recipient. So it was with Nancy and Michael.

There is a thin divide between love and hate and Michael hated two things with a passion: one was onions, the other Kilkenny hurlers. He hated the latter when his love for Nancy saw him transplanted from the rich soil of his beloved Cork into the barren clay of Kilkenny. His red and white flag was a confederacy of rebellion amongst the black and amber. He was a small bantam of a man forced to shout his war-cry above the hiss of cats ... Cork-a-Doodle-Do ... Cork-a-Doodle-Do.

He hated onions; the pungency set him crying and caused his sinuses to act up. But he nevertheless grew them because they were Nancy's favourite.

Each year for the duration of the hurling championship he would hang the tattered flag of his county allegiance high in the chestnut tree beside the road, a defiance to the passing neighbours. And each year he grew onions as big and hard as sliotars and as sweet, to Nancy, in the depths of a wintry stew, as an out-of-season all-Ireland victory.

He nurtured, weeded, ripened and stored these golden aliums. He presented them to Nancy in her kitchen in plaited shanks as if they were Valentine bouquets of the rarest orchids. It was as if the continuous loop of the revolving seasons set its calendar and clock by Michael's onions.

During one season of perfect golden harvest, strangers arrived into the quiet townland of Cappahenry which was home to the couple. Pipemen came who were the contractors tasked with laying a conduit that would pipe the fossilised breath of prehistoric natural gas from beneath the seabed at Kinsale. These men carved a scar diagonally across the landscape that would stretch all the way to the homes and industries of Dublin. Gas would flow under pressure beneath the farms of Cork and Kilkenny, ignoring both county boundaries and hurling rivalry.

For the duration of the pipemen's stay, Nancy and Michael would hear their laughter and music drifting across the evening fields and sometimes the breeze would waft the smell of cook-fires and the unmistakable aroma of frying steak. Within a few days the pipemen were gone, their scar sutured neatly behind them.

The couple liked to take a stroll in the evening between perhaps *Kojac*, *Hawaii Five-0* or *Colombo* and the news. On one such evening when a fingernail sliver of harvest moon hung above them, they returned from their walk. Upon the lean-to shed at the back of the house, Michael had arranged his onions, lined up as if for some souvenir team photograph; in ripening ranks they faced southwards towards Cork, in the direction of the gas field. 'It must have been a bad year for the onions?' Nancy inquired. 'Rubbish, girl,' he boasted. 'That's one bumper crop. We'll be tired giving them away they're so plentiful.' But then he too noticed the cause of her concern: all that remained upon the roof was a scant few stalks ... the onions were gone!

The truth slowly dawned on Michael. He now recalled that the breeze that had wafted from the campsite carried on its breath not just a smell of steak ... but steak and onions.

He rained down curses upon the pipemen. He wished his onions would cause them a plague of gas, that their internal pipework would suffer a pain and pressure no doctor could cure.

He located their point of intrusion beside the ash tree on the ditch, saw the path they had beaten through the wither of late-season dock and nettle and all he could do was glare northwards along their scarred line of departure.

Michael's flag no longer teases the passing cats. The chestnut tree is bare of rebel taunt. One of his last tasks was to spread a summer's harvest of onions along the windowsill, safely away from any threat of predation but still coddled by the southern sun. 'These will last well into winter,' he promised Nancy, and true to his word they did and like all simple tokens of true love they couldn't avoid bringing tears to her eyes.

YOU SHOULDN'T HAVE!

Pat Kinevane

'Scarlet for a week' can only describe how Helen and Paddy felt on opening the box. Like some wicked imp had threaded elastic through their faces, tied it to a car bumper and drove off to imp-land, laughing out his little bum, leaving their expressions ruched in horror like swagged and tailed curtains. Paddy's mother, Nancy, wasn't there, thank God, but had left the first anniversary present inside their double-glazed porch. The card read: 'One year down, one hundred to go. Never fall asleep on an argument, lots of love, Mammy Nancy.'

No fear of a row this time, because they were united eternally in their summation of the said gift.

'Absolutely mingin' ugly.'

Two hideous bedside lamps. The stands were mint green and multi-coloured insects were painted all the way up and around to the switch. That was a grasshopper's leg! The ladybirds, butterflies and exotic beetles were all the more unfortunately brighter because they were glazed to the point of terrific dazzlement. And to top the lot, two fabric shades, in mustard.

All in all, a train wreck. The card continued: 'Will be over soon to see them in situ.'

How could a body not convulse at such terror? Nancy prided herself in her sense of style and adventure. Her own house, where Paddy survived a rearing, was a veritable war zone of knick-knacks, wall plaques and souvenirs from across the globe. Castanets, plates, Eiffel

Towers, snow-shakers and paper fans from the East, all collected under the roof of a two-up two-down circus tent. Helen and Paddy were used to Nancy's taste, but this took the golden biscuit.

'No way!' said Helen. 'I don't know where she got them, or what lunatic sold them, but these are for the bin.' Paddy convinced her to keep them boxed until the royal visit, make it look as if they were part of the furniture, just for that day. They had a good laugh in the end and compared the lamps to the unspeakable set of porcelain hands they got from Nancy the previous Christmas, hands that would hold a nice plant in your hall, or windowsill. Not! Hands that now doubled as an outdoor ashtray when they had friends over for a bite of pasta.

Pandora's box was sealed once more and put under the stairs till further requirement. That night, just before they switched off their own very beautiful Japanese lanterns, Helen had a pang of guilt.

'I'll have a look over the next few days. See if I can spot where she bought them. We could exchange them for nicer ones and tell her the colours clashed. She wouldn't mind Paddy, hah?'

'Who in their right evolved mind would stock the likes of them? You wouldn't find them in a skip. Relax, we'll swap them when she arrives. Night, love.'

And sleep alone was had. The night before was the anniversary. They were exhausted from celebrating, as Paddy recalled as he slipped, smiling, into slumber. 'Good man yourself!'

A week passed. Saturday night, the ashtray hands were in top demand because they had eight people for dinner and a game of *Who Wants to Be a Millionaire* on the PlayStation. A vat of vino was downed. Sunday was a pleasant blur, until about half five in the dusky evening. Ding-dong!

'You get it. I'm not even dressed,' said Helen. Paddy slunk out and the elastic-wielding imp returned to catapult his face to Kingdom Come. Nancy at the door, waving, on her way back from visiting a friend's grave. 'Folly the box' was Nancy's nickname, but that's another story.

'Hi Mam, blah blah blah' from the porch. Helen freaked out and tore to the hall. 'Stall her,' she viciously whispered, passing low behind Paddy, and grabbed the box, legging it upstairs to the oriental bedroom. Nancy spotted nothing, but there continued a blah blah blah between herself and her hungover wunderkind downstairs. Helen was Trojan. She shoved the Japanese lamps under the bed, hauled out the anniversary monsters and with shocking skill screwed on the mustard shades. She positioned the pair, straightened the quilt and picked her knickers off the carpet, shoving them in her dressing gown pocket. A knock.

'Come in.' Enter Nancy and Paddy.

'Where are dey? I'm dying to see dem,' Nancy chuckled.

'Thanks, Mammy, they're really ... unusual.'

'Let's see dem proper,' said Nancy, quenching the main light. Helen felt her way to the bedside switch. Click, and ... behold. The bed appeared to float from the beams that shot from beneath.

Shafts of undermattress illumination and not a spark from the lamps from hell. The Shogun and his Geisha were, once more, 'scarlet for a week'.

WAITING, WITH CICADAS

Peter Jankowsky

My son and I are relaxing on the couch in the living room, feet up, 'chilling out', as he calls it. We're tired and a bit hungover from last night's barbeque, a farewell party for him and his wife from their carefree days and uninterrupted nights, because very soon they will be parents of a little girl. In fact, the contractions have promptly started this morning, the mother-to-be is upstairs in her bedroom, resting, while we, down here, are waiting for things to develop, ready to drive her to the hospital at a moment's notice. But right now it's utterly quiet and peaceful all around us. The wooden house is breathing and whispering in the forenoon's increasing warmth, the light in the room is continually changing, white clouds are being driven by a warm northerly across the Pacific blue of the southern sky. A beautiful day for the little girl to join us on this beautiful planet, to open her eyes to the light 'under the long, white cloud' in Aotearoa, also known as New Zealand.

Utterly quiet, I said it is, but that's not really correct. In fact, it is utterly noisy, but it's a strange sort of noise, one that surrounds and enwraps you until you're almost one with it and hardly hear it any more. It's the song of the cicadas, if you can call it a song, that incessant, intense shrilling, like the sound of a thousand cut-lawn sprinklers, mixed with some glass-cutting and interspersed with rhythmic clicks and breathless drumming. My son had collected me from Wellington airport and had brought me straight to his favourite angling spot on the bay, and when I got out of the car there, at the foot of a wooded slope,

I felt nearly crushed by a cataract of sound that was coming down on me from the trees, a sound-storm. But he had only said: Ah, that's the cicadas, they're everywhere here! And indeed, they were, even in the city centre you could hear them singing in the trees, their voices effortlessly drowning out the traffic noise. Later, on that first day, in one of Wellington's glorious nature reserves, between looming trees and graceful tree ferns, their concert was nothing less than majestic, just as overwhelming and uplifting as an organ playing at full volume in one of our European cathedrals. The sound can have different effects on you, depending on your mental and nervous condition. It can certainly drive you up the wall, this unstoppable whirring, the sound-horizon to everything that happens here. Fortunately they don't intone at night. Right now, though, in the dappled light and summerly warmth of late February, they are a welcome addition to the moment. Time, or timelessness, has acquired a sound, and you can lean back into it.

Which is what we're still doing, myself and my son, the child who will soon have a child, the son who will be a father. The simplest things are the strangest. Slowly, ever so carefully, I turn, lean on my elbow and look into the face of the young man beside me. Do I still find the features I looked at with such delight twenty, twenty-five years ago? Yes, the blue shadows under his eyes which he inherited from his mother are still there, and the eyebrows are still extended like wings. There are some sharply cut lines now running across his forehead. The lips, although surrounded by a beard now, are still soft and shiny, at least now, in his sleep. But when he is talking I know they can sneer with all the disillusionment and sarcasm the experiences in a modern workplace can breed in a thirty-year-old. He's looking forward to the baby with some trepidation, which only shows his sense of realism. I'm looking back to his childhood with memories that give inexhaustible joy. 'May you feel the same in another thirty years!' I think and let myself sink back into the cushion of the cicadas' song. This morning it is totally mesmerising, I'm lost in a cicada trance in which I can't move a limb any more. But after a while I can hear that it is now the young man beside me who moves, he's sitting up, and then a long, contemplative silence follows. It is so sweet to lie still, is all I can think, unable or unwilling to even bat an eyelid. Is he looking at me? And if he does, what does he see in my face? I will never know, because at that moment a pained call from upstairs penetrates the cicadas' song. We both jump up. It is time.

REMEMBERING
BETTY FRIEDAN

Ailbhe Smyth

Growing up in Ireland in the late 1960s and 70s, I was a very confused young woman. Ah well, you might say, weren't we all? But every generation has its own confusions and problems, and of course, just to complicate things, they're not the same for different social groups and classes — and genders. For a young woman like myself, a daughter of the white Dublin bourgeoisie with a university education, the confusion was acute, all the more so since the underlying problem had no name.

There I was, there we were, growing numbers of young women freshly released from our convent schools, flocking or being herded into universities around the country with very little equipment for life except our Leaving Cert results, polite manners and a pair of white gloves. The whole world lay before us, they said, and we innocently believed them. We didn't know then — how could we — that we'd need to ditch the manners and the gloves and reinvent it. For we had an impossible mission: to be educated 'new' women, achieving and succeeding out there in a world which believed we should all be at home all of the time servicing husbands and children and households and what have you. And with hardly a role model in sight. But that's all in retrospect.

I got a degree, got a job, got married and set up house in double-quick time. That it all fell apart just as quickly was a blessing, although it didn't seem so at the time. The difficulty was that without being able to say quite how or why, I knew I was caught in a contradiction I couldn't climb out of on my own. I was getting two messages about who and what and how I should be, so bewilderingly at odds as to make me – literally – ill.

The penny dropped slowly, and for me reading was a crucial part of the process. Some time in the early 1970s, I read Simone de Beauvoir's *The Second Sex*, then Betty Friedan's *The Feminine Mystique*, among other amazing feminist books. They were a revelation and my excitement was immense. I saw that I wasn't mad or bad, or stupid or alone. 'A woman,' Friedan said, 'has got to be able to say, and not feel guilty, "Who am I, and what do I want out of life?" She mustn't feel selfish and neurotic if she wants goals of her own, outside of husband and children.' She named the 'problem that has no name' for women of my generation and milieu, putting her finger on the pulse of those living contradictions, revolutionising how women thought about ourselves and our lives. Above all, Betty Friedan urged us to take the gloves off, to take action to change the world, to stand up and fight for our right as women to independence, equality, justice and human fulfilment.

So, another marker gone, I thought to myself when I heard of her death at eighty-five last week. The twentieth century is indeed over. I didn't agree with all her views – not with the watered-down reformism of her later years, and certainly not when she called lesbians like myself the 'lavender menace'. The phrase makes me laugh now (I love lavender), and she did most apologetically recant.

But caveats are mean spirited. I thought about Friedan's legacy, about the extraordinary debt I owe her and her generation of brave, visionary feminists who taught me, confused and privileged young woman that I was, to think more clearly, to challenge more firmly and to inhabit the world with courage and a passion for justice. Betty Friedan believed in women's right to live fully, creatively and freely. Way back in 1963 when *The Feminine Mystique* appeared, she asked, 'Who knows what women can be when they are finally free to become themselves?'

To be sure, hers was not the only voice, the whole world or the whole story. There was more to come, more work to be done, and there still is, in scads, but she fought the good fight for women with fire and vigour, and I honour her and mourn her passing. May she rest in peace.

And in this twenty-first century, with its myriad new challenges and dilemmas, may feminists have the vision and the strength to go on fighting for women's freedom: for ourselves, for our daughters, for all women everywhere.

TWO CORK PAINTERS

Betty Nunan

Cork's sumptuous fireworks display that opened its European City of Culture year might well have its first great artist, James Barry, turning somersaults in his crypt at St Paul's in London. He would not approve. 'Cork,' he said, 'gave me birth but it would not give me bread.' On the contrary, Daniel Maclise, possibly the city's next finest artist, would have thoroughly approved of the party and spent his night happily sketching its citizens at play.

The story that tells how Edmond Burke discovered his fellow Corkman, young Barry, the talented eighteenth-century painter, is close to a miracle. Burke belonged to the Catholic aristocracy of the county, while Barry was reared in a humble cabin in Blackpool's Water Lane, then the poorest district in the city.

From childhood, the artist spent his spare time borrowing books to read, sketching and drawing. He believed so fiercely in his own talent that when still a mere boy, he walked to Dublin, carefully carrying his first picture under his arm, *Conversion of the Pagan Prince by St Patrick*. It was accepted by the Royal Dublin Society and hung in a remote corner of one of the exhibition rooms, where it was unlikely to be noticed by anyone. But it did not escape the observation of Burke, who asked his secretary who had painted the picture.

'I don't know, sir. But it was brought here by that boy,' answered the gentleman, pointing to Barry, who was standing modestly beside the work.

'Where did you get this picture, my boy?' asked Burke.

'It is mine, I painted it,' said the proud young man.

'That's impossible,' said Burke, glancing at the shabbily dressed youth, whereupon Barry burst into tears and rushed out of the room. Burke instantly followed and soothed him with encouraging words and became his friend and patron. James Barry was the first Irish painter to be elected a member of the Royal Academy of London. He studied and worked unremittingly at his art, perfecting it, even to his final paintings worked in abject poverty. He is now regarded among the foremost neo-classical painters of the eighteenth century.

Many years later, the Quaker family of Cork, whose mansion stood at Glanmire, allowed the young Daniel Maclise, a shoemaker's son brought up on George's Street, to make copies of Barry's paintings and etchings in their library. Maclise left school at fourteen. In time, he would be elected the next Irish member of the Royal Academy in London and awarded its gold medal.

His parents, Alexander Maclise and Rebecca Buchanan, were married in the Old Presbyterian Church on Prince's Street in Cork on Christmas Eve 1797. Late among their seven children, Daniel was born on 2 January 1806. He recalled playing marbles on the Grand Parade with his friend John Hogan, who later became the internationally acclaimed sculptor. The young art students were lucky to be able to study casts of the finest classical sculptures from the Vatican galleries at the Cork Institute on the Mall.

These casts came to Cork with a prestigious pedigree because a pope, a prince and a lord had been involved in their landing in Cork in 1822. Their story begins with Napoleon, who, among his other conquests, looted priceless sculptures from the Vatican galleries. After Waterloo, the British government restored the sculptures to the Vatican, and in gratitude, Pope Pius VII had casts made of the major pieces, which included *The Dying Gladiator*, *Apollo Belvidere* and the *Medici Venus*, as a present for the British people.

Cork owes its gratitude to the last link in the chain, Lord Listowel, a man who actively promoted industry and art in Munster. The Prince Regent did not value the huge sculptures when they arrived in London, so his friend, Lismore, suggested to the prince that he donate them to the citizens of Cork.

Maclise wrote that neither he nor Hogan had ever seen a plaster cast before this collection arrived into Cork. He described 'the effect that the mass of excellence had on their young fancy — beautiful, actual moulds of originals, worshipped by generations, was at first overwhelming, then inspiring', and concluded that 'for years and years by day and night we studied those perfect forms.'

The student friends also attended anatomy lectures in Parnell Place, where Maclise devoted many winter nights to actual dissection.

But I'm jumping the gun. Cork had many great educators in the early nineteenth century. Maclise was fortunate to have attended a school on Patrick's Hill run by the Reverend Hincks, Minister of the Old Presbyterian Church. Hincks had founded the Royal Cork Institute that had opened its first public library on Pembroke Street in 1792. At school, Maclise sketched constantly, drawing irreverent caricatures of teachers until his Latin grammar was profusely illustrated and his reader looked more like an illustrated manuscript.

At fourteen, Maclise was placed in the Banking House of Newenhams, but continued to study art. Soon he was invited to the Newenhams' home in Summerhill, where there was a picture gallery and studio. The Newenham girls and their father loved to paint. In their studio, Maclise discovered colour, canvas and easel for the first time, and with borrowed oils, he worked his first portrait. Newenham's country estate stood beside the Penrose mansion, and in the library there he got to read all of Walter Scott's novels.

Maclise was an athlete too. He would regularly swim from outside Blackrock Castle to Little Island and back. Like so many in Cork, he enjoyed walking along the Lee Fields on Sunday afternoons, or sailing down the harbour in summertime on a friend's yacht, sitting in the stern, sketching the surrounding hills.

The famous novelist himself, Sir Walter Scott, visited Cork in 1825 and came to browse in Bolster's bookshop, near Patrick's Bridge. Scott's Waverley novels of high chivalry and romance had captivated Maclise's imagination. Working all night, he sketched Sir Walter's head and shoulders, and the next morning brought this high-finished pen and ink drawing – it had the elaborate minuteness of a line engraving – to Bolster's, where it was prominently exhibited. Sir Walter was struck with the exquisite finish and fidelity of the drawing. He asked the name of the artist and Maclise was introduced. The novelist called for a pen and signed it, 'Walter Scott'. Bolster suggested that the sketch be lithographed, and 500 copies were sold as soon as they appeared. The sketch is preserved today in the British Museum.

That was the first public recognition of another rising star in the world of art.

MARCH

MADELINE SMITH AND TABLEMATS

Mae Leonard

My Scottish friend and I were in the Robbie Burns Lounge in Ayr, and as I pushed aside my glass to read one of The Bard's poems on the placemat, my friend asked, 'Did ye know, t'was Madeleine Smith set the fashion of using tablemats instead of a tablecloth on the dinner table?'

Now there's a piece of useless information if I ever heard one. But my friend is a history buff and from the smirk on his face I could only deduce that this Madeleine Smith had to be a Scot. Was the use of tablemats her canny Scot's way of saving on laundry bills or did she want to show off her beautiful polished table? And who was Madeleine Smith when she was at home, anyhow?

So in that Robbie Burns hostelry, sipping a wee *deoch an dorais*, my friend – in his best Scottish burr – told me that Madeleine Smith was the daughter of a wealthy Glasgow architect. She was born in 1835 and her life was unremarkable until she reached the age of nineteen. That was when she met Pierre Emile L'Angelier, the son of a seed merchant from the Channel Island, who was working in Glasgow. For Emile it was love at first sight and he sought an introduction to her by a mutual friend, as was the proper custom of that era.

That meeting would soon end the life of one and forever haunt the life of the other.

Madeleine fell madly and hopelessly in love with him too. She was well aware from the beginning that her family would not accept Emile. Secret meetings were arranged. Fiery letters of pure passion were exchanged. I suppose it was inevitable that her father would find out and he forbade his daughter from having any further contact with Emile. Reluctantly she wrote, telling her lover that their romance was all over. However, he managed to contact her again and the red-hot correspondence and meetings continued. Meanwhile, her parents chose a prospective husband for her, William Minnoch, a wealthy merchant. Madeleine liked him and his prospects instantly and accepted his proposal of marriage in January 1857. But what about her Emile? She wrote a letter telling him 'my love for you has ceased ... I did once love you truly, fondly but for some time back I have lost much of that love.'

Emile was perplexed by this turn of events, but he also heard rumours of his beloved's engagement to Mr Minnoch. He insisted that she meet him or he would show her letters to her father. She was thus forced to meet him.

In the early hours of 23 March 1857, Pierre Emile L'Angelier stumbled through the streets of Glasgow towards his lodging house, doubled over with pain. His landlady helped him to his bed and sent for a doctor, but by sunrise he was dead. He had been poisoned. A bundle of Madeleine's letters were found in his room, and added to this was the little matter of her having recently purchased a quantity of arsenic. She was arrested and charged with murder. The trial was held in Edinburgh and lasted nine days. There was huge popular interest in the case and crowds lined the streets every night as her carriage took her back to the East Jail. Madeleine showed remarkable calmness and poise during the trial, even refusing food and water while in court. There is a unique verdict in Scotland that signifies that the accused was not found innocent, but the prosecution had not made a strong enough case to convict – this verdict is known as 'Not Proven', and it applied to Madeleine Smith. She went free that afternoon and returned to her family home. The notoriety of the trial did not cool down and her would-be fiancé, Mr Minnoch, headed for the hills. Madeleine was forced by her family to leave Scotland. She went to London and eventually married George Wardle, who worked with the artist William Morris. They settled in Bloomsbury and became involved in the socialist movement, befriending, among others, George Bernard Shaw. They were noted for their hospitality and their household furniture was so beautifully crafted that Madeleine would not hide her dining room table under a tablecloth – she used lace placemats.

Eventually the pressure of past events took its toll, and after some years of marriage and two children, she and George Wardle separated. Some say that she emigrated to America in 1916 and remarried when she was eighty years old. Official records prove otherwise. More say that she went to Australia and was never heard of again. Poor Madeleine Smith.

THE BLOOMING GARDEN

Cyril Kelly

I'm spending more and more time every day in the — if you'll pardon the pun — blooming garden. I mean I could be out there for half a day and think that barely an hour has passed. It's not as if there's a lot of land involved. Especially in front of the house. What's out there would hardly, in Eamonn Kelly's immortal words, 'physic a shnipe'. A poor Kerry farmer putting a gimp on himself for the sake of the new little wife inside in the kitchen, hoofing the muck from his boots like a bull getting ready to charge, well, such a man would paw twice as much ground as I have out there in front. In aerial photographs that patch isn't half the size of a postage stamp. It wouldn't warrant a wink at a planning tribunal. Yet everything out there has this infernal, eternal habit of growing. Ergo, elemental matters of earth, air, light and water have to be seen to. Each tender tendril has to be supported and sheltered. Even, if you don't mind, cajoled.

But front gardens are not just a matter of horticulture and plant psychology. No indeed. There are many factors specific to front gardens. Apart from the aforementioned, there's sociology, philosophy, not so much theology as spirituality, history, literature. Plus, of course, that evergreen perennial, the birds and the bees.

If I'm out early enough with my watering can, the first people I see, just as the sun looms like a monstrance over the bishop's palace, will be five Philippinos cycling up the road. A bleary eyed, soundless peloton, they pedal past, always in single file. Invariably they remind me of another group of dislocated men. Blasket islanders, conditioned by generations tramping narrow sheep tracks, also trod the streets of Dingle in single file.

By the time nurses from neighbouring flats and houses are skipping down steps, running to the Mater, bussing to Beaumont, I'm usually finishing my watering chores. The lull that follows this early morning flurry gives me a chance to get down to a bit of gardening. Overnight, pansies and busy lizzies have declared jihad. An advance party of pansies, flying bellicose banners of purple, white and psychedelic yellow, has charged into a phalanx of busy lizzies. The War of the Roses had nothing on this. I've no choice but to adopt a policy of 'surrender and regrant', in the course of which I discover an orgy of slugs breakfasting on succulent busy lizzie limbs. Immediately I bag those slimy lechers.

To slug-pellet or not to slug-pellet, that is the philosophical question. Because, for the first time in years, a family of thrushes has nested in a neighbouring tree. Poisoned slugs would hardly help their vocal cords. And as shadows lengthen at the end of the day, a thrush's treetop song is our local muezzin. At dusk, his solitary vespers anoint men's minds with thoughts of eternal things.

Sitting back on my hunkers to take a break, the mid-morning mass-goers are wending by. It's then I catch up on breaking local issues; McKeown's kitty had kittens, Keogh's Sandie is in heat, an outrageous party in No. 32 last night. Then, deep in our Dublin suburb, Mick Treacy from Tipperary leans against my railings, slots his arms between the spikes to rest his elbows. We banter timeless talk of hurling and football till he'll hardly make the recessional hymn at the end of mass.

One of my favourite shrubs is the rhododendron. Pruning it, I think of the romantic rhododendron walk above Howth Castle. Meandering across a rocky outcrop, this path is a secluded tunnel, opening frequently onto clearings of spectacular silence. Trusses of violet, red and snow-white blossoms scorching echoes in the tremulous ventricles of the heart.

Just as I'm wondering if romance exists in this harsh modern age, my erstwhile young neighbour, Susan, pulls up and parks at the kerb. While she's unbuckling her toddler, Daniel, from the baby seat, I recall the time when first I came to this road. On the very pavement where she now stands, hefting her own baby on her hip, Susan used to play house and hopscotch. And there she is now, telling me about her new house in Swords, about her efforts to start a garden. Cyclic life imitating art. Susan's voice is eager, shiny. Shiny and eager to start the infernal, eternal circle all over again.

DIALANN MO MHÁTHAIR

Fachtna Ó Drisceoil

The inscription in my mother's writing on the inside cover of the diary reads: '*Leabhar Shéamais Fhionnbarr, agus Bhríde agus Dhéagláin agus Cholmáin*' – then there is an empty space followed by a question mark and then – '*agus Fachtna.*' Myself, the youngest of five. The empty space represents the brother or sister that could have been, but died in my mother's womb. Strangely, she does not refer anywhere else in the diary to this loss. Yet that empty space between my nearest brother and myself seems more powerful than any written words.

My parents started keeping the diary in September 1960 after the birth of my eldest brother. '*Rugadh Séamus Fionnbharr fé dheabhadh timpeall 9 iar nóin ar an gCéadaoin 21 Méan Fómhar 1960.*' Many of the early entries are in my father's scrawled penmanship, but my mother's more legible schoolteacher's writing soon takes over. Both are in the beautiful old Gaelic script for the first few years. The diary is a battered A4-size hardback ledger, the pages yellowed and stained with age and use.

The proud parents record the daily progress of their first child: '*An 9ú Feabhra 1961: Dúirt Séamus ga-ga. An 10ú Feabhra: Dúirt sé at at agus ba.*' But of course, like all new parents they had their difficulties: '*An 16ú Feabhra 1961. É millte dár linn le iomarca notice. Lig Mamaí dó gol inniu agus stad sé. É go maith ina dhiaidh.*'

Most of the entries are quite matter-of-fact descriptions of every little event in the new baby's life. Now and again the young mother's excitement and pride bursts through the mundane details. The first birthday is announced in large, exuberant capital letters. '*Lá breithe, bliain d'aois. Sceitimíní ar Mhamaí faoin lá. Í ag tnúth go mór leis.*' The presents from neighbours and relations reflect an Ireland far removed from the Celtic Tiger. '*Punt ón Godmother, punt ó Mrs Rodgers, bróga is stocaí ó Nanny, brístí ó Mháire agus Jimmy.*' The excitement intensifies when Séamus, with a great sense of timing that bodes well for later life, chooses the day of his birthday to stand for the first time on his own two feet. As the day draws to a close, my mother reflects: '*Bliain ó anois ag 9pm a rugadh é. A lán cártaí. Brón ar Mhamaí go bhfuil an lá thart.*'

Very little in the later years of the diary matches the excitement of that first year or two. When my sister Bríd is born, her entry into the world is simply recorded: '*5 Meán Fómhair. Glaoch ag Mom go Holles Street. Bríd Carmel ar an saol ar 2.30pm Dé Céadaoin.*' My brothers Déaglán and Colmán follow in 1965 and 1967.

The most animated entry in these years concerns the fiftieth anniversary of the 1916 Rising. How our country has changed, and changed utterly, since those more innocent days, when even a Fine Gael household like ours could embrace this event with enthusiasm. '*Sprid iontach ag borradh le mí anuas. Séamus ag cur aithne ar na Signatories tré pictiúrí agus nuachtáin. P.H. Pearse ar aithne aige. Tomás Ó Cleirigh, Seán Mac Diarmada &rl. É lán de chaint i dtaobh saighdiurí na hÉireann. Brat na hÉireann aige. É ag canadh* "Wrap the Green Flag Round Me".' My father put aside four 1916 commemorative coins in order to present them to his children on their wedding days. He didn't keep one for me, as my parents had neither conceived me, nor conceived of me, at that time. I was not born until the feast of the epiphany, 1972. My mother simply states: '*Rugadh Fachtna. Buíochas le Dia.*' Whether that was gratitude or simply relief, I'm not sure. My sister Bríd, the only girl in the family, cried at the arrival of yet another boy. She wasn't the last woman I was to reduce to tears.

My mother was not as diligent in keeping the diary up to date in later years and the entries are more infrequent. In September 2000 she was diagnosed with stomach cancer: '*13 Deireadh Fómhair 2000: Cuireadh mé faoi scian. Ní raibh sé sásúil. Secondaries sa bhealach.*'

'*Tús na Samhna. Chemo go ceann 6 mhí. Mé ag déanamh go maith as.*'

She died in Harold's Cross Hospice on the last day of April 2001. The last entry in the diary, on 23 December 2000, concerns the death of her brother Dan and the mid-winter journey to his funeral in west Cork: '*Cuireadh é in Inse Geimhleach. Bhí an tír faoi shneachta, sioc agus leac-oighear . . .*'

After that the remaining pages of the diary are blank. Once more, the empty space says more than words can. Some absences will always remain unfilled.

THE *HAKA* FROM IRELAND

Joe O'Toole

The fire in the eyes of the New Zealand All Blacks dancing their ritualistic *haka* with its wild intensity, screaming their words of war, 'we are going to live, we are going to die', is quintessential New Zealand Maori culture.

But even though the wild abandon of the dance evokes an undoubted Celtic response, resonating even with those wild women in *Dancing at Lughnasa*, it never struck me as an Irish story, but Rothaí Móra an tSaoil never stop turning and, serendipitously, while researching a totally different subject, the *haka* became, for me, an Irish story.

The story of the All Black's *haka* begins, of all places, in Galway. The Reverend Dr John Buck from east Galway was a Fellow of Trinity College in the early nineteenth century. Some of his family emigrated to the southern hemisphere. So it happened that his grandson, William, in the magnificence of New Zealand's South Island, fell in love with Ngarongo, a beautiful Maori tribeswoman with a physical disability.

Even though a Maori woman with a *pakeha* man as husband and wife was taboo, breaking all the social codes and norms, true love prevailed, and dismissive of all advice, they married. They met rejection from both cultures, but in adversity, their love only blossomed. Then their desire for a child was thwarted when Ngarongo found it impossible to conceive because of her disability. Pragmatically and lovingly, she selected her Maori cousin for William to impregnate.

Thus, in 1877, was begotten, in the North Island of New Zealand, of Maori and Galway blood, the child Peter Buck.

He was reared by his father and Ngarongo with a full exposure to both European and Maori culture. His father instilled a love of languages and poetry in him and Ngarongo and his Maori great aunt introduced him to Maori lore, customs and history. It was they who taught him the stories, steps and challenges of the Maori dances, the *hakas*. Consequently, Peter spoke Maori and English languages fluently and articulately and found no conflict in believing in the Maori faith while also a practising Christian.

As a young man, his talent flourished. He boarded at an Anglican secondary school where he was an exemplary student, excelling academically, gaining proficiency in Latin and Greek and winning a place in the University of Otago medical school.

Peter Buck holds the distinction of being the first Maori to graduate as a doctor. But far from being restricted to academic superiority, he also proved unmatched in sport, captaining both the college athletics team and the college rugby team and becoming the national long jump champion two years in a row.

But despite his success, he never lost the opportunity to introduce his non-Maori friends to the secrets and joys of the Maori culture. At parties and other social occasions, this tall, handsome and multi-talented young man would, at the drop of a hat, strip semi-naked, leap to the fore and perform an energetic and exciting *haka*. Being a leader and a role model, his impact was extraordinary. He drilled his rugby team in the *haka* to daunt and put the wind up the opposition, then introduced it to other rugby teams, until finally it was taken up by the New Zealand national team.

In the autumn of 1905, when the first-ever All Blacks touring team arrived in Britain and Ireland, they were led and captained by the legendary Dave Gallagher, native of Donegal, who had emigrated to New Zealand as a five-year-old child and now came back to lead his adopted country against his native land.

But before each match of the tour in front of packed stadia, the Irishman, Dave Gallagher, to the delight of the Welsh, English, Scottish and Irish crowds, led them with ferocity and drive as they shouted and danced the *haka* as they had been given by that other Irishman, Peter Buck.

And where was Peter Buck?

Well, he was in Westport — that's Westport, New Zealand — where he was marrying the love of his life, Margaret Wilson, an emigrant to New Zealand from Northern Ireland.

Completing the Irish connection.

Rothaí Móra an tSaoil indeed.

CROSSING THE LINE

John O'Donnell

Ireland's Triple Crown win against England, 2006

Our hopes as high as goalposts; this cabbage patch
So often our graveyard: what was special
About this one? Edge of seat, we perched to watch
In wide-screened homes and heaving bars, *ar meitheal*

As if we might by force of will together
Bring home this rare harvest, beyond our grasp
So many times before. A throaty roar –
Was that ball in or out? Another gasp:

The arc of Leamy; pitched battle then, behind
Till Horgan stretched for whitewash, seconds left.
We waited. God-like from on high, the final word:
You may award the try. At whistle-blow we laughed

And wept, a clear thing sensed; more than a team
At last crossing a line, a bright new green.

SLEMISH

Nuala McCann

Slemish is my holy mountain. Up there, with the wind belting down, it was easy to believe that the huge sweeps of fields and hedges and dry stone walls belonged to me ... Top of the world, Ma!

All Lent we'd hoard and count out the gum drops, the lemon sherbets, safe in the drawer, ready for the glut. With time and grubby fingers, the stash turned sticky but never lost its charm. By 17 March, the one exception in the long Lenten abstinence from sweets, we were baying for the feast.

It all depended on the weather. On the eve, my mother was tortured with hourly inquiries as to whether she thought it might rain and we might not get to climb Slemish. The thought of a day at home, penned in with assorted disappointed climbers, almost drove her to tears.

It was touch and go the year the central heating boiler had the indecency to blow up on St Patrick's morning and our parents emerged, black faced and anxious, from the garage. But they were relieved to send us on our way with a quick douse of holy water.

After early mass and a rallying hymn to our native saint, they drove us to the foot of our holy hill and let us loose like stray cats, scratching and mewling to get out to the fields and hare up the slopes.

Rough and free and gawky as mountain goats, we scrambled through the furze, anchoring ourselves on the gorse and yelling to each other in voices whipped away by the wind. Up on top, wheezing and laughing, we owned the view.

It is so long ago that I can't remember if the stone on top was painted green, white and gold or red, white and blue. We couldn't care less. We pitched camp and gorged ourselves on the saved Lenten sweets. The first mouth was manna, the last, a sickly glut, lumpen in the stomach.

Then it was down past the old woman with the moustache, jangling bottles of lemonade given free by a local farmer, and on to the ten-mile walk home, singing and fighting.

We four together – friends, enemies, companions, schoolmates – slagging and dancing and laughing – caught forever in a freeze frame on a country road, slapping sticks along the hedges.

The local priest drove by and our friend said, 'You cannot get into the car, he may be carrying the Holy Eucharist and you cannot engage him in conversation.'

But he stopped because he was kind and we all piled in with the Holy Eucharist and he tried to chat and we were all struck dumb.

I glanced back at the mountain and remembered the teacher talking about Patrick alone with just the sheep for company, gorse scratching his bare ankles and his escape, followed by the voices of the Irish in a dream, crying, 'Come back to Ireland.'

Suddenly, I felt unbearably alone.

That is all thirty years ago now. I want to leave the four friends, carefree forever on the country road, plucking hedges and making jokes.

But St Patrick's Day shall always be a reminder of certain sorrows – the close friend who died cruelly long before her time or the child who was never to be. Some of the four friends got more than their fair share of sorrows.

Now, I know that my Slemish, my holy mountain, is really only a bit of a hill. But from the top, the world still looks distant and beautiful. I imagine that perhaps God has pitched camp on a very high peak and, from there, creation looks pretty damn wonderful. But sometimes, God, I want to whisper … just sometimes … it is a different story on the ground.

ICONS

Peter Sirr

In the Dublin Writers Museum the curious visitor can admire Oliver St John Gogarty's driving goggles, Brendan Behan's Painters and Decorators union card, James Joyce's trousers and other fetishes, all earnestly establishing the disappointing materiality of writers. And if they tire of this they can pop next door to the Dublin City Gallery The Hugh Lane to gaze at the faithfully recreated disorder of Francis Bacon's studio. Or they could catch a plane to the British Library to experience the exhibition 'The Writer in The Garden'. Among the exhibits is poet Philip Larkin's lawnmower, together with a seventeen-month correspondence between the poet and a lawnmower company. Readers might remember Larkin's poem 'The Mower' and his distress at his inadvertent killing of a hedgehog in his garden. But who needs poetry when you can have the real thing, in this case a letter indicating that the poet was so upset he couldn't bear to use his Qualcast Commodore any more? And nor did the replacement he bought from East Yorkshire Mowers do the job either. 'I am still not happy about the Webb lawn mower that I bought from you last month. The blades continually jammed and I had to finish off the lawns with my old Qualcast Commodore.' The problem was, as we all know, 'longish grass, wet grass or moss'. Moss is bad news all right. Three lawnmowers later and the saga continued, but there's no need to rely on the letters; you can examine for yourself the blue Victa Powerplus 160cc super two stroke, the final mower the poet owned before his death in 1985 and occupying pride of place in the exhibition.

Lawnmowers, letters, laundry bills all go to show that what our particular portion of historical time values is the 'life' of the writer. Part of our fascination with the life of the artist has to do with the fact that the life is evident, whereas the imagination is mysterious. You can look at a lawnmower, examine the blades; you can read the letters or the transcripts of the divorce court. But how can you explain this brushstroke or that sudden illuminating flash of language?

In its lovingly reconstructed confusion, the Francis Bacon Studio tries to show us the mind of the artist at work. In this poem I imagined the same process being applied to a writer, an imaginary museum for an imaginary writer.

The Writer's Studio

They've been worrying for ages —
how best to show your chaos.
Two days from the opening
a curator re-arranges papers,
spills ink on the floor, half eats an apple
and throws it in a corner, but still
the disorder comes to order;
the flung pipe, the forgotten shirt
sculpted and composed, with the notebooks,
the scrawled on walls and mildewed postcards.
It's all there, through the peephole,
this reconstruction of your mind
From which you are entirely absent.
You're in heaven cursing the dullness of angels,
throwing your clothes around like clouds,
prowling the fragrant avenues
for a fight, a drink, someone to talk to
or sleep with, and if some freak wind
planted you here among your own things,
you'd sweep the lot from under our eyes,
tear it all down, rip the postcards, the T-shirts,
rob the till and drink it dry and float
back up to your high bed and wake up
having forgotten everything. We

who so loved your life we made a fetish of it
will stand in the air, hoping to catch
whatever falls: broken crockery, a smashed cloud,
we'll see your hand in the wind and rain,
hear your voice in the roaring streets,
follow you from porn shop to pub
and back again. And then a tree will fall,
or a leaf, someone lean out a window,
a cat slope
down a laneway
and at last
we will understand you.

CONTINUITY

Ted Sheehy

I'd like to make a confession ... there are at least seven working radios in the house at home and often there might be three of them on at the same time. Even my youngest daughter has had her own little radio since she was seven. When I upgraded my mobile phone last year I just had to have the fancy one with the built-in radio. Let's face it, it is a problem, but I know you'll agree that as habits go it's not the worst because I take it, speaking from the radio, that I'm talking to the converted.

I've been listening to the radio all my life, but it was only in a B&B in Galway one morning a few years back that I realised that the relationship between radio chatter and time is a fairly complex thing. Two radios happened to be on in the background as I was having the breakfast bit of the B&B. Both were tuned to the same station and it dawned on me during the weather forecast that the sound was coming from one marginally ahead of the other, as if the time zone shifted a split second between the kitchen and the breakfast room. The news was marginally less newsworthy where I was sitting. I poured another cup of coffee and wondered, how could this be?

Now I know science has the answer – my experience in that Galway B&B was probably due to the radios being tuned to different wavelengths – but how interesting is that? I was (and still am) less interested in the science than in following the thoughts prompted by the realisation that a voice, or sound, or picture carried by a radio signal is not trapped in or by the time or place it is heard.

It's obvious, of course, but I'd not thought of it before that moment, that the sound was there in radio wave form, whether I heard it or not. Just as you can hear my voice now, coming from your radio. You can turn off the receiver, but the signal is still in the air about you. And though your radio may be plugged into the wall, it's the signal that reminds us why it's known to an older generation as 'the wireless'. It's a more apt name for what it is that a radio actually does.

This signal is skipping toward you through space and you have tuned it in from among a vast invisible babble of radio traffic. Taxis, aircraft, mobile phones, radar, radio and television stations, motorbike couriers, military communications, shipping, air traffic control, baby monitors, pagers, satellites, wireless broadband, walkie-talkies, emergency services ... the list is endless.

And even if all the receivers in the world were turned on and tuned in, they couldn't swallow up all the signals we send. They bounce around the planet before careering off into the space-time continuum. I recall reading somewhere that early radio traffic from Earth has travelled fifty light years' distance through space, and it's still travelling. The surge in global television output has already reached twenty light years away.

Any day now, some extra-terrestrial Universal Environmental Protection Agency may drop by to give us an enormous fine because we're using space as a dump for our used radio waves. For all we know, we could be killing distant life forms with noise pollution. Or maybe an alien species that consumes radio waves like we drink beer might see Earth as the biggest free bar in the universe.

But how was it that one minute I was listening to the news on the radio in a Galway B&B and the next I was thinking about aliens using humans the way ants use aphids? Well, it's almost certainly my mother's fault that I'm never more than a foot away from a radio, and it's probably also her fault that my mind strayed into the realms of science fiction over breakfast.

My mother read a lot of science fiction and passed on books and stories by the likes of Isaac Asimov, John Wyndham, Philip K. Dick and Ursula LeGuin to me. I learned early on that aliens, androids and sub-atomic universes were just as valid as the subject material of literature as the social mores of Jane Austen's novels. And radio? Well, radio was what my mother did for a living. For many years she was a continuity announcer, heard by many on this frequency but usually unnamed, as was the style of the time.

I'm sure the thought would amuse her, fifteen years after her death, that her voice may still be heard – introducing a programme, or playing 'Hospitals Requests' – out beyond Cassiopeia, across the darkness of space among the unnamed constellations. Perhaps, as I speak, being decoded by life forms beyond our imagining.

So here now is my voice, coming after hers. I listen for her among the radio chatter like I did as a child when I would hear her say, 'Here is the news, read by Charles Mitchell.' Hello mother, it's me. I'm surfing the radio waves in your wake. I'm twenty light years behind you ...

AGNES MARTIN

Mark Joyce

In the arts, what is perfection? For the majority of artists, perfection is an unattainable ideal. Artists compose and edit their creations as best they can, in a real-life context. They usually have to make compromises to communicate with an audience. The price of perfection is just too high. There are, however, a few artists out there who are annoyingly persistent in their pursuit of perfection.

The American abstract painter Agnes Martin spent her life in pursuit of ideal forms, which are as close to perfection in the visual arts as we may see in this era.

She was born in 1912 in the town of Macklin, a province of Saskatchewan, in Canada. Her father, a Scottish Presbyterian farmer, died when she was two years old. It was a pioneering and religious childhood, and the Bible and *Pilgrim's Progress* were her first books.

After training as an art teacher in the 1940s, she moved to Taos, New Mexico for its breathtaking landscapes and Native American culture. The bohemian ambience of the town also appealed to her, as it had to writer D.H. Lawrence twenty years earlier. It was in Taos that she met the influential New York gallery owner Betty Parsons, who told her she would take her on, but only if she moved to New York City. So in 1957 Agnes Martin moved into a derelict sailmaker's loft on the East River in Lower Manhattan. This was her living and working space for the next ten years. Her neighbours in the warehouse included many great American artists of that period, such as Ellsworth Kelly and Jasper

Johns. The subject of her paintings had always been the New Mexican terrain, which she had known since the 1940s. She had developed an abstract language based on the exquisite flora and fauna of the south-western desert, its purity of light and the dry earth-scape.

At the beginning of the 1960s, Martin made a fateful decision. She started to use a grid as an organising motif in her paintings. The poet John Ashberry noted that her grids were handmade, and not mechanical. They were intimate distillations of her experience of the world. She dated her own artistic maturity from this time, linking the simple grid motif to the pursuit of the ideal forms of Plato and the topography of the western plains she knew so well. Indeed, there is something of an American 'plainness' in this work, an ingenious directness and simplicity in the tradition of American literature, music or indeed, furniture, as so clearly expressed in the Shaker style.

In the 1960s, Agnes Martin was included in the defining exhibitions of that decade. She found herself being co-opted as part of a young art movement, Minimalism. All of the other minimalists were half her age.

In 1967 she turned her back on this late artistic success, travelling for a time through Canada and the western United States in a pick-up truck. She came to rest back on a remote mesa in New Mexico, where she built herself an adobe house. She didn't paint during the following seven years. Instead, she wrote a searing examination of her artistic practice and a Taoist exploration of existence, experience and the external world. When Agnes started to paint and draw again, she was sixty-two years old. The final thirty years of her life were organised around the creation of a constant and unbroken stream of masterpieces of modern art.

Her daily routine was simple. She rose at six in the morning in the retirement home she lived in to draw and paint on six-foot by six-foot canvases, which she made herself. After three and a half hours she went to lunch in a favourite diner, often with friends or strangers who sought her out. She went to bed at six in the evening. She said of herself, 'I get up with the light and go to bed when it gets dark, like a chicken.' She never married and didn't buy a newspaper in fifty years. She listened to CDs – Beethoven's *Ode to Joy* was a particular favourite. Her only material indulgence was a brand new white Mercedes 230E which she drove herself about in.

She said the best part of painting was when it was finished.

To stand in front of an Agnes Martin painting is to be enveloped by the exquisite proportions of the horizontal graphite lines which divide up the painting and the closely toned acrylic colour, which evokes the very air around the viewer.

This year, visitors could see a number of the works of Agnes Martin for themselves in the 3x Abstract Drawing show in the Irish Museum of Modern Art. They can also experience the vertiginous attempt at perfection, the plain and direct poetry of an Agnes Martin painting at the reopened and newly named Dublin City Gallery The Hugh Lane in Parnell Square in Dublin.

Agnes Martin died in Taos, New Mexico in December 2004. She was ninety-two.

HUGH LANE

Judith Hill

In the Hibernian Hotel in Dublin on the afternoon of 11 January
1907, the wealthy young London art dealer Hugh Lane received the
tribute of a portrait of himself by the great painter John Singer Sargent.
It shows a slim, immaculately dressed man with a pale oval face, nervous,
a slightly withdrawn expression in his large hooded eyes and Edwardian
moustache. It also portrays the self-reliance that underpinned his
success. 'I have,' his aunt, Augusta Gregory, often heard him say, 'nothing
but my taste.' It was the *fin de siècle* spirit, which valued subjective impressions and put art over life. Hugh Lane believed that a well-placed vase
was more important than a good meal. He was quick to take offence and
was the victim of nervous attacks, which epitomised many manifestations of his spirit. He was also in striking contrast to his flexible, well-
rooted aunt, with her ability to work pragmatically towards a well-
defined goal.

Since making his fortune, Lane turned his attention to Irish art, then
severely undervalued. He would later remark that with Lady Gregory for
an aunt, he was compelled to think of Ireland. But it was also true that,
being self-taught, he was keen to extend his influence by acting as a
patron and, eventually, to secure an official position in the art world. He
also had a strong desire to see art displayed in public. It was not his way
to think in general terms or to speak of the public interest, but as
Augusta Gregory quickly realised, her nephew was on a trajectory that
could contribute to the Irish cultural revival. She would define him as a
'fellow-worker', dedicated, like herself, to Ireland.

The portrait of Lane had been presented to him in recognition of his proposal to set up a gallery of contemporary art in Dublin. He had inaugurated a purchase fund with an exhibition of pictures, including his own collection of paintings (he was one of the first people outside of France to collect the work of the Impressionists), and he had promised to donate this collection of paintings when a suitable building had been found.

A year later, a temporary Municipal Gallery of Modern Art was set up in Harcourt Street in Dublin. But Lane's gift of pictures was conditional on the acquisition of a permanent structure. Adamant that the design should be of the highest quality in the best possible location, he set his heart on a building designed by the foremost architect of his day, Edward Lutyens, in Stephens Green. When Lord Ardilaun, who had presented the square to Dublin, objected, Lane, angry and resentful, divided his gift into two: the 'Lane Gift' was formally presented to Dublin, while the thirty-nine known as the 'Lane Collection' would be withdrawn by January 1913 if a 'new suitable gallery' had not been decided on.

In the early months of 1913, the issue of the gallery was rapidly becoming politicised. William Butler Yeats's poem 'To a Wealthy Man' was printed in *The Irish Times*. It criticised Lord Ardilaun and damned the people of Dublin who had not supported the idea. Having implicitly set the aristocracy against the poor, the poem provoked the nationalist William Murphy to condemn the gallery in *The Daily Express* as an unnecessary luxury at the time, when the priority should be slum clearance. Thus, when Lane proposed a graceful Lutyen's design for a gallery on a bridge over the Liffey, there were vociferous objections, strengthened by the nationalist abhorrence for an English architect. Lane responded with bitter invective and patrician scorn for what he called the 'Goths and Vandals' of 'bad taste'. When Augusta Gregory tactfully suggested alternative sites, his 'bitter tongue' was turned on her as he accused her of lacking aesthetic standards. Later that year, the corporation, which, although deeply divided, had until then supported the bridge site, voted against it. Lane was required to leave both site and design to the corporation.

Even before this defeat, Lane had made a formal loan of the thirty-nine pictures to the National Gallery in London. When he drowned as a passenger with the sinking of the *Lusitania* in 1915, Augusta Gregory discovered an unwitnessed codicil to his will that left the pictures to

Dublin. It had no legal status in England, but Augusta, undaunted by setback after setback, spent the next seventeen years trying to persuade the British establishment that there was a moral case to answer. She failed. The majority of the pictures have since returned to Ireland, but the moral point has never been ceded.

LEONARD COHEN AT SEVENTY

Catherine Ann Cullen

There's a cracked black-and-white photograph between the pages of a book in my parents' sitting room. It's a head-to-waist shot of a moody-looking man on a stage. His hair is dark and his eyes are half-closed as he sings into a bare microphone. He's holding an acoustic guitar, and you can see by the bend of his fingers that he's plucking the strings.

The singer is Leonard Cohen, and the picture was taken in March 1972 in the National Stadium in Dublin. My parents were there to hear him sing what were already classics, songs like 'Suzanne' and 'So Long, Marianne', as well as his first public rendition of 'Kevin Barry'.

In those days, my father took hundreds of photographs and developed them in a makeshift darkroom, the cupboard under the stairs. I used to gaze at Cohen's picture and imagine how pleased Dad must have been to see his image swim into life, with its stark shadows and its sense of smoky atmosphere.

Like Bob Dylan, Tom Paxton, Johnny Cash and The Beatles, Leonard Cohen was part of our growing up. In the sitting room where that photo is now a buried treasure, my father would pick out 'Suzanne' or 'Bird on the Wire' or 'Hey, That's No Way to Say Goodbye' on his guitar, and when the extended family gathered for a singsong, one or other of the uncles would add 'Chelsea Hotel' or 'The Sisters of Mercy' to the repertoire.

When I picked up a guitar myself at the age of twelve, those songs were among my early party pieces. Their distinctly unparty-like gloom gave them adolescent cred, but it was the romantic lyrics that appealed to me.

And though I loved Shakespeare and worshipped John Donne, it was Leonard Cohen who inspired me to write my first sonnet. I bought Cohen books for my dad for a succession of birthdays and Christmases, conveniently allowing me the pleasure of reading them myself. I especially enjoyed *The Spice Box of Earth*, published in Canada in 1961 but not in Europe until 1973. It contains many fine poems, several of them finer than my teenage favourite, 'Travel'.

The theme of 'Travel' is one that runs through so many early Cohen songs – a love that is compelling but temporary, that Cohen can't live with and can't live without. The poem ends with a holistic description of the way in which the love he has left stays with him: 'Horizons keep the soft line of your cheek, The windy sky's a locket for your hair.'

I'd always thought of 'Travel' as the sonnet that inspired my love of the fourteen-line form. But when I went back for a sentimental read on Cohen's seventieth birthday, I found that the poem had sixteen lines. Maths was never my strong point. Maybe I should stick to myths.

So I fished out that old photo, and held it in front of my dad. 'Joe took that,' he said, 'in the National Stadium.' (Joe is Uncle Joe, who's now a professional photographer in Drogheda.) 'Did ye enjoy the concert, anyway?' I asked. 'Well, I always loved Leonard Cohen,' my dad said. Then my mother chipped in. 'He was a bit – *leadránach*,' she said, using that great Irish word that even in English works onomatopoeically to sound long drawn out and tedious.

But there's one family link with Leonard Cohen that can't be shaken. His seventieth birthday came just a few weeks before my dad's. Happy birthday Mr Cohen, poet and pop icon and sometime *leadránach* writer of more-than-sonnets. I'm glad you're here to see seventy with the moody eyes that stare out of a photo that my father never took. And happy birthday, Dad.

COMHAIRLE PHÁDRAIG DO THADHG AN DÁ THAOBH

Tadhg Ó Dúshláine

Anois teacht an Earraigh beidh an lá ag dul chun síneadh is thart ar lá le Pádraig beidh Éireannaigh ag tarraingt ar Cheltnam –

Nó sin é an leagan nua den seanamhrán curtha in oiriúnt don oilthireacht seo thar sáile d'Fhéile na gcapall an tráth seo bliana – ceithre lá de spórt is spraoi is ragairne – faoiseamh ó na híobairtí idéalacha, an troascadh agus an tréanas sin go léir, a chuirimid romahinn don Charghas. Is maith mar a thug an file Sean Ó Riordain, an chon-trarthacht san idir tíriulacht agus spioradaltacht 'nar gcarachtar mar Éireannaigh faoi deara, sa dán magaidh ina labhrann sé leis an stail cháil-iúil sin Tulyar:

> Nach doigh leat é bheith ait
> Ceardau ded cheird, ded chlu, ded chleacht,
> A theacht ag cleachtadh ceirde anseo in ár measc
> I dtír na n-ollamh, tír na naomh
> An tír a bheannaigh Pádraig féin?

Agus go deimhin, sé an capall siombal agus sampla Tadhg an dá thaobhachais sin ionainn, an choimhlint sin idir saoirse an choirp agus srian an anama. Siombal gleoite soineanta na háilleachta agus na buaine a mbímíd faoi dhraíocht aige le linn na hóige, is ea an capall agus a mbaineann leis.

Airíonn an leanabh fuaim an chapaill, a deir an file. B'aiseann sé fuaim an chapaill ar son fuaime féin. Agus éisteann leis an bhfuaim ag dul i laghad agus ag titim siar isteach sa tost. Agus briethníonn sé cosa deiridh an chapaill agus déanann ionadh dá n-údaras is dá seandacht. Agus líontar an saol de chapall-alltacht agus de shodardhraíocht. Sin bheith – bheith faoi ghné eile. Agus sin, dar liom, filíocht.

Ach ní ar an fhilíocht amháin a mháirimid agus bíonn an gnáthbhraca laethúil prósúil go maith, codarsnacht nár mhiste, mar go cuireann sé beocht sa tsaol, faoi mar a thugann an mórfhile eile le fios: *if all the year were playing holidays, to sport would be as tedious as to work.*

Ná ní bhíonn rith maith leis an each i gcónaí, agus ba mhaith mar a thuig aspal mór na hÉireann gurb í an tsíorchoimhlint seo idir capall an choirp agus marcach an anama an dúshlán mór a bhí roimhe, tar éis teacht inár measc dó. B'é teagasc Phádraig dúinn na go gcaithfidh an t-anam a bheith i gceannas, faoi mar a bheadh marcach, ar chapall an choirp, má táimid leis an gcraobh a bhreith linn i ndeireadh na rásaíochta go léir. Bí an oidhreacht a d'fhág sé againn ná go bhféadfaimís an gheallúint seo a bhí sa chapall dúchais a thabhairt chun foirfeachta, le trenáil is le treoir. Agus is chuige sin a bhí criú Phádraig, faoi mar a chímead sa dán cliste a chum an sagart, d'fhonn a theachtaireacht a chur abhaile ar lucht na gcapall. Tosnaíonn sé amach faoi mar a bheadh sé ag gléasadh capaill: 'Cuir srian lem chorp, a Dhia', a achainíonn sé, agus leanann air ag cur adhastar na haithrí, béalbhach na déirce agus srathair an chreidimh faoin ainmhí chun an teaspach ann a cheansú. Anuas ar sin buaileann sé díolait an dóchais agus srian na collaíochta chun barr feabhais a chur ar an dtraenáil.

Ba mhaith mar a thuig Pádraig go gcuireann an capall ionann stailc suas, go n-imíonn ar ruathar aonair agus go dtagann amach ar fad ón gcairt ar uairbh fiú. Agus thuig sé, ar an láimh eile, go dtéann an marcach thar fóir uaireannta chomh maith, ag lascadh agus ag ceangal an chapaill chun go ndéanfaidh sé a réir. Is maith mar a thuig Pádraig an fiantas ionainn nuair a thug sé éisteacht d'Oisín ag cur síos ar mhianta Fhionn Mhic Chumhaill:

Mian mhic Chumhaill ba hárd gnaoi:
Éisteacht le faoidh Droma deirg,
Fleadh Almhaine i measc na ndámh,
Ba hiad sin go brath a mhian.

Agus is maith mar a chuir sé ar ár súile dúinn ná beidh rith an ráis i gcónaí linn agus mar ná bíonn tréan buan:

A Oisín, 's fada do shuan / éirigh suas is éist an salm.

'Se tá le baint as san go léir ná gur i dteannta a chéile is fearr iad – capall an dúchais agus srianta an chreidimh. Lá dár saol inniu, Lá le Pádraig, lá maíte is mórtais – faoi thuairim ár seanaigne déanaim ólachán; éistimís le mianta an dúchais agus amárach, casaimís an athuair ar dhéanamh ár n-anama.

AT THE HEART OF THE RIDICULOUS, THE SUBLIME

Josephine McArdle

I came across Lawrence Oates in the lines of a poem, and ever since then I've been haunted by the enigma of his famous valedictory remark. He was just going outside, he said, and may be some time. That was on the nineteenth of March 1912, and, in his stockinged feet, he crept out of his tent, in blizzard conditions of less than minus forty degrees. It was his thirty-second birthday.

Derek Mahon's poem 'Antarctica' celebrates the self-sacrifice of the weakest man in Scott's polar expedition who went willingly to his death, in the belief that it would give his comrades a better chance of getting through. His portrait of Captain Lawrence Oates once again elevates him to the realm of true hero.

But who was this man? Why had he chosen to explore the frozen landscape of Antarctica? And who did he leave behind him when he boarded the *Terra Nova* in Cardiff on 10 June 1910 and sailed towards the Southern Ocean, the most dangerous waters on Earth?

Lawrence Oates was not a man who craved the spotlight. He was a quintessential reluctant hero. A cavalry officer in the Inniskilling Dragoons, having trained at the regimental headquarters in the Curragh of Kildare, he was in service in India when he learned of Robert Scott's intentions to reach the South Pole and claim the honour of conquest for Britain. He paid a thousand pounds for the privilege of being a member of the historic party. He would take care of the ponies what would haul the sledges across the frozen surface.

Horses were his greatest passion. As an Eton schoolboy, Titus, as he was affectionately known, came alive on the sports field. He was dominated by his mother, Caroline, who believed that an expensive public school education would guarantee academic excellence for her baby boy. However, the young Oates struggled with dyslexia and his scholarly record was pitiful and humiliating. His sole ambition was to forge himself a career in the army. His taste for adventure was inherited from his father, who himself had followed in the footsteps of Livingstone on lengthy journeys of research deep into Africa. After the death of his father, Laurence, at sixteen years of age and the eldest of four children, became the lord of the manor at Gestingthorpe in Essex. However, he never became more than a notional head of the family, since his mother exercised rigid control of the family expenses.

By the age of nineteen he was the very essence of the tall, dark and handsome Victorian gentleman. It was around this time that he met Henrietta Learmont, the thirteen-year-old daughter of a master builder and a former domestic servant. Whether or not his mother had heard of his dalliance with young Henrietta is unclear. However, the following year, around the time Henrietta secretly gave birth to her little girl, tucked away in a remote part of Ireland, Laurie's mother whisked her son off on a tour of the Caribbean.

The little girl was raised by two former nurses in a special home for unwanted children of unmarried mothers in north London. She was named Kathleen Gray. In time, Henrietta put the experience behind her and married well. She changed her name to Toby Cooper. Kathleen grew up watched from a discreet distance by the wealthy patron of the Wright-Kingsford Home, none other than Mrs Toby Cooper herself. Kathleen, or Kit as she became known, was brought up in the belief that both her parents were dead. Only after her marriage in 1926 did she discover the true identity of her father. She immediately tried to establish contact with the Oates family, but when she arrived on Caroline Oates's doorstep in Gestingthorpe and confronted her with the news that she was her son's child, the stern woman refused to entertain her or see her again. Kit kept the secrecy of her parentage for over thirty years. She had a son, John, and a daughter, Gill, both of whom she brought to see Charles's friend's film *Scott of the Antarctic* at the Odeon in Leicester

Square, London in 1948. On arriving in the foyer they were confronted by life-size cut-out figures of Scott's ill-fated polar party. Unaware of the family connection, they were nonetheless immediately struck by the stark likeness between Captain Oates and the young John. It was a strange experience, Gill recalled years later: 'It could have been John standing there in cut-out.'

It is a deeply tragic and poignant tale, the story of a young officer who never knew of his own daughter's existence, and the young woman who guarded the secret of her identity, tight lipped and resolute, in memory of a great man.

Derek Mahon concludes his poem 'Antarctica' with the words:

> *He takes leave of the earthly pantomime*
> *Quietly, knowing it is time to go.*
> *'I am just going outside and may be some time.'*
> *At the heart of the ridiculous, the sublime.*

THE TALLEST LEPRECHAUN IN IRELAND

Brian Thunder

For four years running, I held the record of being the tallest leprechaun in Ireland. I stand at a height of six foot two and a half inches in my bare feet. Add to the equation a tall stovepipe hat and the high heels of my brogues, and as a leprechaun, I was close to an impressive seven foot. I held this record on St Patrick's Day as a performer in the Dublin parade, working with a company called Theatre of Fire. The first project we did involved leprechauns, and every year after that we included a leprechaun element no matter what theme the parade took.

The thinking behind this was that leprechauns are a quintessentially Irish phenomenon and deserving of celebration, and that by incorporating them every year we would produce some kind of brand image for our element of the parade: we would be the pageant that always had leprechauns. From year to year our leprechauns would always reinvent themselves. They were themed to the float they would accompany.

We had aviator leprechauns accompanying a giant bi-plane, playboy bunny-girl leprechauns accompanying a Las Vegas magician being pulled out of a hat by a giant rabbit. The possibilities were endless.

I'm certain I was the tallest leprechaun during all that time, as I came across only one other one in the whole parade and he was considerably shorter. In the last few years, I have been a commentator at one of the grand stands on the route and can confidently claim that my record stands, as I have not seen a single leprechaun in the parade since I stopped performing in it.

So where have all the leprechauns gone?

My personal theory is that we are embarrassed by the imagery of them. This is unfortunate, as here is a rich part of our culture that is unique to us. Bríd Mahon, in her 1992 memoir *While Green Grass Grows*, of her time spent working for the Irish Folklore Commission, displays a particular fondness for the leprechauns as the author of a popular children's book called *Loo the Leprechaun*. The Irish Folklore Commission was established at a time when the richness in our culture was in danger of being lost. While the work of its collectors has preserved our knowledge of this culture, unfortunately our living links to much of it have all but disappeared. For the people who shared their stories and traditions to the Commission, leprechauns, the little people or the *Sí*, were not some imaginary works of the imagination. Many of them firmly believed in their existence. Building on fairy rings or cutting down a white thorn tree were considered not just superstitious but dangerous courses of action that would antagonise the little people into seeking revenge.

Mythology shares confusion between historical fact and fanciful imaginary distortion. Many people today have no problem imagining that Cúchulainn, Fionn Mac Cumhail and the Fianna must have their origin in some fact. The mythology of leprechauns probably cannot survive when no one is prepared to admit that a race of little people ever existed. And yes, leprechauns might just as well have had their origin in the low-statured people of the Tuatha De Danainn who were supposed to have lived here before the arrival of the Celts.

In her book, Brid Mahon relates a crucial moment when our accepted image of the leprechaun was redefined by American culture. In 1946, the Irish Folklore Commission was visited by Walt Disney, of all people. He had come on a visit to Ireland with the express purpose, according to Mahon, of meeting a leprechaun. The Commission indulged Disney's request and its director, Seamus Delargy, accompanied him on a trip around Ireland, introducing him to people whose belief in the existence of leprechauns was as strong as Disney's. Ultimately, he was disappointed in his quest to meet a leprechaun, but he did return to the United States with his knowledge of the little people increased and a copy of Mahon's children's stories. For some time she harboured hopes of this book turning into a Hollywood movie. Her book was never used and Disney's trip ultimately resulted in the production of *Darby O'Gill and the Little People*, a film saved only by the performance of Jimmy O'Dea as Brian, King of the Little People.

Disney's image of the leprechaun prevails to this day, and surely it is long overdue for us to reimagine them. My own favourite has been that of a Hell's Angel leprechaun on a miniature motorbike chasing St Patrick on a giant Harley Davidson.

WILLIAM DARGAN'S HOUSE

Cathleen Brindley

Our present preoccupation with public transport brings to mind the name of William Dargan, the great builder of our railways. In 1851, Dargan saw a house and fell in love with it. It was perched on a hill near Dundrum, County Dublin and was surrounded by beautiful gardens. The late-eighteenth-century house had originally belonged to Lord Trimelston and had been called Rowbuck Hill, but had passed through the hands of several owners by the time Dargan saw it. The name of the townland on the 1836 Ordnance Survey Map was Mountainville, later to become Mount Anville, which is what the house is called to this day. As soon as he bought it, Dargan set about enlarging and improving it. With the help of his railway architect, John Skipton Mulvany, he turned an eighteenth-century house into an Italianate villa. The most striking addition was a campanile, or more precisely, a viewing tower from which uninterrupted views could be had over the whole of Dublin Bay, towards the mountains behind, as well as over the magnificent gardens and woods of the estate itself.

One of the high points of his ownership of the house came in 1853, when Queen Victoria, in Dublin to visit the Great Exhibition on Leinster Lawn, which had largely been financed by Dargan, decided to pay him a visit. In early September 1853, carriages carrying the queen, the prince consort, two of the princes, the lord lieutenant and other notables trotted up the drive to call on Mr and Mrs Dargan at Dargan Villa, as he then called Mount Anville. Everything was just right. The day was fine and the tide was in, so Dublin Bay looked at its best. The queen, in a green silk dress, primrose gauze bonnet and a favourite white shawl, skipped briskly up the stairs of the tower, followed by the whole party. They were charmed by the view and before leaving she offered a baronetcy to William Dargan, which he politely refused. She then planted a tree, a sequoia, in front of the house which is still there today, a towering giant.

Unhappily, in 1865, failing health, the result of a fall from a horse, forced Dargan to sell his beloved Mount Anville and to return to his house in Fitzwilliam Square. The new owners were the nuns of the Sacred Heart, a French order invited to Ireland some years previously by Cardinal Cullen. They built on a school wing which in no way impinged on Dargan's magnificent house. When I was at school there, we children did not penetrate the old house except on Sunday afternoons, when parents and family visited and we were summoned to the 'parlour', as the beautiful reception rooms were called. These rooms were full of light, as their windows looked out over the terraced gardens, with their urns and cast-iron balustrade. The impressive entrance to the house is through a Doric-style portico into a small outer hall, which in turn leads into the most striking feature of the house. This is a large inner hall with a grand staircase to the right. This inner hall rises to the full height of the house and is lit by two domed roof lanterns. A gallery runs around the hall at first-floor level, which gives access to the bedrooms.

But it is the gardens with their exotic planting which remain in my memory. First and foremost, there was the Cedar Grounds with a number of cedars of Lebanon and a huge deodar tree, its boughs sweeping the ground and forming a large room-like space where we juniors invented all kinds of games. Beyond the cedars was a tulip tree, a mulberry, walnuts, arbutus, Spanish chestnuts and many others. A raised walk, called the High Terrace, gave an overview of the gardens, and further down the grounds was an avenue of many varieties of holly.

The exotic planting certainly predated Dargan's ownership of the house and can probably be dated to the Trimelston family. Sadly, though inevitably, there are changes to the gardens, which I probably saw in their original state. In 1965 the cedars had to come down as they were in a dangerous condition. The High Terrace made way for a retirement home for an ageing community. Much of the land was sold, so that where once the terraced gardens looked out over fields and woods, the roofs of houses are now visible. But there are survivors. The deodar tree under which we played still stands sentinel, though deprived of its lower branches. The mulberry whose berries we picked off the grass to eat is still there, as is the avenue of hollies.

Dargan's spirit must be glad that his house is still in perfect condition, and I feel that the great transport entrepreneur would have been fascinated by our newest form of transport, the Luas, which runs not far from his house, Mount Anville.

'IS GLAS IAD NA CNOIC ...'

Pat Butler

Ní gach lá den tseachtain agus mé ar bharr sléibhe – ach go háirithe ar an seachtú lá déag Márta, i bhfad i gcéin, 12,188 troig ós cionn an Atlantaigh. Gile na gréine, munarb í a teas, ina lóchrann beannaithe – caidhp Dé timpeall orm. B'fhiú tréigint na dtránna dubha gainí agus boigeacht na haeráide cois cuain don léargas a shín amach ós mo chomhair.

Ní im aonair a bhíos ar bharr Tenerife an Lá le Pádraig naofa sin. Thóg scata turasóir eile an seáp minibus intíre liom – teangacha forleathna na hEorpa ar a mbeolaibh – chun barr Sliabh Teide a bhaint amach. Dá mba eachtra dóibh siúd é – oilithreacht a bhí ann dom. Isteach linn sa mboth-chábla chun an míle go leith troig deiridh a chur dinn. Lá i measc na gceithre bhfichidí a bhí ann, sinn crochta ós cionn an tsléibhe is airde sa Chomhphobal.

Agus leothaine fionnfhuar na nGaoithe Trádála um thionlacan, ligeas uaim, ós íseal, admhaím, leath véarsa cúthalach de 'Dóchas Linn Naomh Pádraig'. D'ardaigh mo mhisneach fán dtráth go dtángas chomh fada le 'Sé do chlaoi na draoithe', agus ligeas amach go dásachtach é. Níor Shliabh Mis ná Cruach Phadraig a bhí agam, ach thug beann volcánach Teide altóir choisricthe dom an lá céanna.

Bhraitheas níos fearr ina dhiaidh sin go raibh ómos ceart tugtha do phátrún spioradálta an Náisiúin Ghaelaigh. Níor thug mo chompánaigh aon cheann don mbriseadh amach ceolmhar seo – ní folair nó go bhfuair béasa agus carthannacht araon an lámh in uachtar ar a mbreithiúnas!

Agus siar liom ar aistear samhlaíochtúil sa minibus ar ball agus sinn ag tabhairt aghaidh arís ar na hóstáin chósta as a dtángamar ar maidin. Bhíos ar ais i gcistin na hóige, ina raibh an deatach móna mar thúis bheannaithe inár dtimpeall, tráth a mbíodh deasghnáthaí seanda eile á gcomhlíonadh againn, sceitimíní orm féin is ar mo dheartháir fá choinne na féile le teacht.

Réitigh Bridie na boscaí beaga seamróige chun iad a cur an cuan amach thar lear chucu san ar linne iad – Mary agus Bridget agus mo sheanathair William i Londain – an tSiúr Rosario – Molly a thugadh mo mháthair riamh uirthi – ar dualgas saoil le hOrd na Toirbhirte ar ardchlár Dhubh-Chnoic Dakota Theas; Humphrey, an 'Boston Labouring Boy' – Nora bocht, nár réitigh Nua Eabhrach léi in aon chor, agus John, an siúinéir ab fhearr i New Jersey – an peata deartháir ba ghoire do mo mháthair riamh anall. Thugadh sí suntas speisialta dá bhosca siúd, an seamróg ba úire istigh ann, an craobhóg ba dheise díobh ar fad.

Sna caogadaí agus sinn óg, chaithimís lá amuigh fán dtuath ag seilg na seamróige. Lá le sean-spiúnóga, sceana agus forcanna chun fómhar an phlanda dhraíochta a bhaint is a cur isteach. Níorbh fhada gur foghlaimíos an difríocht idir seamróg agus seamair. 'Tá an tseamair i bhfad Éireann níos má ná an seamróg,' deireadh Daid, 'níor mhaith linn na gaolta a mhaslú le fiaile gharbh thuatach in áit na seamróige néata.'

Bhí sé tábhachtach na préamha a thabhairt slán, an cré ina alt timpeall orthu – cothú don aistear fada thar sáile. Leagtaí na craobhóga mar dá ba leanbh leochailleach gach ceann díobh, ina sraitheanna sínte ar leaba féir i mála, coisriche le deora uisce fá choinne an aistir abhaile chun na cathrach ar bhus Bhun an tSábhairne. Bhíodh na fuinneoga tais le ceofrán ón dteas istigh agus ón bhfuacht lasmuigh, agus ligtí domhsa, an páiste ab óige, suí in aice ná fuinneoige agus laoch mo roghasa – Dan Dare, Desperate Dan, Korky the Cat, nó, agus me níos críonna , Biggles agus Algy ag troid in aghaidh na Huns a tharraingt lem mhéar ar thaise na fuinneoige …

'Sin La Gomera amuigh on gcósta,' a deir tiomanaí an minibus, 'bhí teach ansin ag Colombus agus is as a chuir sé chun farraige ar a aistear cinniúnach go Meiriceá … '

Briseadh ar mo aislingiú – bhíomar ag tarraingt ar chósta theas Tenerife agus ní raibh ach fiche neomat idir sinn agus compórd cúig réalt an óstáin. B'shin an tráth seo bliana anuraidh.

Táid uile anois ar shlí na fírinne – Mam agus Daid, mo dheartháir Liam, na haintíní is na huncail go léir, gach éinne imithe, seachas Bridget i Londain. Raghad amach inniu le mo ghar-iníon Saidbh ag seilg na seamróige arís. Seolfad chuig Bridget í, aintin a bhfuil an ceithre scór go leith aici. Ráiteas beag na féiniúlachta ath-múscailte, ar son na muintire a d'imigh romhainn, ar son an leanúnachais, ar son Bridget, ach, go príomhga, ar mo shon féin …

APRIL

FREE STATE

Gerard Smyth

for John McGahern

Saying Goodbye at the airport
you speak of destinations on that far shore,
of distance that wearies the jet age traveller
and the long journey ahead
through all the beautiful cities.
Cities like stories waiting to be read.

But I am happy
motoring through the Free State,
the Glebe Road where O'Carolan dragged his harp,
the hilly landscape where on some days
the lake is radiant and very still.
On other days it is like a page
of thumbprints, dull and marked
by cloud shadow
and the meadow-dust of Leitrim.

BECKETT COUNTRY

Tim Carey

I can't claim to be a literary aficionado. In fact, I got a middle C in honours Leaving Cert English – twice – and my first serious book purchase was only made when I was eighteen after winning £37 in a late-night poker session. The next day the coins were strewn across the counter of a Dún Laoghaire bookshop as I clutched my trawl of paper-backs.

The interest I developed in literature comes partly from my mother, friends and teachers. But I also think it comes from the fact that I live in what is possibly the most literary county in Ireland. Dún Laoghaire-Rathdown, a makey-uppy county created in 1994 out of the break-up of the old Dublin County Council and Dún Laoghaire borough, is not one that rolls off the literary tongue. But it is a unique literary landscape.

A quick tour will give you some idea. Looking north to Booterstown, Blackrock and Monkstown, there is Frank McGuinness and the Marsh, grenades thrown by Paul Carson in Blackrock, *The Quiet Man* Maurice Walsh, the house where Flann O'Brien wrote *At Swim Two Birds*. Looking further there is Leo Cullen, Gerald Dawe, Marian Keyes, Sarah Webb, Marita Conlon McKenna, Val Mulkerns, Nuala Ní Dhomhnaill, Martina Devlin, Eamon Delaney, Liam Ó Muirthile and so many more. Walk south past the Mariner's Church where the grand-father of another local writer, Julie Parsons, was once canon. Then move on towards the Mecca of Irish literature, Joyce's Tower in Sandycove, inland a few paces to where L.A.G. Strong spent glorious summers, then a short hop to where Hugo Hamilton, *The Speckled Boy*, grew up and Joseph O'Connor, who often passed the speckled boy. Up the hill beyond Fitzgerald's pub, pass the road where Denis Johnston lived, another where Synge lived and Monk Gibbon. Move on to Dalkey for the second chapter of *Ulysses*, and where Hugh Leonard was *Home Before Night* and *Out after Dark*, where Flann O'Brien proposed his molleycule theory of bicycles and police, and where George Bernard Shaw lived part of his childhood. Then go up to Killiney and Paul Murray's *Evening of Long Goodbyes* and down to Deansgrange and Clonkeen Road where Colum McCann was born and raised ... a unique literary landscape, all in an afternoon's walk.

At the top of Clonkeen Road, you could continue another mile up Cornelscourt Hill from Cabinteely to Cooldrinagh, the home of Samuel Beckett. But what had Beckett to do with these surroundings? There is little to root him in a geographical reality. He was a man of ideas who, at times, would not even let his actors move on stage. A closer reading of Beckett's work reveals the remarkable influence of this part of Dublin in particular. It occupies a paramount role in what Eoin O'Brien has called 'Beckett Country'. As Beckett revealed late in his life, 'the old haunts were never more present' and 'I walk those backroads with closed eyes'.

A significant landmark used by Beckett to evoke an experience at Greystones Harbour that would change the direction of his writing is Dún Laoghaire's East Pier. There, Beckett recounts in *Krapp's Last Tape* the struggle to establish himself as a writer and where, one spring equinox, came the revelation, 'suddenly I saw the whole thing', that Beckett would use himself as his own literary subject.

Malone Dies reaches its macabre climax when a party of lunatics take a boat trip to Dalkey Island. The events in *All That Fall* occur on the day of a race meeting in Leopardstown racecourse, with much of the action taking place in Foxrock train station (known as Boghill station in the book). Although he was careful not to pinpoint a precise location for *Waiting for Godot*, the often bleak and windswept landscape he encountered on his walks in the Dublin Mountains must have been an inspirational mood setting for it. The quarries at Glencullen and Barnacullia are remembered in *First Love*.

Beckett tramped the hills, fields and lanes of the Dublin Mountains with his father. They would climb the Glencullen Road. The first thing they had to do, of course, when they got to the top was to admire the view, with special reference to Dún Laoghaire, framed to perfection in the shoulders of Three Rock and Kilmashogue, the long arms of the harbour like an entreaty in the blue sea. It is just a few miles from these peaks to the coast of Dún Laoghaire-Rathdown. Surely there can't be any area more densely populated with writers, their memories and works than these.

SAMUEL BECKETT AND GEORGE REAVEY

Sandra O'Connell

The Closerie des Lilas was a little off the beaten track from the popular cafés in Paris's literary quarter, Montparnasse. Unlike Le Dôme, La Coupole or La Rotonde, which were buzzing with young and hopeful avant-garde writers and artists, the Closerie was an ordinary workman's place. It had been a favourite haunt of Ernest Hemingway, who described it in his memoir *A Movable Feast* as his 'nearest good café' where 'no one was on exhibition'. There among the regulars – in Hemingway's words 'elderly bearded men in well worn clothes who came with their wives or their mistresses' – one could frequently spot two young Irishmen in the early 1930s engrossed in a game of pool – Samuel Beckett and George Reavey.

Reavey, who had arrived in Paris in 1929 (a year after Beckett) after graduating from Cambridge, came from an intriguing cosmopolitan background. The son of a Northern Irish father and a Polish mother, Reavey had been born in 1907 in Russia, where his father had made a career in the booming linen industry. The October Revolution and ensuing civil war forced the Reavey family to return to Belfast, before eventually settling in London. In Paris, Reavey lived a precarious existence, sharing a studio in an artists' commune with the English painter Julian Trevelyan, who later wrote that they 'cooked each other great meals of spaghetti' and that 'Sam Beckett was a constant visitor'. The red-headed and red-bearded George Reavey was an experimental poet and a literary enthusiast. Not only was he a steady companion during Beckett's first years in Paris, he was also to have considerable influence on Beckett's development as a writer.

Within a few years of his arrival, Reavey had set up, together with Russian émigré Marc Slonim, a literary agency in the heart of Paris's Left Bank. The appropriately entitled European Literary Bureau was busily signing up authors from the French Surrealists to the Russian Futurists, which Reavey and Slonim placed with British publishers. Owing to his growing literary influence in Paris, Reavey was able to recommend his friend Samuel Beckett when the American publisher Samuel Putnam looked for contributors to his ambitious anthology of Modernist literature, *The European Caravan* (1931), and when Edward Titus required a skilful translator of French Surrealist poems for his magazine, *This Quarter* (1932).

'Fed up with English publishers at the time ... [who] were always turning down books of poems, not only by me, but by various other of my poet friends,' as Reavey explained in an interview with Beckett biographer James Knowlson, he 'decided to see what [he] could do about it' and started his own publishing house, Europa Press, in Paris in 1935. One of Reavey's first projects was a collection of poems by his friend Beckett, entitled *Echo's Bones and Other Precipitates*. Although Beckett had published a Proust monograph in 1932 and a collection of short stories, *More Pricks than Kicks*, in 1934, his London publishers turned down his poems, as did several others. The publication of *Echo's Bones* was, however, highly important to Beckett, who tried to break away from the perception that he was purely an imitator of James Joyce. For example, Richard Aldington, an influential writer and critic at the time, described Beckett as a 'splendidly mad Irishman who was James Joyce's white boy'.

In November 1935, Reavey's Europa Press published *Echo's Bones and Other Precipitates* in a small but beautifully produced edition of 327 copies. While Beckett was delighted with Reavey's achievement in seeing the book through, he grew increasingly frustrated when copies failed to appear in bookshops, as his biographer Deirdre Bair reports:

> Beckett was livid with anger ... and fired off a series of
> caustic letters to Reavey demanding to know why the book
> had not been distributed. Reavey sent soothing but evasive

replies, saying copies had been sent to all major stores in England and Ireland, and that all appropriate periodicals had been flooded with review copies as well.

Yet their friendship survived these turbulent times and, in 1937, Beckett turned again to his friend for advice when he sought a publisher for his novel *Murphy*. Beckett had written and set the story about a down-and-out and prostitute in a London bed-sit. After sending the manuscript unsuccessfully around several publishers, he turned to Reavey for help. Reavey undoubtedly brought new energy to Beckett's frustrated efforts but he faced a difficult task, as a succession of publishing houses regarded *Murphy* as too obscene, too obscure or too complex in its form and narrative. Others expressed initial interest but demanded that Beckett cut (what they considered) offensive content and phrases. In all, forty-two publishers rejected *Murphy*, and according to Deirdre Bair, Beckett kept 'first in jest, then grimly … a neat, handwritten list of publishers who had rejected the novel'. Bair, who met Beckett in person on several occasions during the research stages of her biography, recalls that 'the intensity of his anger and hurt at its continuous rejection was such that he could barely bring himself to talk about it as late as 1973.'

George Reavey finally succeeded in persuading the English literary and art critic Herbert Read, who had started as a reader with the London publishing house Routledge, to take on the book. When *Murphy* finally appeared in 1938, the publishers were anxious to advertise the book's humorous Irish side, telling readers: 'This novel comes from Ireland, but it is written in a more pungent, hilarious, ecstatic style while still displaying the characteristic waywardness and charm of the Irish.'

Despite forty-two rejections, Reavey defended and promoted a work that was perceived as difficult and obscure at the time by many of Britain's and America's literary leaders, but that he regarded as exceptional. Following Reavey's move to New York in the late 1950s, he began once more to promote his friend's work and was instrumental in the first American publication of *Murphy* by Barney Rossett's Grove Press.

The publication of *Echo's Bones* and *Murphy* is a testament to Reavey's dedication to Beckett and his expert judgement as a literary agent and publisher. Reavey's untiring, selfless efforts earned him Beckett's lifelong friendship, admiration and enduring loyalty.

THE FATE OF FELTRIM HILL

Arnold Horner

It had been known to the ancients as Faoil Druim, the Hill of the Wolves, and in the unhurried decades around the start of the twentieth century, it was well known to exploring cyclists and walkers. In one of his earlier works, Samuel Beckett sent Bellaqua and Winnie walking there. He describes the view from the summit through their eyes. It is the landscape of north County Dublin.

Although less than 200 feet in altitude, Feltrim Hill, near Swords, has had a prominence that belies this statistic. This was partly because of its local status as a focal point enhanced by the great windmill on its summit. Some authorities indicate that the windmill was built with Dutch brick around 1668. But there was also an earlier windmill, as this is shown on William Wright's Down Survey map drawn in 1655.

When I was first introduced to Feltrim, forty years ago, it was because of its geology. The Feltrim limestone, I was told, was highly rich in fossils and dated from the carboniferous period in geological times – roughly 3,000 million years ago. More specifically, it was being described as a 'Waulsortian reef-knoll', of which there are a number in the Dublin area. Today, I am told that it is more correct to describe Feltrim as a carbonate mud-mound, not a reef-knoll. For me, at least, it is fascinating to think that, although identical in their formative processes, carbonate mounds of a size comparable to Feltrim are still in active formation. Recent off-shore mapping has revealed the existence of such mounds as huge underwater hills on the continental shelf off Ireland.

Today, the landscape around Feltrim, and indeed Feltrim itself, has changed greatly from that survey by Bellaqua and Winnie. Now you see less the tessarae of small fields, and more a vista increasingly fractured and pockmarked by a mish-mash of building – housing estates, bunga-low villas, warehouses and sheds and, of course, the construction cranes – the hallmark of an encroaching Celtic Tiger.

And the hill itself is changed utterly. Its landmark windmill, long disused but nonetheless a feature that had stood for over 300 years, is now no more. During the night of 23 October 1973 its collapse occurred in mysterious circumstances – an act of destruction which, though trivial compared to the fall-out from the Middle East war then in progress, was nonetheless something of a local landscape disaster.

All that's left of the windmill is its base, and all that is left of Feltrim Hill is a much-scarred rocky crag. Small quarries had long been in use on the hill to supply needs, but over the last sixty years, these have expanded and merged, and Feltrim Hill has been carried away to supply the needs of a voracious building industry and a booming city.

Today, the limestone of Feltrim, formed by the accumulation of countless small organisms on the mud-mounds of 300 years ago, are spread out across the housing estates of north Dublin. They lie under motorways and under the runways at Dublin Airport. Most of what was once the Hill of Wwolves has now become a large hole, in places perhaps 150 feet deep. Feltrim Hill has made the ultimate sacrifice by providing trillions of atomised particulates in the interests of progress.

If he were alive today and were to contemplate the Feltrim Hill he once described, Samuel Beckett might surely permit a flicker of expres-sion to penetrate his blankness. Like the fate foreshadowed in Beckett's *Endgame*, much of Feltrim Hill is now specks in the void, in the dark, forever.

A RELIGIOUS EXPERIENCE

Leo Cullen

The plan that Good Friday was for my brother and me to ride the ponies to Mullinahone Church. There was where Father Sweeney, the most interesting curate in any parish of Ireland, ministered. There he kept his stable of ponies. There, in the village of Mullinahone, beneath the mountain of Slievenamon, where Charles Kickham based his great book of *Knocknagow* or *The Homes of Tipperary*, there we were to take the ponies.

Knocknagow may not have meant a lot to me right at that time of my life, but Father Sweeney certainly did. As well as stabling ponies, in the summer months he also stabled boys like me, like me and my brother and the sons of other horsey men, who he coached in the elements of horsemanship. And we had a ready supply of tutors to show us the finer points of sitting firm in a saddle, for there he also, at all times, stabled a few broken-down jockeys, small, wiry men broken with bad wind or with drink; men who threatened violence on him because by confining them to base he prevented them bursting out for a cure, threats that had about as much effect on him as the breezes that blew past the VW Beetle car he whined around in all day. With all these activities, did he ever have time to say mass? He did. Every day he said mass, but he was often last to arrive for his own service and often you could see his riding jodhpurs beneath his vestments. And what else was there about this attractive figure of my early days? He had a brilliant smile; his face lit up when he smiled, for in his mouth glowed a gold tooth. Yes, and at funerals I often saw him: that sense of humour of his, with which he could drag grief-stricken mourners at gravesides back to the land of sanity.

So we were riding two ponies to Mullinahone. We would tether them at the church gates and nip in for the vigil, where we would be joined by the rest of my family, who would have driven there. That was the plan.

My brother Edward was a good horseman. He kept a firm seat in his saddle and he wore his hard riding-hat with enthusiasm. I would not wear a riding-hat. I was embarrassed that friends might see me on the road. Edward did not care about that sort of thing. Edward rode the bay cob, more horse than pony. Edward could hack a mount along at a good and steady pace, and that he did. I rode Grey-boy. I was a timid horse rider. Horses like to have confidence in their riders, like to know who is boss, and Grey-boy, a flighty if well-bred animal who shied from his own shadow, did not have confidence in me. But on this Good Friday, breezy day that it was, road dry and hard, my Grey-boy was behaving himself and I trotted happily along as I watched the cob swish her tail before me. Clip clop, clip clop. 'Hello Mister, hello Missus' I was able to say to people who watched as we passed by, was able to wave at the cars that slowed down for us. How peaceful it is to ride upon the road, I was able to say to myself. My, I may even have had time to reflect on the sombre hour that was approaching: the ordeal of our Saviour.

Then I saw it. A long way up the road, I saw it lift in the breeze and come floating, like a Turkish carpet, around the bend out of Mullinahone. Dry and wafting in the breeze, a large sheet of newspaper, the page of a Sunday newspaper it must have been, at just about the level of a pony's head. I twined the reins around my fingers and said a prayer, 'Calm now, Grey-boy,' and I just knew that Grey-boy was going to shy and that Edward's cob was not.

When the page floated into his vision he bucked like a rocket across the road, and even as his hooves skidded like on glass I was on my way out of the saddle. Up, and out, my bare head plunging into the road. Stars, yes, there were stars, as I heard the deep core of the earth echo within my skull. Edward grabbed at Grey-boy's reins even as my head spun in a strange ellipse. I remounted and rode into Mullinahone and felt the cold grip of day like never before.

Father Sweeney was arriving at the church gates. He disentangled Grey-boy's martingale and bridle, come undone by my fall. 'Whoa boy,' he said and looked searchingly at me.

We knelt. It was all wood, Mullinahone church – balcony, floors, pulpit, pews, made of wood. The service began, the statues hidden behind their purple drapes for the holy hour. All was muted. But then, just when it should have come to the darkest moment, three o'clock, the sun beamed in the window. My headache rang through me. I swooned as I beheld the figures of the holy vision, as the sun that was not supposed to begin its dance until Easter Morning took off on a mad skite. And I passed out.

Then Father Sweeney was standing before me, my father, mother, brothers, sisters all standing around and I was seated on a tombstone outside the church. 'What happened, young horseman?' he asked. I told him of my beatific vision. His fingers trawled across the top of my head like he was reading Braille and he felt the lump there, now at its most engorged.

'Whoopee,' he whistled and he smiled and that gold tooth in his mouth caught light. 'Young horseman,' he said, 'you have had a religious experience.' Then he pressed hard on the painful lump. It was his way of saying something to me and I knew it; his way of saying that unless I held a firmer seat on my pony's saddle, life would hold further religious experiences for me.

EASTER MYSTERIES

Mary Coll

I've always felt more than a little outraged on behalf of Easter, over-shadowed as it is by the showy excesses of Christmas, with all its pres-sures and hype, when in fact it has far more to offer and comes at exactly the right time of year. From a Christian perspective the events of Holy Week are far more dramatic and mystical than the relative simplicity of the nativity. Dark, intense rituals, full of powerful symbolism, statues covered in purple cloth, empty tabernacles, the washing of feet, the veneration of the cross, Pascal fires, and then the extraordinary finale of the Resurrection. No wonder some of the best festivals and carnivals in the world centre around them, with cities and towns across Europe and Latin America coming to a standstill for Easter processions that make the onlooker feel as if the Middle Ages only came to an end last Thursday. All this magic, and without the need to buy presents, send cards, decorate the house, dance around your handbag with the new trainee from accounts, plus four to five days' paid leave and a licence to eat chocolate. It's impossible not to feel that somebody somewhere hasn't utterly failed Easter as far as marketing is concerned.

Christmas is all about conformity, doing it by the book, eating certain things at certain times with certain sauces or else the sky will fall, whereas at Easter you can eat soggy tomato sandwiches up a tree for all anyone cares, once you find some way of celebrating the first real holiday of the new year, with its promise of summer just around the corner again.

For me it's a certain smell that does it every time, not the cloying, sticky scent of pine cones, mulled wine and dried fruits, but the musky fragrance of sand and sea water dried into the fibre of rucksacks and bags as they're dragged out from the back of wardrobes, or down into daylight from the dark attic after their long winter hibernation. Then there's the inside of the summer house opened up again after its solitary contemplation of the ocean in our absence, a little damp, a little musty, salt and peat in the air, nothing matching, and inky darkness outside after nightfall. Every Easter for as long as I can remember our thoroughly overextended clan has been gathering in Achill like the Kennedys in Cape Cod, with the same affinity for extreme sports but without either the wealth or the weather, although sometimes for internal politics and conspiracy theories we just might give them a run for their money. It's a tradition my parents started in the early 1950s, arriving by bus with their bicycles in the boot and an enthusiasm for fresh air, high seas, heavy wind and regular downpours. They were also deeply fond of Lough Derg and Croagh Patrick, so it's not surprising we find ourselves more at home on Achill than stretched out under sunshades on the sands of Lanzarote. We head west, year after year, with grim determination and the kind of equipment one might pack for a jaunt in Antarctica. Wetsuits, windbreakers, fleeces, hats, gloves, scarves, rainwear, swimwear, sunscreen, sunglasses, lip balm, hiking boots, sandals, blankets, hot water bottles and whiskey, lots of whiskey. Every year I resist, just a little, traditions; even the really good ones don't sit well with me. I struggle to find a faster route, and the best place to break the journey before the journey breaks me. I question the apparent need for bicycles, surfboards, body boards and canoes, and try to lay down the law about PlayStations while sticking a few DVDs of my own under the car seat. Then we turn left just after Mulranny, and it's as if we have managed to drive off the world as we know it and onto another landscape where the time zones have shifted into reverse, light comes filtering through entirely different prisms and the lid of cloud and sky above our heads is raised to infinity. By the time we reach the bridge at Achill Sound, I am ready to swim across if necessary.

It's not just the heart-stopping beauty of the place, the way it haunts you like a love affair that has never been resolved, the way you can never claim to know it fully because it is never the same from hour to hour, let alone day to day – you tend to take all of this for granted after a few decades. What draws me back is the bigger picture we tap into there every Easter, the sense that daylight is now ready to resume its confident flexing and stretching against darkness, that chairs and tables can once again be carried tentatively out into the garden at even a faint glimpse of sunshine, the way that everything seems suddenly lighter, and we can emerge into the open once more to seriously flirt with the real business of living. These are vows worth renewing, wherever we find ourselves at Easter, even the impossibly cold waters of Achill at first light that blessed morning, and try as it might, Christmas can't even begin to hold a candle to them.

THE CONFESSIONS OF AGIMET OF GENEVA, CHATEL, OCTOBER 20TH, 1348, RECOUNTED BY A WITNESS

Mary O'Donnell

Lent being over, he was despatched after Easter
to Venice for silks and other wares. The snow
had melted. Content to make the journey, he rested
In the spring nights, safe beyond the towns and hamlets
Of Black Death. Now screaming, he faltered through
The vile story of a secret encounter with
Rabbi Peyret of Chambery, chief conspirator
among poisoners of Christendom, teacher of their law.
Willingly he took a package half a span in size, wherein
lay venom from snakes of Africa, the edges
sealed with a woman's angelic stitching, he said,
all in a leather bag. *For the wells*, the rabbi whispered,
for every Christian cistern and spring in Venice,
that the plague will claim the butchers, tanners
and nobles who borrow freely, then resent our gold.
Pour carefully, then cleanse your fingers
lest the particles are carried to your lips.
Let the Christians sip their last!

For this, rewards beyond all dreams. Thus Agimet
Lightly bore poison to Venice; eyes glittering,
He scattered it into wells and fresh, sweet water.
Of his own diligence he left at once — spurred
By a Rabbi's promise! — for Calabira, Apulia, and poisoned
many cisterns. Nor did he demur before the fountain
of Toulouse where Christians clamour in the late sun,
and women and children fill ewers, and all the wells
near the Mediterranean Sea. This, the profligate poisoner
declared true enough for him to lay his soul on the five
Books of Moses if proof were needed. All this
I heard and more, after torture, a little,
eased the truth from his breast.

THE MAN WHO LIVED ON A PILLAR

Mary Russell

The landscape north of Aleppo, in Syria, is scattered with white stones that gleam cheerful and bright in the morning sun. Two donkeys, drawing a plough, leave a turf-brown ribbon of upturned earth behind them. As I walk along the road, people call out to me — *ahlan*, they say, in Arabic — welcome, come and have a cup of coffee, but it's another eight kilometres to where I'm going so I accept one very welcome coffee and then press on, for I am a woman on a mission — to find the pillar on which Saint Simeon is said to have spent nearly forty years of his life.

San Samaan, as they call him there, was an eccentric, a holy hermit or a total head case, depending on your point of view, though it is possible, I suppose, to be all three at the one time.

Anyway, Simeon was born in nearby Antioch in 390, and after becoming a Byzantine monk he engaged in some very strange habits, such as burying himself up to his neck in earth or wearing a belt studded with points so sharp they drew blood.

It was the sort of thing that people loved, and in no time at all he had acquired a large following who all wanted to touch the hem of his garment. To prevent this he ascended a pillar three metres in height, and when this failed to deter the would-be touchers, he raised it again and again until finally it was eighteen metres high, on which he positioned a substantial platform with a railing around it.

When he died in 459, his body was eventually spirited away to Constantinople, but his Byzantine followers immediately set about building a magnificent basilica in his honour. The ruins of it are still there and so is the pillar – a bit the worse for wear, but definitely there.

Now here's the intriguing part of the story: about five years ago, I learned that there was a man, Aphraim, a priest of the Syrian Orthodox Church there, who had ambitions to emulate Simeon and spend a bit of time up a pillar, and I set out to try to find him. Aphraim had studied briefly at Maynooth, but though they remembered him there, no one was sure where exactly he'd gone to next. My search wasn't paying dividends and I more or less gave up – which is usually a good thing to do in such circumstances, because then the answer comes when you're least expecting it.

And that's what happened only a few months ago. I was in Aleppo, visiting the Syrian Orthodox Church, which still conducts its services in Aramaic, which was the language used so long ago, by Christ. It's a bit like Arabic, but at the same time it isn't, if you follow me.

When I bumped into the local bishop he invited me to come back that evening for vespers. We have a man here from the States, he said, who once studied at one of your universities, and I knew this had to be Aphraim.

Vespers was a great show – masses of candles and red lights, lots of kissing of the bishop's ring, clouds of incense wafted about by small boys wearing white gowns with red crusader crosses on them. And a lot of chanting – in Aramaic, of course – and there was Aphraim, resplendent in his black robes and thick black beard, wearing an ornate and beautiful silver cross – and a huge smile.

Hi, he said afterwards and beamed at me, and I could see that given his generous girth and possibly the good life lived in America, his plans to spend a bit of time up a pillar had had to be shelved, for Aphraim now lives in Teaneck, New Jersey – just across the river from Manhattan – and is the Syrian Orthodox Archbishop for the eastern part of the US.

When I returned again to San Samaan's quiet hilltop, I thought of how far away New Jersey seemed. Here, the air is fresh and a warm breeze lifts the leaves of the trees. The sandy-white dirt road lined with poplars curves away down the hillside and the morning sun lights up the

Kurdish villages that populate the land, stretching away towards the smokey-blue mountains of Turkey.

Even as I have these thoughts, the voice of the muezzin soars up from one of the minarets below, calling the faithful to prayer, and as his voice dies away, the hilltop is once again returned to silence and silence. To a time before religion. To a time before history itself.

REFLECTIONS ON A PHOTOGRAPH

Elaine Sisson

There is a famous photograph taken at 2.30 on the afternoon of Easter Saturday, 1916 which shows Patrick Pearse in his official role as Commandant General of the Army of the Irish Republic surrendering to Brigadier-General Lowe of the British Army. The photograph was taken at the junction of Parnell Street and Moore Street and shows Pearse in a long military coat wearing a slouch hat tied under his chin. Even though he was over six feet tall, Pearse seems small. His hands are clasped behind his back and he looks straight ahead, his familiar side-profile distinguished under the unbecoming hat. In his hands General Lowe holds a sword-stick and a pistol in a holster, both of which belong to Pearse. They were given over in addition to Pearse's pouch of ammunition and his canteen, containing two large onions, as part of the ceremony of surrender. General Lowe is smartly dressed with a peaked military cap, knee-high leather boots and displays the impressive paraphernalia of rank. Records tell us that he was mannerly towards Pearse, treating him as a military peer, a courtesy Pearse appreciated.

While the focus of the picture is on Pearse and Lowe, there are, however, two other people in the photograph. One of them is hardly there at all. If you look closely at the bottom of Pearse's trench coat, you can see four legs: Pearse's boots, and beside him two small feet in sturdy shoes disappearing into a light-coloured skirt. This anatomical mystery is easily explained. The legs belong to nurse Elizabeth O'Farrell, who had walked with Pearse to the top of Moore Street as part of the conditions of surrender. It was Elizabeth O'Farrell, dressed in her nurse's uniform, who carried the white flag. You'd have thought that her role in history deserved to be remembered in a photograph. But, for whatever reasons, Elizabeth O'Farrell was hastily airbrushed out of the photograph, which appeared in numerous newspapers the next day. It was obviously a quick editorial decision, as her neatly shod feet and the hem of her uniform remain, visible yet unseen, like the trace of a ghost. Maybe it was considered unseemly to surrender in the presence of a woman; maybe it was considered unseemly for a woman to be involved in military combat. It's impossible to know. In recent years the recovery of women's role in our history has been underway and perhaps one day it might be possible to restore Nurse O'Farrell's torso, arms and head to her proper place beside Pearse.

There is also a fourth person in that photograph. He is a young British soldier; handsome, dark, tall and slender in boots and light-coloured breeches. He's looking at Pearse's letter of surrender, which he holds in his hands. His stance is casual, even nonchalant. His name is John Muir Lowe and he's the Brigadier-General's son – it's possible he's only holding the letter so that his father can take charge of Pearse's belongings. John Lowe was a seasoned soldier; he was a Second Lieutenant with the 15th Hussars and had served at Gallipoli during the 1915–16 campaign there. Sometime after this photograph was taken, he must have ended back in combat in France, as he spent time as a German prisoner of war. Yet after the First World War ended he stayed in Germany to run a pickle factory. It was probably during this time that he changed his name from John Muir Lowe to John Loder, possibly because it sounded more Germanic. But his real love was acting and he appeared in a number of German films, some by the director Alex Korda, during the 1920s. Leaving pickles behind forever, he moved to America and appeared in the first talkie for the Paramount Studio in a 1929 film called *The Doctor's Secret.* That year alone he appeared in ten films and his career seemed to be on the rise. However, he returned to England in the early 1930s and featured in over forty films over the next eight years, including *Lorna Doone* in 1934, Hitchcock's *Sabotage* in 1936 and *King Solomon's Mines* in 1937. For the most part, however, he played secondary or even tertiary characters; occasional roles with little importance.

When war broke out in 1939 he left England promptly and returned to America. He had probably had enough of war and at forty-two he was still young enough to serve. During the 1940s he found work in B movies under the name John Loder, playing stiff-upper-lip types. His six-foot-three frame and ageing, debonair looks made him perfect for playing decaying aristocrats. His profile increased, however, and he appeared in some major hits of the day, including *Now, Voyager* with Bette Davis in 1942. It was probably by moving in these circles that he met the Viennese-born film star Hedy Lemarr. Lemarr, one of Hollywood's most beautiful and glamorous leading ladies, married John Loder in 1943. Lemarr was his third wife, he was her fourth husband. By the end of their lives, between them they chalked up eleven spouses. They had three children together, but they divorced in 1947. Loder later married an Argentinean heiress called Alba Larden and semi-retired to her ranch. He wrote a book called *Hollywood Hussars* in 1977 and died in 1988, aged ninety.

If you happen to spot that picture of Patrick Pearse, Elizabeth O'Farrell, Brigadier General Lowe and John Loder on the corner of Moore Street and Parnell Street, then look carefully. Look for a nurse's small, tidy feet sheltering underneath Pearse's coat and a debonair, slightly bored twenty-year-old who was dreaming of Hollywood at a pivotal moment in our history.

MISS PEARSE

Bairbre O'Hogan

My connection with the Pearse family began before I was even born. While trying to improve his Irish, my father read *Íosagán agus Scéalta Eile*, a collection of short stories and poetry by Pádraig Mac Piarais. One of the stories in this book was about a wooden doll called Bairbre, who was bald, had a gamy eye and only one leg (the other having been bitten off by a dog). Despite these physical deficiencies, Bairbre was much loved and accompanied her owner in all the tasks of a five-year-old's life. The name appealed to my father, and it was agreed that if the imminent baby were a girl, she would be called Bairbre. And so I was.

In turn, I was introduced to those same stories in school. I loved them, and found it easy to imagine the people Pearse described: children running around barefoot, a sickly boy watching the swallows arrive and leave, an old man who hadn't been to mass for more than sixty years. We took part in a class play when we performed *Na Bóithre*, about a little girl who envied her brother's freedom, cut off her hair and ran away. Our teachers taught us his poetry in Irish and in English. On a family holiday, we had visited his house in Rosmuc, County Galway and I was familiar with the names of the Connemara townlands and parishes that he threaded through his writings. And when a 1916 veteran came to our primary school to mark the fiftieth anniversary of the Easter Rising, I was only interested in hearing about Pearse the writer, not Pearse the patriot.

We had a great family friend, Sr Denis, who was a Religious Sister of Charity in Linden Convalescent Home in Blackrock, County Dublin.

She was a tall, imposing figure, dressed in black from head to toe, but with a gentle voice and a mischievous sense of humour. She asked me if I would like to meet Margaret Pearse, or Miss Pearse, as she called her – the elder sister of Patrick and Willie, who was in her ninetieth year and was a resident in Linden. I was thrilled. I decided I would recite 'The Wayfarer' for her and practised it night and day at home to ensure I was word perfect.

I only knew one other nonagenarian – a neighbour who travelled into Bewley's on Grafton Street every day by bus, and who lived a very busy and fulfilled life on her own. I was therefore taken aback slightly to be brought into Miss Pearse's bedroom in Linden and to see this tiny, white-haired lady propped up on pillows and only able to whisper her greeting to me. It was difficult to picture this little lady as a serving Senator in the Oireachtas and as a teacher in the famed St Enda's. She looked so frail, so fragile, that I felt my ten-year-old voice might shatter her delicate frame, and so our few words were whispered to each other. Then Sr Denis mentioned that I would like to recite a poem for her. I began 'The Wayfarer'. Though my voice shook with nervousness, I made no mistakes. I was word perfect.

When I finished, I looked at Miss Pearse. Tears were trickling down her face. I didn't know what to say. Should I apologise? What had I done that made her cry? She thanked me for coming. I asked her to sign my newly purchased autograph book, and then Sr Denis ushered me out.

Almost forty years on, I can still feel the shock of seeing this famous woman cry. I wonder what exactly she was thinking about.

A WREATH FOR
TWO PLUNKETTS

Tony Quinn

I see His blood upon the rose, and in the stars the glory of his eyes,
His body gleams amid eternal snows, his tears fall from the skies.

Those lines from his renowned poem about the divine presence in nature helped to ensure Joseph Mary Plunkett's place in Irish folk memory. The poet became a patriotic and romantic icon when he married an artist, Grace Gifford, in Kilmainham Gaol just before his execution after the 1916 Easter Rising. That heroic story of ninety years ago is recalled in a patriotic ballad: 'O Grace just hold me in your arms and let this moment linger.'

Joseph studied at UCD and was active in literary and nationalist societies. He travelled in Europe to improve his health and went on secret missions to Germany seeking help for the planned rebellion. Despite delicate health, as a member of the Irish Republican Brotherhood, Joseph planned the military strategy for the Rising. He had learned army techniques with the Officers Training Corps when he was a pupil at Stonyhurst, the Jesuit upper-class school in Lancashire.

During research for my book, *Wigs and Guns: Irish Barristers and the Great War*, the Plunkett family background intrigued me. Joseph's family were wealthy Catholics and his father, George, was known as Count Plunkett because the Pope had honoured him. The Count's father, Patrick, remarried years after his first wife died. Patrick's second family included Gerald, who was Count Plunkett's half-brother because they had the same father but different mothers.

Joseph Mary Plunkett was the same age as his uncle, Gerald, as they were both born in 1887. They attended the Jesuit school, Belvedere College, but the closely related men took different paths, as the Plunkett family had divided loyalties.

Gerald, an Oxford graduate and barrister, was a baritone, a fine musician and keen yachtsman in Dublin Bay. A volunteer in the Naval Reserve, he was posted to the Royal Naval Division in Gallipoli in 1915.

Before the third battle of Krithia, Sub-Lieutenant Gerald Plunkett arranged for chaplains to comfort and provide spiritual solace for the men in his platoon of the Collingwood battalion. During high summer 1915, laughing and joking, Gerald gallantly led his troops towards the Turkish trenches. Shot in the head, he died instantly, aged twenty-seven. Turkish machine guns wiped out the Collingwood battalion, which, according to military reports, 'fell like a field of corn under a reaper or a ship sinking with all hands'.

Gerald Plunkett has no known grave but is named on the high memorial at Helles in Gallipoli. Placing a floral wreath beside Gerald Plunkett's name, I recalled the stories of two talented young Irishmen and close relatives, Gerald and Joseph Mary Plunkett. Each died in violent conflict as heroes for diverse causes, cut off in the flower of their youth.

Joseph Plunkett attained an honoured place in Irish history as an executed leader of the 1916 Easter Rising who signed the republic's proclamation. In comparison, Gerald's memory was forgotten. A new memorial at Belvedere College, however, remembers all its past pupils, including both Plunketts killed in twentieth-century conflicts.

Describing the ill-fated campaign in Gallipoli, the author Compton Mackenzie contrasted the scent of orchids and other wild flowers there with the stench of dead horses. During my visit to the former battle-field area, I reflected on the stories of two Plunketts in a serene place now planted with laurels and rosemary for remembrance.

1 SEATOWN PLACE

Conor O'Callaghan

For a country not renowned for snow, Ireland has produced more than its fair share of polar explorers: Kildare's Ernest Shackelton's race with Scott to the South Pole has been captured for the small screen by Kenneth Brannagh; Annascaul's Tom Crean can be seen nightly on a television commercial mumbling 'The Kerry Dances' in a snowbound cave, dreaming of one more pint of famous stout. Arguably Ireland's greatest polar explorer, however, does not enjoy such popular renown. There are no dramatisations of his heroism, and he does not feature in any marketing campaigns. I know about him only because he came from my hometown, Dundalk.

A little over ten years ago, myself and my wife moved back from Dublin. Between the jigs and reels, we ended up buying a new house in the oldest section, called Seatown. I fell in love with name and place. It is on reclaimed land and has a feeling of being both here and elsewhere, moored and adrift all at once. The short walk to the centre of town passes a Georgian terrace. The last house on the left has a blue plaque with a knighted name, nineteenth-century dates and a description of a profession that intrigued me so much I went researching.

Sir Leopold McClintock was born in his family home, 1 Seatown Place, in 1829. His father was the inspector of taxes. He was educated at Dundalk Grammar School until, at the age of twelve, his uncle secured a naval commission for him. In 1845, when McClintock was still a young officer, Sir John Franklin captained the *Erebus* in an attempt to become the first known ship to navigate the Northwest Passage: that fabled sliver from Atlantic to Pacific across the uppermost coast of Canada. For fourteen years Franklin's whereabouts remained a mystery. McClintock, having been in the crew of two previous failed rescue voyages, captained a third commissioned by Lady Jane Franklin. He departed an ambitious young officer and returned two years later one of the most celebrated men in Victorian public life. In the interim, through chattels found littering the barren landscape and Inuit sightings of strange men battling the elements, the last days of the crew of the *Erebus* were pieced together.

After Sir Leopold's father died, his mother moved to Gardiner Place in the town and 1 Seatown Place went out of the family. When we arrived back ten years ago the house was in flats, then a B&B. Its most recent and current incarnation is as a hostel for asylum-seekers from other continents. Some evenings I walk past with my kids and they are sitting out on the steps: talking, laughing and beneath it all probably wondering what strange twist in fortune has washed them up on this shore. Occasionally I have a strong urge to tell them who once lived in their present home, if only to give them hope. Perhaps they know the story anyway.

Upon his return in 1859, McClintock was knighted by Queen Victoria and granted the freedom of London. One month later, at a civic reception in Dundalk, he accepted an award from the townspeople and told them he would 'cherish it always more than any other honour, as it comes from the town where I spent my youth, from the friends of my boyhood days, from my home.' He died in 1907 at the age of eighty-eight and is buried in Westminster Abbey. To this day a giant stuffed polar bear he shot can be seen in the Natural History Museum on Merrion Row, Dublin. The strip of water between Victoria Island and Prince of Wales Island in Arctic Canada now appears in every atlas as McClintock Channel.

I write all this in that golden no man's land between late spring and early summer. The evenings are getting warmer and brighter. As I write, I can hear the faint echoes of gospel music wafting over Seatown. This is a new song in these parts, and one I welcome. It suddenly occurs to me how fitting it is that 1 Seatown Place now houses those who have travelled several continents to find safety and new lives. I like to think Sir Leopold McClintock, a man who made his name in search of the lost, would have approved.

THE MAGIC FLUTE MYSTERY

Val O'Donnell

When Mozart's masterpiece, *The Magic Flute*, was recently presented in Dublin, I spared a thought for an adoptive Dubliner who played a significant part in the first presentation of the opera, by Emanuel Schikaneder's theatre company in Vienna, in September 1791.

The Dublin connection centres on the unlikely figure of Sir Charles Lewis Giesecke, the first professor of mineralogy of the Royal Dublin Society. Giesecke was born Johann Georg Metzler in Augsburg in Germany in 1761. He abandoned university studies in 1783 and joined a travelling theatre group, adopting the name Carl Ludwig Giesecke. Later on, he became associated with Schikaneder's theatre company.

Little is known of Giesecke's career in the theatre, but the evidence points to a talent in writing for the stage in addition to performing. He is credited with an early German translation of *Hamlet* and with a number of librettos for operas, including one for the opera *Oberon* by the Viennese composer Wranitsky, which was presented at Schikaneder's theatre in 1789. So it is hardly surprising to find the name of Carl Ludwig Giesecke appearing against the part of the First Slave in the first production of *The Magic Flute*. That's a far cry from the principal part of Papageno, the bird catcher, which was created for the versatile Schikaneder. But the story of Giesecke's connection with the opera goes further.

In time, Giesecke became disillusioned with the theatre and went on to attain international distinction as a mineralogist – notably for his discoveries in Greenland, where he endured great privations during a seven-year period spent exploring the mineral resources of that inhospitable land. In later life he referred to his 'arctic cough' as a legacy of those years.

While at Edinburgh in 1813, in difficult circumstances, Giesecke learned that the Royal Dublin Society had advertised the position of Professor of Mineralogy. Friends persuaded him to apply and conveyed strong recommendations to Dublin on his behalf. Giesecke was successful in the competition, despite the fact that he was initially unable to lecture in English. Professor Giesecke came to reside in 14 St George's Place, beside St George's Church in the north inner city, in a house purchased soon after his arrival in 1814. He was regarded as extremely charming and witty company in Dublin society, and was sought as companion by all who knew him.

But Giesecke's passion for travel was not fully satisfied. In 1817 he obtained leave from the Royal Dublin Society for an extended visit to Europe for personal and professional reasons. During his sojourn, an encounter in a Viennese café with some former opera associates led Giesecke to claim that he was the main author of the libretto of *The Magic Flute*, which is widely believed to contain sympathetic allusions to Freemasonry.

Although Schikaneder is routinely credited with authorship today, many musicologists have been convinced that Giesecke did indeed play a significant part in writing the libretto, given his close association with the Schikaneder company, his talent for libretto writing and his lifelong membership of the Masonic Order.

Also, Giesecke possessed a personal interleaved copy of the libretto, still preserved today. This would suggest that his involvement in the first production of the opera went beyond appearing in the part of First Slave in the chorus.

It seems unlikely that the full story of Giesecke's role in the first production of *The Magic Flute* will ever be determined. However, one clue that could help to resolve the mystery may be languishing in a forgotten trunk in a Dublin house. Sir Charles Lewis Giesecke died suddenly in 1833, at the house of his friend, the architect Charles Mulvany, in what is now Parnell Square. His impressive commemorative mural tablet can still be seen in nearby St George's Church, where he was buried.

After his death, Sir Charles's personal effects were auctioned in Dublin. They included albums he maintained throughout his life containing autographs, quotations and illustrations recording encounters with a wide range of individuals. Two of these albums came into the possession of the National Museum of Ireland in 1909. They reveal crucial time gaps pointing to the existence of a further album of the years 1781 to 1800, covering the period when Giesecke worked and socialised with Mozart, Schikaneder and other leading theatre figures in Vienna.

If such an album were ever found, it could shed important light on the mystery of the authorship of the libretto of *The Magic Flute*. In any event, it could be worth a fortune!

PADRAIC FIACC

Gerald Dawe

In a year of important literary commemorations, it might be timely to recall one Irishman who has largely slipped from view.

Patrick Joseph O'Connor was born on 15 April 1924 in Elizabeth Street in the Lower Falls district of Belfast. His early years were spent in the house of his maternal grandparents in East Street in the Markets district of Belfast. On both sides of his parents' families, the political impact of the Irish Civil War, the backdrop to his own birth, was immediate and long lasting.

His mother's family, the McGarrys, had been driven from their home in Lisburn, their furniture, including a piano, burned. His grandfather never recovered from the ordeal. His grandmother, like his own mother, would loom large in the young boy's imagination as powerful figures of spirited resistance. His father, Bernard, came from a prosperous family of shopkeepers from County Cavan. Like many before him and since, he went to Belfast to make his own way, working as a barman, and became active in the IRA. In the late 1920s, in the tense and economically insecure atmosphere of post-Civil War, partitioned Ireland, exhausted by almost two decades of political upheaval and military campaigns, the father, again like thousands of others at the time, emigrated to America, to New York. He was reluctantly joined in 1929 by his wife, Annie Christina, and their three sons, including the eldest (and first surviving child), Patrick, who was five.

The family made headway to begin with as the father's grocery business prospered and another son and daughter were born, but with the fall-out of the Great Depression and the ensuring slump of the Thirties, the O'Connor business collapsed and with it the fabric of the family life started to unravel, with tragic results. The father began to drink heavily. His wife turned her vengeance on America and yearned for home, identifying with the eldest son an intense and romantic sense of Irishness mediated through her reading of Yeats's poems to the impressionable boy.

From these early experiences, first in Manhattan and eventually in Hell's Kitchen, Patrick Joseph O'Connor was schooled locally and wrote profusely. Under the influence of the Irish literary revival's iconic figure in America, Padraic Colum, and his wife Mary, the poet 'Padraic Fiacc' (O'Connor's chosen nom de plume) was born, modelling, to quote his editor, Aodán Mac Póilín, 'his work on the technique and style of Gaelic poetry, although much of his early work was written in an identifiable American idiom.'

By 1941 Fiacc, now a somewhat precocious teenager, studied for the priesthood at the Franciscans in St Joseph's Seraphic Seminary in Calicoon in upstate New York. He left St Joseph's partly as a result of a disagreement over a sequence of poems which he wrote in memory of a fellow student who had drowned, but continued his studies with the Irish Capuchin order at Holy Oak in Delaware. His time there lasted for five years, when in 1946 he left America, returned to Belfast and worked as a night porter in the Union Hotel, a well-known, and shady, place at the back of the City Hall.

The voyage home aboard the Swedish *Grispholm* was through the still-mined Atlantic waters. By this time the twenty-two-year-old Fiacc was carrying the experiences of his New York years – the cosmopolitan, modernist, bulging, exuberant city, the ghetto-world of ethnic districts, the clerical and spiritual exercises of a seminarian conversant in several languages, the post-war 'shock and awe' and the bravado of victory and a sense of fulfilling his own mother's desire to return home. His brother, however, had returned from war profoundly damaged by the experience. It was quite a lot to handle for a twenty-two-year-old.

Now, almost sixty years later, Fiacc, the 'Troubles' poet, survives and still resides in his native city of Belfast, where this year he celebrated his eightieth birthday. His life story, the life story of the darker side of the road to peace in Ireland, is contained in the urban, edgy film noir of his poetry, such as the powerful poem below.

First Movement

Padraic Fiacc

Low clouds yellow in a mist wind
Sift on far-off Ards
Drift hazily …

I was born on such a morning
Smelling of the Bone Yards

The smoking chimneys over
the slate rooftops
The wayward storm birds

And to the east where morning is
the sea
And to the west where evening is
the sea
Threatening with danger
and it
Would always darken suddenly.

BELFRY

Pat Boran

If you wanted to get high in Portlaoise about 1972 or 73 (and you were still only ten years old), you joined the altar boys. Someone said that from the red-brick belfry of St Peter's and Paul's Church – the town's periscope, as I used to think of it – you could see right inside of the prison, just a few hundred yards away. If they were out in the exercise yard, you might even see the prisoners themselves in their manacles and chains, in their grey two-piece suits with the black arrows pointing to their heads, the way they did in comic strips. It was a fascinating idea, that the biggest mystery in our town, in our world back then, could be exposed even partially by simply climbing up into the belfry of the church. And because everyone wanted to see inside the prison, everyone wanted to be an altar boy.

And so, the day the little puppet-frail parish priest came into our national school and made his tour of the classrooms, talking to himself in that whispery, sibilant way he had and playing with his hands in the manner of someone delicately untying a knot, I forced the image of myself dressed like something from a Christmas card to the back of my mind, and instead concentrated hard on the possible view of the town, my town, that would spread out below me. And, like most of my friends in the classroom, I put up my hand.

Somehow, as we sat there with the blood draining first from our fingers, then from our wrists, so that we had to draft in our left arms to help hold the right ones up, somehow we managed to force to the back of our minds the thought of all the early mornings and late evenings that would lie ahead, all the hanging around outside and waiting, at funerals especially, among upset people, all that traipsing to and from the overheated vestry to the ice-cold church, as our brothers and fathers, and fathers before them, had done.

And the truth was that yes, there were cold evenings, and colder mornings. But the belfry of St Peter's and Paul's was worth it. From the second- or third-floor windows of its concrete, red-brick-encrusted tower, you could see a town that was breathtaking, captivating and, if you were like me and suffered a little from vertigo, dizzyingly so.

You could see Main Street, the lower part at least, starting its gradual rise and swing up away from the not-yet-overgrown Triogue River, still alive with pinkeens. You could see, running up through what had once been our back garden and was now picked out by two lines of sulphurous yellow sodium lights, the great four-lane curve of the town bypass, or the link road as it was locally known (in preference to the somewhat cumbersome James Fintan Lawlor Avenue). You could see Rankin's Wood to your left, the bloated crowns of the trees obscuring their trunks and branches below so that the whole wood looked like a single entity, which it was, a living creature even then struggling to survive at the edge of an expanding town. And over to your right, out the opposite window, the Burying Ridge, the town's oldest graveyard, changing shades of green as its long grass was blown this way and that. As if the spirits of all the quaintly named townsfolk of 100 or 200 years before – the Ramsbottoms, the Hendersons, all those mellifluous names – had never quite gone to sleep.

On a cold funeral evening, you might be standing in the cross-winds of that belfry for twenty minutes or half an hour, watching out for the first sighting of the hearse and cortege on their way in from the hospital. And it would be *bitterly* cold up there. But once the polished chrome and hood of the hearse came into sight, all thoughts of the cold disappeared and it was time to approach the bell.

And if you were lucky, and one of the older boys was too busy smoking, or was down somewhere outside the church chatting to some young one, you could grasp that huge, barely flexible rope that hung down through the middle of the bell shaft, lean out over it to draw down with what little weight you had, then relax on the slight recoil to draw down even harder at its apex, over and over, feeling the pull of the bell and getting a sense of the rhythm, taking the weight and measure of it, the way someone digging turf has to, or someone digging a grave; until, with no effort whatsoever, and no resistance, suddenly you're in the air, lifted off the flat, lifeless concrete surface your feet have been gummed to for the last twenty minutes, to have everybody else now suddenly below you, shouting up and laughing, and urging you on, to 'look at the prison, can you see the prison?', and you just clinging on and willing the next flight higher, soaring above yourself, the town, the world, in a literally ecstatic, almost religious moment, in which you understand at last the real meaning, the real significance of the word *belfry*. The bell. Free.

MORNING POEM

Enda Wyley

To wake to this.
If we had known
we would not
have slept so long.
Mist has fought and won
its battle against the sun
and all is murky grey.
The spider's frail line blows
from the sycamore
to the cottage hedge,
while across the lane,
dew looks dense but breaks
like bubbles at a touch.
The fat brown birds
are not afraid of our steps
along the gravelled way,
of our fingers
stamping berries.
Oh purple hunger!
The baby dips
in and out of wonder,
twirling the soft air,
testing the sky

with her sounds.
Geraniums wake bedraggled
in their window beds
and yesterday's paint dries
at last on the red wooden door.
To wake to this.

SURE WHAT IS 500 YEARS AMONG FRIENDS?

Bernard McGuckian, S.J.

Thomas Williams died on 23 February 1983. He wasn't Welsh, as his name might suggest. He was American. Contrary to what you might expect, he wasn't born in Tennessee. He was born in Mississippi in the town of Columbus on 26 March 1911, to Cornelius Coffin Williams, a shoe salesman, and his wife, Edwina Dakins Williams, daughter of a line of Episcopalian clergymen. Religion of one kind or another ran in the family from way back. It was only as an adult that Thomas styled himself Tennessee. By the time he died a month short of his seventy-second birthday, any one of the more than fifty American states would have been happy had he chosen to call himself after it.

Even the very names of his plays catch the imagination: *A Streetcar Named Desire, Cat on a Hot Tin Roof, Rose Tattoo, Glass Menagerie.* He had hardly broken onto the theatrical scene in the middle of World War Two when the biggest names of stage and screen were tripping over each other to get into his roles. Elia Kazan could pick and choose for his stage production of *Streetcar*. He settled for Marlon Brando and Vivien Leigh. Only Paul Newman and Elizabeth Taylor were good enough for the film version of the *Cat*. Williams's work is set in the Deep South of the United States, but the themes he deals with are universal. He explores family tensions and feelings of frustration, especially in women. As with all great classical work, his plays touch something deep in all of us. There is something of both the evangelist and the rebellious non-conformist in Tennessee Williams. Much of his early life was spent traipsing around rectories with his mother to visit her relations. Many of these were either Episcopalian clergy or their wives. Perhaps an explanation for the evangelical fervour he brought to the theatre may have percolated down through the generations from the spirit of one of the more remote but arguably the most distinguished of all his clerical ancestors.

His rebellious streak may be traceable to another dimension of his family. A number of them were deeply involved in the American War of Independence. Tennessee Williams tells us in his autobiography that he was a direct descendant of Valentine Sevier (pronounced as in the English adjective 'severe'). Valentine was a less-celebrated brother of the more famous John Sevier, who was the first governor of Tennessee. On 7 October 1780, these brothers joined with about 1,000 other American patriots in the Battle of King's Mountain, South Carolina, where they overwhelmed the British. This battle was a turning point in the Revolutionary War.

These Sevier brothers, John and Valentine, were grandsons of a John Sevier who married a lady called Smith in London around the year 1700. This particular John Sevier had made his way from the region of Navarre to England in the wake of the Revocation of the Edict of Nantes in 1685 by Louis XIV. With a number of other members of his family, he had become Huguenot and felt he would be safer in Protestant England. While in London, he had anglicised his name to John Sevier from Juan Xavier, or in Dublinese, X-avier.

This Juan Xavier, alias John Sevier, was a direct descendant of Juan de Jasso, who married his wife, Maria, a few short years before Christopher Columbus set out on his fateful westward voyage. Besides bringing a castle as a dowry, she also made it possible for Juan to style himself the Lord of Xavier. She bore him six children. The three eldest were girls and the three youngest were boys. The youngest boy, Francis, was born on 7 April 1506. About twenty years later he ended up sharing digs at the Sorbonne in Paris with an older and more mature student, who became his mentor in things spiritual. This man was a native of Loyola, another small town in the Basque country not too far away from Francis's own home place. The pair of them, with five other students from the university, formed the small group that gave birth to the

Society of Jesus, or more popularly, the Jesuits. Together, they were canonised on 12 March 1622 as St Francis Xavier and St Ignatius of Loyola. Speaking of Francis, Ignatius said that he was the toughest dough he ever tried to knead. The end result was worth all Ignatius's efforts. Even people of other faiths consider that no one since St Paul himself has ever embodied more perfectly the ideal of a Christian missionary. In this five hundredth anniversary of his birth there will be celebrations on all five continents, especially Asia, where Francis died, exhausted after his Herculean labours, on an island a few miles off the coast of China.

A few years ago, after seeing Fionnuala O'Flanagan in a Gate Theatre production of *A Streetcar Named Desire*, I made the short walk up home to St Francis Xavier's in Gardiner Street, Dublin. At the time, I little dreamed how small the world really is, nor had it struck me so forcibly that 500 years is no more than the span of five healthy lives placed back to back. Tennessee Williams knew that he was a 'Sevier'. I only learned recently that he was a Xavier. To this day I do not know whether or not he knew this himself. He knows now.

MAY

I LIKE LILAC

Jennifer O'Dea

May was the Month of Mary. The first day saw the May Altar ritually assembled in the corner of the classroom with a piece of white lace, a prayer book, a statue of herself, of course, but most crucially, a vase. The climax of the following four weeks was when it was your turn to bring in the fresh flowers to adorn the altar. We were assured that it didn't matter what kind of flowers you had, even a bunch of daisies would be appreciated by Our Lady. Shame on the girl who believed that. There were all colours of roses and rich-looking foliage, bunches of tulips that wilted before the day was out, dainty mauve cowslips that you could slip your fingers into when no one was looking, and of course lots of cherry blossom. Some of the rich girls' mummies even *bought* flowers – an unbelievable extravagance in 1970s Ireland.

In our house it was always lilac. We had a single lilac tree in the back garden that yielded a handful of blossoms a year. The boys had no interest in them, but my sister and I eyed each bud as it slowly unfolded itself into the early summer air. We pestered my mother on a daily basis to cut them down sooner rather than later so we could bring them to school. Finally the day would come when she would circle the tree and announce that she would cut. Oh, the joy of that morning! She would go to work swiftly and unmomentously, snipping the flowers and handing them down. The scintillating aroma of freshly cut lilac would fill the air.

Walking to school that morning was a religious experience. My flowers proudly held in both hands, I was a single-handed procession, a postulant going to the altar for the first time, a saint tending a graveside, a child at an apparition; I was Mary herself.

I would walk preciously into the classroom and go straight to the altar to dispose of the old flowers, which had barely started their decay – but there were no prisoners in this war. Then they would be shown to the *múinteoir*.

I never understood how anyone could be so indifferent to something so beautiful. She never appreciated them properly. She didn't understand. Lilacs were special. There were only a few of them in the world – you only got eight or nine if you were lucky, and you had to share them with your sister. Alas, the moment of glory was always too short lived. Within two or three days the beautiful pale purple would be ousted in favour of a new arrival, a batch of carnations or a peony rose. Mary had a voracious appetite for flowers.

In those days May meant lilac and hymns. It held the promise of a long, hot summer of bicycles and ice creams and beautiful smells in the garden. Of staying up late and playing cards with parents. Of spending the night in cousins' houses and pitching tents in the garden. Of midnight feasts and dressing up. And no school. No worries.

Later on, May was a worry. When the lilac appeared in our garden it acted as a deadly reminder of the march of time. The flowers bloomed and faded on the tree, unpicked. No pleasure in them any more. They made me realise the Inter Cert was on its way and a couple of years later reminded me the Leaving Cert was a reality. Each day in May ticked louder than the last. A clock turning into a bomb. The weeks went by until the dreaded June appeared and all hope was gone. Exam day after exam day loomed ahead.

Years later, when I was at university in London, I had no garden. At the end of my first year I had a subliminal sense of relief that this May wouldn't be characterised by floral fear. Then one day in the top corridor I saw an open door where there had never been an open door, daylight pouring in. I approached with curiosity and looked outside. There I saw students sitting around on wooden picnic tables, drinking coffee without a care in the world – it was a *roof garden*. Every year at the same time the door was thrown open to the summer and I knew I was lost. This roof garden was my new lilac tree.

I still get a vague sense of unease at the onset of May. I fantasise that I might get a letter in the post from the Department of Education advising me that due to a confusion I will have to resit my Leaving Certificate — *honours* maths this time. Or, with much apology, a notice that my college finals have been lost and that I will have to retake them. Then always the great relief descends and I heave a deep sigh of contentment that they can never get me again. And as I gratefully relax with my daughter in the new room, I look into the garden and think —

'We must plant some lilac.'

FIRST HOLY COMMUNION

Joseph Woods

I came across this image some years ago while flicking through some family photos – a mixed bundle, unarranged, covering a few decades and mostly in black and white. As is usually the case, in our family and probably with most, no one had bothered to scribble a name or a date on the back of the photo that caught my eye. Such is the present and snap-shot sense of the photograph that no one imagines a day will come when there will be no signifiers, when hardly the year of the photograph can be guessed and even family or descendants will not be able to identify the sitter.

It was my mother who readily identified that the girl in the photo was a cousin, distant, and from a side of the family we'd lost touch with. It was obvious, too, to both of us that she was photographed on the occasion of her first Holy Communion. And the time? Guessed to be somewhere in the very early 1960s. What was odd was the drama or setting of the photograph. It made me chuckle, so much so that my mother said I could hold on to it.

The circumstances and setting of it reminded me of those poses in photographs you see at the turn of the nineteenth century when, after the explosion of the flash, a minor phosphorous bomb, everyone fell at ease coughing and spluttering in the smoke. Something we can only have witnessed from movies when lovers have their photos taken, usually before he departed to the front or some expedition to the Antarctic. Tragically, never to return again, the movie pans out with the photo of the two of them, the only tangible thing when all was innocent and the journey had only begun.

In my cousin's photo she is standing on an empty road, too raised to be a bog road, but lean and winding – the kind of road that bends or turns for no reason, in moonlight to darkness, in sunshine offering up bubbles and trickles of tar. The road behind her is empty, bleak in a black-and-white fashion and framed by a few hedges. Centred in the middle of the road is my cousin, standing in her communion dress and veil looking slightly grumpy and at variance with her required pose.

One can understand why, when one sees she is holding a crucifix half her size on an occasional table that has been draped by a neat white tablecloth in what appears to be the middle of nowhere. Maybe the taking of the photo took too long on her special day, that rigid pose, holding her crucifix straight for the camera, or perhaps it was simply a freezing cold Irish day?

What strikes me as odd is where the table, tablecloth and crucifix were procured from. Were they carried in the boot of a car until a suitable location was found? If so, surely the road as I have described was a bit incongruous or lonely for a happy occasion? There is a certain art in artlessness and I have kept this photo as some icon of the past, something of the decade into which I was born.

MISSED KODAK MOMENT

Denise Blake

At a month's distance Ian, what do you remember?

It was the school concert; the two lines of thirty one
fifth-class boys herded in to assembly, song sheets held up
you seated at the front, nursing your guitar, strumming
the broad Donegal version of 'Always Take the Weather'.

Do you remember what came next?

The Master remembers the taste of sheer relief;
after all the practising, weeks spent teaching an Oasis song,
facing the risk of trying modern instead of hymns;
they did raise more charity money than having held the cake sale.

Brian remembers how he held the music-sheet in front of his face
so no-one saw him; Joseph remembers steering the pretend
car-wheel for 'Baby You Can Drive My Car'; for Darren it's the beep
-beep part of the song; and Packie, how well he air-guitared.

You do remember being nervous beforehand, but afterwards?

Your dad remembers that familiar smell of Lysol and stale
farts wafting and how boys sang 'Sweet Home Alabama'

in an American twang. Eoin and Thomas remember that all their friends saw their big cousin playing guitar and they said 'he was really brill.'

You did say; when it was over, 'the boys thought it was great craic.'

I remember this, as I left the hall, just at the corridor corner,

I looked back. You were still seated, this mass of pupils had moved to be near you. I tried to take that picture, but the camera jammed. So Ian, I remember them around you in adoration, you the messiah of rock. Your smile. You had been nervous. Now you are the man.

MEETING RAY IN A ROUND-ABOUT WAY

Mick Rainsford

My daughter, my mother-in-law and I were on Route 101 about ten minutes before my mother-in-law broke the silence. 'We'll be passing through Port Angeles, you know,' Babara said – Barbara's my mother-in-law's name. 'We could stop if you'd like.'

Why would I want to stop at Port Angeles? I thought, preoccupied as I was with the scenery sweeping past: heavy belts of pine through which glittering stretches of blue water occasionally flashed. Little shops, roadhouses, gas stations that looked like somebody just threw them together along the side of the road.

Then it hit me; Port Angeles was where the writer Raymond Carver spent the last years of his life. Those last ten sober years. 'Yeah,' I said. 'I'd like that.' I wasn't sure exactly what I intended doing there. I just didn't think it right to drive straight through.

Hunger got the better of us outside Sequim and we pulled into a diner. Soon after we were on the highway again, soon after that, rolling through the outskirts of Raymond Carver's adopted home.

Sandwiched between the Olympic National Forest to the south and the Strait of San Juan de Fuca to the north, Port Angeles is one of those cities that seems built on the edge of the world. It's not a very big city by American standards, around 20,000 inhabitants. It has those things common to seaside towns the world over: the expanse and smell of salt water. Sandy shores, souvenir shops.

I found myself hankering after fish and chips: I always do within smelling distance of the sea. There was a tiny playground across from where we'd stopped, about fifty yards from the seafront.

'Why don't you take a stroll?' Barbara suggested. 'I'll look after the little one.'

'You sure?'

'Sure,' she said. 'Go ahead.'

I didn't go far. I just walked around three square blocks, wondering how often Raymond Carver might have covered the same ground. My daughter and I were heading home in a few days so I was searching for last-minute souvenirs. The seafront in Port Angeles has its fair share of souvenir shops, replete with nautical knick-knacks, military memorabilia. The Marine Corp shop was closed. A second store sold Zippos which had seen service in Vietnam, the inscriptions they bore testimony to the humanitarianism of their owners. 'Death is my business,' read one of the most popular, 'and business is good.'

I stepped in next door. 'Welcome to the Blue Dolphin,' an elderly man in a captain's hat called. Most of the souvenirs that caught my eye in the Blue Dolphin I could not afford. In the end I bought an aluminium wind chime shaped like a puffer fish.

'Are you a native of Port Angeles?' I asked as I handed fifteen dollars over.

'Oh yeah,' the man said. I wanted to ask if he'd ever met Raymond Carver. Instead I just took the change and left.

When I got back to the playground, Barbara was chatting with two young women who had a little boy with them. The women were talking about some store they worked in, saying how Barbara really ought to visit it. It was then I asked about the population, just to have something to say to them.

'Did you know,' Barbara asked suddenly, 'a very famous writer once lived here with his poet wife, Tess Gallagher.'

The women's faces crinkled into smiles. 'We know her!' they cried simultaneously.

'No way,' I said.

'Sure,' they told us. 'She comes into our store all the time. She's a real sweetheart.'

DOING THE LAUNDRY

Sharon Hogan

There's lots of clothes washing and laundering to be done here in
Australia. Strangely enough, I'm absolutely loving it. I'm holidaying in
Perth, with my brother and his wife and three stepsons, and doing their
laundry each day has been my way to make myself useful while I'm a
visitor in their extraordinarily full lives. It turns out doing the laundry
is also proving to be a meditation.

Picture this: three growing boys, needing a full array of clean clothes
in both my brother's and his wife's ex-husband's houses, plus two hard-
working adults: daily clean clothes for school and for after-school, for
football-playing, bicycle-riding, beach-going, barbecue-making, eating,
working and sleeping – in a country where temperatures reach 40
degrees centigrade! It turns what in my little flat in Dublin is a gentle
weekly chore into a daily campaign against a veritable dirty clothes
mountain. John and Jules hate doing it, set at it when they get in from
work with gritted-teeth determination, when what they really want to do
is eat something, chill with the kids and wind down slowly. Luckily for
all of us, the combination of the sheer volume of clothes to be washed,
the fact that I'm left alone with the job during the day while they're all
out at work and at school, and the wonder of knowing that something
wet can be dry in the heat of that antipodean sun in a matter of an hour
is bringing out a domestic devotee in me that I never knew existed!

Here's the way it works: first, there's filling the washing machine with
things of the same colour, like whites (mostly little things, bras,

knickers, teacloths, the boys' boxers – it's really quite a cute little load), or reds and golds (big towels, floor mats, bright T-shirts – a good, robust load, that one), or blues and greens (John's work shirts, Jules's silky blouses – a more discreet, tasteful kind of load). And when they're washed, there's organising everything onto the clothesline (big towels on the back lines, lighter shirts and nice flapping shorts on the middle lines, little fluttery jocks and socks and bras and things on the front lines). And then the sun beats down, drying the clothes before my very eyes, and the neighbour's wind chimes sound in deep, sonorous tones, and a soft sea breeze just takes the edge off the heat.

It's a moment. The senses are wide open and all there is in the whole world is the smell of clean clothes; and bending and straightening and reaching towards the bleached-white line; and lifting light and heavy fabrics from a red plastic basket; clipping clothes in rows, with snappy little pegs of pale green, sky blue, canary yellow, tomato red; the rich clang of the wind chimes wafting in and out of hearing; the elusive touch of salt just flavouring the occasional breeze; the brilliant duck-egg blue of the cloudless sky. And in the middle of the activity, of the sounds and movements and colours and textures, there is quiet. Within the physical and sensorial variousness, there is utter silence. I love it.

Who knew I'd like a career in a launderette? Who knew my real role model would be Dot Cotton? What was I thinking, wanting to wear a chiffon frock and win an Oscar or a Pulitzer, when there's such quiet in doing the laundry?

A GOOD CONNECTION

William J. Cook

When I was growing up in the tiny coastal village of Martinsville, Maine, the family telephone was a large wooden box which was screwed to the dining room wall. Constructed of finished oak, it had a substantial presence. It was like a piece of built-in furniture in the heart of the house.

On top of the box was a metal cradle which held a heavy black receiver, and on the side was a crank for summoning the operator. Her name was Violetta and she sat at a switchboard in her house nearby. Violetta connected everyone's calls by hand, and knew everything. If you wanted to place a call you had to pick up the receiver and listen to make sure that no neighbours were already talking on the line. If indeed no one was (or if they weren't saying anything interesting), you braced yourself with one hand on the box and turned the crank handle rapidly for a second or two. It had a curious resistance, and sounded as if you were churning a cavity of felt-covered marbles.

On the bottom of the box were two bells like those on a bicycle. A clapper in the middle blurred furiously between them when a call came in. When the phone rang we needed to listen carefully because it also rang in all the neighbours' houses. Each family had a different ring so that you could differentiate between yours and theirs: two short peals, for example, or one long one. Ours was one long and one short, which was rather hard to identify, especially if you were watching TV or practising the piano.

Once we were sure that the call was for us, there would be a scattered chorus from various corners of the house. 'I'll get it!' and then silence, while each of us waited to see if someone else was closer. As my older sisters began to get calls from boyfriends, there was less hesitation. In fact, there was often a race between them and me to see who could answer it first; a mad dash that ended, if I was wearing socks, in a long and satisfying slide across the waxed floorboards. When relatives called, on Thanksgiving or Christmas, whoever answered would yell and we'd all gather round the dining table, eagerly waiting for our turn to talk.

Eventually, of course, we got a more modern phone. It wasn't quite as substantial, but we hung it on the wall where the old one had been. One by one my siblings went away to boarding school and they'd call home. Those of us remaining would hurry to the dining room. It was good to hear their voices, but it wasn't till later that I realised just how comforting it must have been for them.

It was 1972 when I first travelled abroad alone. I came to Ireland on a bicycle tour, and I must have been terribly homesick, for one of the things I remember most clearly about the trip was phoning home. I'd been ill in Killarney. It was dismal weather. I remember the chunky pay phone in the guest house; the way the overseas line crackled, and its hollow ring. Suddenly my mind leapt across the ocean to the dining room in Maine. I could see my parents heading for the phone, and even before they answered, I felt better. I realised that I wasn't just calling to chat. I was making a connection to home.

My father lives alone in the house now. We children have moved on, Mom is in an Alzheimer's ward and my wife and I are finally living in Ireland. We like it here, but I still get homesick from time to time, and then I call my father. As soon as the line starts to ring, I'm right back there in the dining room. I can see him walking across the well-worn floorboards, and when he answers, I can picture him clearly. I'm glad he doesn't have a mobile phone like everyone else nowadays. I don't have to ask, 'Where are you, Pop?'

He's right there next to me ... in the heart of home.

IN MEMORY OF FRANK HARTE

Catherine Ann Cullen

Oh where, oh where is the voice of Frank Harte?

When he sang there were two crowds:
One that gathered to listen and one he conjured out of the air.
He peopled the streets with Zozimus and Moses,
Summoned Billy in the Bowl,
Launched a flotilla of ships up the Liffey, led by the Calabar.

Dublin made him and he in turn
Built his city out of old songs,
Resurrected heroes, restored lost bridges
So the ghosts could cross back to us.

As a child he heard old soldiers from the Dublin Fusiliers
Who'd gone from Chapelizod out to Flanders
And they talked of killing snipers
In a place that they called 'Wipers'
And Frank sang of all the lives that battle squanders
With his whack fol de di dol right tan tan te nah.

His voice was anguish echoing in an empty cell,
His voice was a keening for dead trades and dreams,

His voice was a passion kept in check
Or a rebel blast across shivering rooftops.

He sang of lost worlds with lost words:
Tabinets and twangmen, waxies and swaddies.
There was a love that laughed in his telling
Of a scrimmage in Kimmage, a rumblin' in Crumlin,
Of oul' wans and bould wans and blackguards and all.

Oh where, oh where is Frank Harte now?
He is sat fornenst a hawthorn bough.
He's unlocking Kilmainham, he's opening Mountjoy,
He is sending home safely a rosy-cheeked boy,
He is following someone he called Henry Joy.
Sing whack fol di die dol right tan tan te nah.

He remembered the lot of the labourin' man:
The wasted navvies, the Paddies hoking spuds,
The lads who held hods, turned sods,
Were crushed under wheels of industry or state.

He called up James, he called up Jim,
When History lived, it lived through him,
With failures, achievers, with lovers and leavers
In the whirr of the loom of the Liberties weavers.

Oh what will he leave us? — The sun and the moon,
And the air when it carries an old Dublin tune.
Sing whack fol de di rol di all the day long,
Sing Frank Harte the weaver has spun his last song.

MATINÉE AT THE ABBEY

Val Mulkerns

It concentrates the mind wonderfully when I realise, in this, the centenary year of the Abbey Theatre's foundation, that when I was first taken there as a child of eight or nine, the theatre was a bit less than forty years old. W.B. Yeats was still alive and still appeared sometimes at the top of the parterre steps on Saturday afternoons to 'count the house', as my father said. Even at that age, I thought the long silvery hair and the exactly matching shade of the beautiful silver suit of clothes very dashing. Sometimes he sat down at the end of a row, murmuring to himself, and once he sat right in front of us until the first interval. But mostly, having counted the house, he went away.

If he counted us among the paying customers, he was greatly mistaken. Nellie Bushell could have told him that. She was a quiet-spoken little Dublin lady who sold programmes and showed you to your seat. She seemed to me very much older than Mr Yeats, and she always wore black. She had a tiny face under the wispy grey hair, and small eyes which were usually watering from hay fever, and frequently had to be mopped with a damp handkerchief. My father – she called him Rajah – always had a chat with her at the interval, and once he took her home to Inchicore by taxi in order to find out what was the trouble with her fuse box, which kept plunging her house into darkness on unpredictable occasions. My father knew Nellie Bushell as a trusted friend since the days of the Rebellion (as they both called the Rising of 1916) and he told me she was only a young girl at the time, and whizzed around the city delivering important dispatches on her bicycle. Her house, where she made us tea and gave me Hadje Bey's Turkish delight, was wallpapered with old playbills and photographs – and she had a cat which accompanied me from room to room when she invited me to look around. Only once again was I ever to see a house so full of photographs of faces familiar to me from the stage, and that was, you might say, at the other end of the timeline in the seaside home of the actress Shelagh Richards. There was a photo of *her* too in Miss Bushell's house, as one of the sisters in *The Constant Nymph*.

However, the person who amused me most on one of those Saturday afternoons was not on the stage. It was a full house that day, for Lennox Robinson's *The White Headed Boy*, and the loudest laughs came from a tall young man who apparently wasn't able to get a seat because he hadn't come in time. He sat on the floor at the end of our row, with long legs curled around one another, and his high shouts of laughter stood out among the rest. My father and he exchanged a word or two on the way out, and later, I asked who he was. 'Lennox Robinson,' my father said, shaking his head and laughing again. That was what gave me the notion that as a grown-up you couldn't have a more enjoyable job than writing plays.

The wonder is I never tried it.

In my experience you never actually see anyone reading a novel of yours, although once on the bus I saw a man in front of me folding his *Evening Herald* and beginning to read a weekly column I used to write for it. Unfortunately, he read no more than fifty words or so before turning to the sports page. Oh well, I'd only abandoned my bike that day because of the incessant rain. It would have been better to get soaked to the skin really, because there are some things it would be better not to find out.

But actually being one of the same audience which is falling around laughing at your play – now that must be something!

VINYL

Conor O'Callaghan

The older I get, the more I believe that 'music' and 'youth' are synonyms. Time was when I had a huge collection of LPs or LPs recorded onto tape by a friend who scoured the obscure shops and market stalls of London for the latest indie offerings. What I hadn't actually heard, I'd usually heard enough *about* to bluff along.

Then me and my girlfriend, with whom I once bopped at gigs, did all those bourgeois things we swore were not for us. We got married, had kids and moved out of the city. By the time thirty had long since passed through town, the CD revolution had come and our music-playing hardware (once state of the art) had the air of collectors' items. Tapes stopped arriving from Camden. One day one very nice kid wore a Smiths T-shirt into my tutorial. This was just my patch. Was he, I enquired, a big Smiths fan?

'Yeah,' he replied hesitantly. 'But they're kind of ... *old.*'

There then ensued a pre-class conversation, excluding the tutor, about a band the tutor once revered. They viewed The Smiths the way me and my generation viewed, say, The Beach Boys: ancient but admirable, purveyors of cheesy pop that must have seemed vaguely radical in its day. The conversation came to a grinding halt when one of the guys, the one with the pierced tongue, made reference to the stash of 'big black CDs' his old man kept under the stairs.

'LPs,' I interrupted.

They looked at me, quizzically, in silence.

'They're called *LPs*.'

They smirked at one another, looked at their feet and thus our class on poetic metre began.

On the strength of that chat I went looking for a new needle for my wife's stereo. She got it from her brothers and sisters for her twenty-first, and it still worked. Last I recalled, however, the needle was in bits. So one afternoon, with an hour to kill in the capital, I called into a shop on O'Connell Street that someone told me was the likeliest spot. Sensing my mortification, the assistant shouted up the shop, 'This gentleman wants a STYLUS for his hi-fi.'

The rest of the staff came down to our end, and just stood, arms folded, with something like a mixture of wonder and pity. I felt like that Japanese soldier who emerged from the jungle to be told that the war had ended years ago. The assistant sold me a one-size-fits-all model that looked more like a masonry nail, and walked me to the door.

A couple of Sundays ago my wife and me had a bottle of Chablis with our lunch, fitted the infamous stylus to the infamous hi-fi and wired the plug. We dragged the box of 'big black CDs' from the attic and cranked up the volume. We took it in turns to choose a song at a time. I went first. That moment, when I lifted the needle from its rest over to the record, was almost unbearable. When I let it go, the flack of dust and feedback crackled though the speakers. Within seconds it was circa 1983 again: the New Romantics, all button-up shirts and synth solos and lipstick. We winced, giggled a bit when we realised we still knew all the words and squabbled over the next track.

It was great fun. Simple Minds when they were still an underrated arthouse pop band from Glasgow; Horslips's glamrock reworking of 'The Táin'; Miles Davies letting fly in Carnegie Hall, May 1961; Thin Lizzy fighting the good fight; the mop-heads of Tavares from the original soundtrack of *Saturday Night Fever*. It was like being a teenager again, a momentary sensation in which our kids were more than happy to play their parts. Eve flung open the door and demanded that we turn that racket down. I was just then on my knees on the study floor, playing air guitar to the accompaniment of Mountain live in California circa 1972. I opened my eyes to find a delicious contempt on the face of our nine-year-old daughter. I got to my feet, apologised and reduced the volume. When she closed the door again behind her, we rolled our eyes and picked up where we'd left off, louder than ever.

Music, as the English poet Philip Larkin once wrote, 'shows us what we have as it once was, blindingly undiminished.' My younger brother says that turntables are making a comeback, that many of the hipper bands are releasing on vinyl too. Stick around long enough and fashion is certain to pass through your street again. Suddenly you find yourself once more being cool, if 'cool' in a vague, retro kind of way. And that thing you thought you'd mislaid in those fallow years may still be there or thereabouts and not quite as diminished as you assumed.

TEA IN MISS MAC'S

Gerry Moran

I knew her only as Miss Mac — the name my mother always called her. In fact I was so young and naïve then that it never occurred to me that Mac was short for anything.

Her full and proper name was Margaret McSweeney and she was my mother's best friend. Miss Margaret McSweeney, a very single, very gracious and very elegant lady. Indeed, for as long as I live, my concept of a lady will be that of Margaret McSweeney.

Miss McSweeney was tall and thin as a whip. She walked carefully, proudly, her chiselled face held upright and straight, her wispy hair sometimes in a bun, other times covered with a silk headscarf. And always she seemed old to my childish eyes, old and fragile as a piece of antique furniture, her thin features, hollow cheeks and occasional glasses confirming the notion in my mind.

Miss Mac and my mother had worked together as bookkeepers in the local Smithwick's Brewery. They were the best of friends, the best of chums. They suited each other like hand and glove. Miss Mac a good listener, my mother a good talker. Miss Mac the placid one, my mother the feistier of the two. Even when my mother married and went on to rear a family of five, they never lost sight of each other and always kept in touch.

Every so often Miss Mac came to tea in our house and always it was an occasion. The best delph was brought out, the good tablecloth laid and the food was always that bit more dainty, delicate and interesting.

An even greater occasion was going to tea in Miss Mac's. My mother did this once a month or thereabouts and would bring one of her brood of five in tow. Being the youngest, my turn didn't come for quite a while, but when it did I was never disappointed. Dressed like a new pin, my mother and myself set off one fine evening for tea in Miss Mac's. It was enchanting – her sitting room was full of personal effects, bric-a-brac, old photos, fine china, tawny lampshades and plush armchairs spared from the tossing and tumbling of a family of five children. The table was elegantly set – starched white tablecloth with gleaming cutlery, iced cakes, biscuits and little triangular-shaped sandwiches. It was a feast in more ways than one – the delicacies, the soft lamplight, the cosy calm and the exotic surrounds all made for a warm, intimate, magical experience.

The magic, of course, faded as I grew older and hurling on the green proved more alluring than tea in Miss Mac's. She never lost touch, however, and nearing my wedding day I drove my mother and herself to Dublin to kit themselves out for my big day. Later that evening we had tea with Miss Mac and my mother, this time in the plush surrounds of some fine hotel. A few glasses of sherry, some ale shandies and ham sandwiches found us in a jovial, reminiscent mood and for a few brief moments we could have been back in that snug sitting room of hers. Miss Mac, as it happened, was most definite about her wedding present for us: a good old-fashioned clock for the mantelpiece, one that chimed. She was adamant that it had a chime. When I pressed her as to why, she gently squeezed my arm and said, 'So you'll think of me whenever that clock strikes the hour.'

That clock hasn't chimed in a long, long time, I'm afraid, but we still have it. And whenever I look at it, perched high on a bookcase, I think of Margaret McSweeney, Miss Mac, and those magical tea-times in her cosy room that has long since yielded to progress and the voracious JCB.

A PRIVILEGE

Dermod McCarthy

You could drive down Grafton Street then. I was near Bewley's that Friday evening in May on my way home to Arran Quay when I first heard an ambulance siren somewhere in the distance, then another, and another, and they all seemed to be getting closer. As I reached Switzer's a fire engine swept up from the Trinity College direction and sped around the corner into Nassau Street.

I switched on the car radio and froze on hearing the news flash. Three bombs had just exploded in Dublin. City streets were strewn with dead and dying. Ambulances were ferrying the injured to the city's hospitals, heralded by a cacophony of sirens. Rush-hour pedestrians stood back, rigid with shock and disbelief.

I was a chaplain in the Richmond Hospital at the time. Along with Jervis Street, it later became subsumed into the Beaumont Hospital of today. The Richmond was particularly renowned for the treatment of serious head injuries. I got there as fast as I could. And so began a night that is forever lodged into the hard drive of my memory.

An hour later a fourth bomb exploded in Monaghan. In all thirty-three people died and 258 were injured that evening in 1974.

They were already carrying stretchers and trolleys into the Accident and Emergency entrance of the Richmond as I got there. To this day the images are unforgettable — pale frightened faces everywhere, no buzz of conversation, the trained efficiency of nurses and doctors, an endless succession of ambulances, operating theatre staff who had gone home for the weekend rushing back to scrub up for a difficult night's work ahead.

What on earth could a chaplain do in the midst of all this horror and chaos? I never felt so helpless. Where was God in all this, and why? But of course the big questions had to be left aside for the moment as I looked into pleading eyes and struggled to find words of comfort and calm, words to soothe and encourage.

There were no mobile phones then. I lost count of the telephone calls I made throughout the night from nurses' stations or corridor payphones to worried families — with good news and bad news. There are no words to explain to distraught parents of a beautiful young woman with an engagement ring on her finger that although she is alive and will survive, she will be different now as she tries to cope with life without a limb and an eye.

Memories of that dreadful night came flooding back a month ago on hearing news of the accident near Navan when five young women lost their lives. Once again ambulances rushed dying and wounded young people to nearby hospitals. Once again anxious parents awaited news from operating theatres and emergency departments. As the whole nation grieved with the families who had lost their children, in every home where students are bussed to school the first thought was 'they could have been ours'.

And remembering my own sense of helplessness in the Richmond Hospital all those years ago, I salute the clergy of the home parishes of those girls. Even though they were as shocked and horrified as everyone else, they impressed us both by the sensitivity with which they conveyed the pain of their people, and the poignant dignity with which they enabled the bereaved families to bid a public farewell to their daughters in the glare of national publicity.

Some might say it's all part of the job of a priest, chaplain or minister. And yes — so it is. But it is much more than that. It's a privilege to be there, to be allowed to share in the lives of people at their most critical times. It's a privilege to be called on to sit by the bedside of a dying man or woman, to help a family put words on their prayers, and perhaps even to enable the person in the bed to gently ease open the door to eternity — without fear.

THE ANCESTORS

Grace Wells

Over the table in my mother's kitchen hung a portrait fifteen feet high and eighteen feet long. Its frame was of thick gilded wood and plaster of Paris that chipped and fell away at the slightest touch. Its vast oil canvas portrayed a nineteenth-century drawing room in which nine brothers and sisters had been artfully arranged, robed in exquisite evening dress.

They were known as 'the Ancestors' and they came from my mother's side of the family, from some much larger house in a grander time, handed down through generations to rest on our wall.

As young children, my sister and I rivalled over the beautiful dresses in the portrait. Because she was older than me, it was her prerogative to choose her favourite first. She always laid claim to the beautiful pink silk skirt and cream lace of the woman who stood just left of centre, carefully arranging flowers.

I was left then to pick from the less elegant white gowns of the three girls clustered by the grand piano, or take the sapphire organza of the woman on the sofa, or the sky-blue taffeta of the lady who played the candlelit harp.

We never much noticed the men, with their long sideburns and their dark suits that blended well into the dark drawing room walls.

We wiled away hours staring up at the unimaginable luxury of those clothes, never once noticing the finer details of the picture, not seeing how badly the oriental carpet at the Ancestors' feet had been painted, nor that the four legs of the brown and white dog who looked on lovingly had been finished entirely without perspective.

Our mother loved *The Ancestors* and her love for it seemed to grow in direct proportion to the sense of embarrassment that began to wax in me. For as I grew into the world it became increasingly obvious that *The Ancestors* was some sort of anomaly. None of the girls I went to school with had ancestors who had swanned through life in ball gowns and no one we knew owned fifteen-by-eighteen oil paintings.

My shame grew and my mother's pride swelled and visitors who entered our kitchen would sooner or later ask about the extraordinary picture that dominated our lives.

My mother, with an air that was part Royal Curator and part Queen Elisabeth herself, would regale what she knew of the painting. Thus distant cousins and maiden aunts and sea-dog uncles would be informed. But my mother drew no boundaries. Delivery men, cleaning ladies, plumbers, carpenters, electricians, school friends, prospective brothers-in-law, anyone and everyone would be trapped beneath *The Ancestors*, held fast by my mother's oration.

I was mortified. I would will myself invisible, disappearing far within to a place where none of this was happening. For *The Ancestors* was slowly becoming the symbol of everything I disliked about our upper-middle-class life.

Still, my mother went on telling perfect strangers how we were descended from Dudley, the man in the centre of the portrait. She would go on about blond-haired Frank, go on about the little she knew of the women.

'You can tell,' she would say, extending a well-practised arm, 'that the three girls at the piano haven't "come out" yet, for their hair is still worn in ringlets while the other ladies have their hair up. And you can tell by their dresses they haven't been to court yet, for they are all still wearing white gowns.'

I didn't just cringe and blush: I turned away. I ran. I rejected everything *The Ancestors* and my mother stood for. I threw aside their snobberies of accent and language, their silly notions about the 'right' public school and the 'right' way to hold a fork and the 'right' way to ask for what must never be the toilet, but always the lavatory. I threw off my upbringing in search of a more honest way to live.

In time I would come to put as much distance between *The Ancestors* and myself as I possibly could. I erased their standards from my life.

But I was too young and rash to see the babies that went with the bathwater; to notice that with the one oil painting went all art; with my rejection of their splendid drawing room went architecture and great literature and a whole host of other achievements of civilisation.

Ultimately, I moved so far away that I came to be living in Ireland, in a semi-derelict thatch cottage. On its smoke-stained walls hung icons of the Madonna and John F. Kennedy. Over time and with the renovation of that home, those pictures came down and drying flowers and herbs went up in their place.

Some years after I had left that cottage, I rented an old two-storey farmhouse in the heart of the country. Above its flagstone floor hung the lamp of the Sacred Heart and a portrait of Jesus holding open his wounded hands. Out of respect to the owners of the house and to the country I lived in and to the old ways that were so evidently dying all around me, I left Jesus there to watch over us.

But on the day my five-year-old daughter asked me, with tears in her beautiful brown eyes, 'Did they really hammer nails into Jesus' hands, Mummy?', I replaced the picture with one of her own colourful works of art.

Here in my latest home, I hold off putting up pictures. My partner brings me Islamic calligraphy and Iznik plates and illuminations of ancient Istanbul that gild our walls. I begin to welcome civilisation back into my life. And this year the last of my brothers and sisters finally left home. My mother moved to a smaller house. She offered me many of the possessions that would not fit in the new place. I was happy to receive an oak desk and a green armchair and was glad I had no walls large enough for *The Ancestors*. But I was gladdest of all that my sister in Berlin wanted to take them. It pleased me to hear of their journey across Europe.

I like to think of them gracing the walls of her elegant house. I like to think they will be handed on in time to a niece or nephew; on down the lines of our family.

Last night in a dream I saw my mother's old kitchen broadcast on the screen of a television. There was our old table and behind it the great portrait exactly as it had always hung. Excitedly, I yelled for my partner to come and see the image my family had eaten three meals a day beneath, the image that was backdrop to our Christmases and Easters and our long summer holidays and all the minute details in between.

In the morning my sense of excitement stayed with me. I woke knowing that *The Ancestors* had finally entered my dreams invoking fondness. I had at last stopped running from it; stopped being ashamed. I had come home to live beneath my own skin.

BED

Nuala McCann

'You know it's time to return to the day job when you look out on a windy day and think: "Oh quick, must get a set of sheets on the line",' jokes my neighbour.

Me? Sometimes I go out to our back yard and walk straight into the big white duvet cover flapping on our line. So that it drapes me, enfolds me, blots me out — a ghost of a woman in white — just for an instant.

Is this what it feels like to be two sheets to the wind, pushed by a whoosh of breath from heaven? Is this what it feels like to disappear?

It is 1968. I am seven years old. Neil Armstrong hasn't walked on the moon, threepenny bits are still knocking about and mothers are generally the stay-at-home variety.

My mother has pillar box red lipstick and a floral housecoat; most of them did back then. She wears stiletto heels and pretty hats, but not when we're making the beds.

And we are making the beds in our house, she and I. She is a champion ironer. Her beds are crisp cotton. You sink into them and rest like you're flat on your back in a field full of daisies.

'You lift the corner and you fold it over, a kind of envelope shape,' she says. And I fiddle at my corner of the bed. (We are still waiting for the invention of fitted sheets). But she is no bossy matron. She is patient. We work together from one corner to the next. And the bed is so fresh and new and inviting that I want to crawl in and hibernate.

And now it is 1977 and my father is in hospital. He is very ill. His face is the shade of the coarse white cotton sheets. Two blue eyes peer out. The rest is camouflage.

Shipwrecked on his hospital bed, he tries hard to chat. But you can tell he is in pain and the cotton of the sheets is harsh and rough against my fingers.

I want to whisper, 'Come home to us, we have bed covers like summer meadows, warm daffodil yellows, soft pinks. Come home and we'll wrap you in crisp sheets and bring you back again.' And he does and we do.

So that when the day comes that the best, white linen sheets must be taken from the drawer of the carved wooden cabinet and someone fetches the white candles and the crucifix, I cannot believe that this is how it must be.

The snowdrops bow their heads in the small glass vase. No amount of coaxing or freshly laundered sheets will bring him back this time.

And then it is spring again and our new son is tossing about in his cradle. It is week six. Our eyelids would need to be sellotaped open. My mother comes up to our house to stay the night, armed with bed linen. She will make up a fresh, crisp bed for us, she says.

'I'll sleep downstairs with the baby, you get a good night's rest,' she says later.

And we thank her a thousand times for the chance to close our eyes. We dash up and snuggle under our crisp, fresh duvet and reclaim blessed oblivion.

Now, eight years later, my son and I are making the beds together. At the last minute, he jumps onto the mattress and shouts to me to whisk the duvet high in the air and bring it down on top of him.

High, high, I shake it out and bring it down so that he is all covered up, the silhouette of a laughing, heaving mound kicking his feet on my fresh, new bed.

'Do it again, do it again!' he shouts. And I do, again and again, as I have done since he was a baby and just able to crawl into the middle of the bed.

Nowadays, he is too cool for pictures of summer poppy fields on cotton duvets. He is a navy blue, striped kind of a boy-man. And I have no heavy iron to press into corners, smoothing out wrinkles to crisp perfection.

When you grow up, you see how little you can make perfect. Some things can never be solved by smooth sheets. But I bless my mother for her crisp, fresh beds. For the care she took into making them just right. For all the love you can gather onto one four foot, six inch bed.

THIS LITTLE PIGGY

Leo Cullen

There was a time with my father when after our mother died and we went to live in Dublin, as well as having to cut his hair, and his toenails, I also had to cut the fingernails of his right hand. He was hopelessly right-handed, that was why. Holding the scissors in his right hand he could get at the fingers of his left hand all right, but because his left hand had nil dexterity and could not manipulate the scissors, the fingers of his right hand were out of bounds to him. And he hated dirty finger-nails, in any of us, especially himself. As for his being unable to cut his toenails, well, having to look down at his toenails, he said, made him dizzy.

At least where the cutting of the toenails was concerned, he always bathed his feet in the basin for a while beforehand. Our housekeeper hunted the children from the kitchen and ran the basin and placed it at his feet and then he said, 'ouch, ouch,' and she added dribbles from a jug of cold water until she got it right and then, unless there was a phone call, he left the feet in for about fifteen minutes. If there was a phone call, which generally there was, for he got a lot of phone calls, he had to hop out to the hall to take it. But he always stuck the feet back in the basin on his return. Without his knowing it, the footbath in the basin relaxed him.

His feet were all pearly and dimpled then when they landed out on the newspaper for me to dry and manicure, the toenails so softened by the footbath that the scissors was well up to its task and the shavings fell onto the paper perfect as crescent moons. Only thing was, I didn't like to take the scissors too near the toes for fear of cutting him. And then he complained: 'Do you want to leave me with hooves like a donkey,' and I had to trim around all over again.

The right hand was the big problem: in order to get a grip of one of those thick fingers I had to grapple with him like we were wrestlers. He was so uncooperative. 'What are you doing, you're hurting me,' he squealed. It reminded me of when I was young and he used to recite as he squeezed, one after another, not my fingers, but my toes:

> This little piggy went to the market
> This little piggy stayed at home
> This little piggy ate bread and jam and butter
> This little piggy ate none
> And this little piggy went weeky, weeky, weeky, all the way home.

Now he was that little piggy.

'I can't do it,' I said then. 'Your nails are too thick.' You see, I knew that to do the job properly, to get a cutting edge, I had to place the cutting part of the scissors, not the blunt part of the scissors, inside the nail. That involved a very complicated manoeuvre of me coming at him from beneath his armpits, coming at him, you could say, in a sort of a half nelson. The struggles. The shouts:

'This is the last time I ask you to do my fingernails.'

'Well don't then, that suits me.'

The nails of his hand were like spades, hard and growing thicker with each cutting.

Then one day I had an idea: I advised him to bathe his right hand in the basin along with his feet.

'It'll only make me dizzy and wouldn't I look a right fool,' he said. 'I've never heard such an idea.'

But he did it. He was like an ostrich, with his head down and his hand in the basin. Until the phone rang and he gave a start and got tangled in himself and fell into the basin, upending soapy water all over the floor.

We didn't do that again. But he continued to ask to have his nails cut.

And then he didn't ask any more. I don't know when that happened. Other issues, like being grown up, had come into my life and I didn't notice.

I don't know how he managed after that.

When he died and he was laid out in the hospice, what amazed me most about the dignity of his lying were his feet. They were neat and small and pearly. And I couldn't help noticing the evenly cut toenails. I don't remember seeking out the fingernails of his right hand for examination. I don't think I did. I probably just knew some patient soul had ministered a benign and peaceable trimming to him, hands as well as feet.

THE COLLECTOR

Peter Jankowsky

It's when the little worlds we call our own collapse, in natural or in manmade disasters, that the colour grey comes into its own: lava and volcanic ashes, floodwaters and mud, dust and dirt are all grey, and so are the remains of our cities anywhere in the world when our wars have ground them up into rubble. Colours which had made our surroundings appear splendid and in good order have been thrown together like all the colours of a child's paint-box, and the result is a ghastly grey, the hue of destruction. Afterwards, children who have survived the cataclysms may have to discover the colours of life all over again, and will never again take them for granted.

When Berliners, in 1945, came out of their cellars, bunkers and air-raid shelters, they found their world turned upside down in every sense. So the adults, that is: the women started to clean up the mess, and we, the children, went about making this new and dangerous playground our own by collecting things. Shrapnel, for instance, held a fascination for many of my playmates, spent cartridge cases, too, and even live bullets. Both my father and stepfather had been killed by these, so I kept well away from them. Shrapnel especially I found repellent, its torn, murderous shapes, its glinting, razor-sharp edges. I had come across something more to my liking, something smooth and shiny and, once you had removed the dust, glowing with colour – a broken tile.

Many of the houses in Berlin wore socks, so to speak, for three or four feet up from the pavement they were tiled, as were many of the hallways. If you looked for them, you could find pieces of these tiles in many places now, and that's what I did. Soon I had a little collection together. It was lovely to sit on the pavement in the great heat of this first post-war summer, my back to the wall, famished and weak to the bone, and to hold one of those smooth, cool surfaces against my cheek, to squint at the crackled glaze, the marbled colour, as the light brought out all its depth and beauty. Yes – beauty. I had discovered beauty in the midst of ugly chaos. Smitten, I now wished for all the colours of the rainbow, but that was not easy; dull colours were much more common than good, clear ones. On one occasion I found walls of the most luminous cerulean blue in the hallway of a house some distance away, and my obsession got the better of me: I started to hammer away at one of the damaged tiles in order to loosen it from the wall. The next moment the door of the ground-floor flat burst open and an old man came out, waving his arms, shouting, giving out about children who were destroying the little that had been left intact by the bombs. I turned tail and for days felt miserable about my crime.

Indeed, I must have had doubts about the whole thing, because I did not bring my collection home to my family. That meant that I had to find a hiding place for it somewhere on the street. And there was a brilliant one, I thought, right beside our house. By now, reusable bricks had been salvaged and stacked up in enormous heaps along the pavement. If you removed one of the bricks, reached into the hole, pulled out another one, and so on, you ended up with a brick-sized passage with a chamber at the end, at arm's length, large enough for my treasure of maybe a dozen broken, colourful tiles. The entrance was easy enough to conceal by simply putting the first brick back in its place. I was so taken by my invention, and so anxious about its security, that I returned to it several times a day to check whether my hoard was still there.

And one morning it wasn't. No matter how much I fumbled and searched inside the stack of bricks, my tiles were gone, definitely gone – stolen! I can still recall the shock in my guts. My beautiful treasure, a part of myself, had been taken away! I could not understand it. Even today I still can't, but I'm not surprised any more. As a six-year-old I felt I was walking about in a grey fog of incomprehension. It took me some time to get over my loss. What I hadn't lost, however, was my attraction to beautiful colours and shapes. The things I collected next I could safely bring home. There was nothing untowards or even earthbound about them, they were uplifting in the truest sense: the feathers of birds are both beautiful and mysterious, in shape and colour, aren't they?

JUNE

THE BLUE NOTES IN RORY'S HEAD

Joe Kearney

It was a time when we needed heroes. It was a time when being Irish in London was not the most favoured or fashionable thing to be. While we were legitimately creating holes and trenches in the landscape of England, some others of our countrymen, with materials far more dangerous than picks and shovels, were doing similar and more deadly work in the name of 'the cause'. We, however, kept our heads down, said nothing and just continued swinging our picks. When we were not digging the heavy clays of England we hung out with our own maudlin company in the coldwater bed-sits and homesick taverns that pockmarked the ghettos of Cricklewood, Kilburn and Camden Town.

However, it was during this time, in the late 60s, that we finally found one of our own to look up to and admire. Rory made you proud to be Irish, made you proud to be associated with the land that spawned him. Rory Gallagher, lead guitar player and vocalist with Taste (that's Taste with a capital T for those few who might not have heard of the greatest progressive blues band that ever lived). Rory was one of our own; a working man when he loped his long strides onto the stage. Kitted out in lumberjack work shirt, jeans and construction boots, he wielded his battered Stratocaster guitar like an axe. No rambling quasi-philosophical intros between numbers, he just got down to the job, playing the blues. And the blues were what he understood. Over time,

Rory had tuned his ear to the music of the universe and had locked onto its fleeting and obscure wavelength.

There is music in the heavens for those who will listen, for those who choose to hear the tinkling of celestial spheres, the whispered rush of galactic winds and the oldest sounds of all, the sad notes that seep up from the belly of the world and are moved to form hieroglyphs in the clouds of heaven – the blue notes.

He caught them in his head and threw them back at us along the strung, corded tension of his guitar, those electric ghosts of old sorrows. He captured the sighing pain of the broken, the defiant chant of the dispossessed and the frustrated howls of the sufferers of injustice and maltreatment. These ghosts touched his living soul. He was the conduit through which the voiceless could articulate themselves, in the sound of the blue notes.

We, who dug for a living, knew these chords for what they were. When we sunk the pick deep into the earth, strains of this music vibrated up our arms and lodged itself close against our hearts for comfort. Our straggled clutch of navvies might have been a chain gang in Alabama or cotton-pickers beside the great Mississippi delta instead of just mere lads from Ennistymon and Mullinahone, lost and largely forgotten in London.

Our heads were wired with the complex solos we knew by heart, the thrilling riffs and the ornate flourishes we would one day come to recognise in the great baroque music of Vivaldi and Teleman. Our cheap plastic record players scratched dementedly at the vinyl of Taste's three albums until our minds included the clicks and skips of the warped shellac surfaces in the score of the music.

Sitting on the edge of some half-excavated trench, gnawing on the hunger of our loneliness, we saw jet trails above our heads and they were the strings of his guitar.

The wind howled in the trees and it screamed out 'Born on the Wrong Side of Time'. In the jostling flatbed of one of Murphy's, McAlpine's or Enright's trucks, the rhythm of 'Dual Carriageway Pain' rocked through our tired spines and re-energised us for another day.

Rory died on us twice. The first time was in 1971 when he disbanded Taste and we, his most devoted of fans, believed the world had come to a premature end and we searched the skies over London for other dark portents. The second time, unfortunately, was for real. On this week in June, ten years ago, Rory Gallagher passed away at the young age of forty-seven. He has left us with the noble legacy of his music, but most of all with the memories of that shy and gentlest of bluesmen who lifted our heads out of the clays of England and filled our souls with the old music of the world – the long, lingering, distinct howl of the blue notes.

SCHOOL TOURS

Vona Groarke

There weren't too many school tour venues close to Ballymahon. That meant a good long journey, and that was fine by us. We liked Dublin because that gave us a good two hours either way. Anywhere except Birr Castle or Clonmacnoise, which were too close to home.

One year, we went to see Oliver Plunkett's head in the church in Drogheda, lining up single file to pay our dues. Michael Ryan said on the bus that the girls all had to kiss it, but when we saw it, we were glad it was safe in a glass case.

After that, we went to Laytown for a spin on the beach. Probably most schools wouldn't think of going to the beach for their school tour, but we came from Ballymahon, bang in the middle of Ireland, as far from the sea as it is possible to get. There might even have been one or two of us who had yet to see the sea.

It rained. Michelle got lost and we searched everywhere until she was spotted up at the chipper van, chatting to the man inside, cadging a free bag. Sister Joan confiscated it and sat up on the low sea wall with Sister Paula, the two of them chatting and laughing away, polishing off the whole bag by themselves.

We all brought money, despite being warned, as we were every year, not to. There was always a gift shop open for us to stock up on our annual supply of china seagulls (for our Mas), keyrings in the shape of Guinness pints (for our Das), pocket knives and sticks of rock with a slip of paper that had the town name on it. There weren't any sticks of rock with 'Ballymahon' on them, so these were pretty exotic. The fact that you couldn't really eat them anyway meant that you could afford to leave them somewhere for Sister to sit on, just like she did every year, to great fuss.

I always had 50p and I always knew exactly what it would be spent on: a ball as pink as I could find so that maybe this year my brother wouldn't mess with it and have it burst by sundown of tour day.

The boys played football everywhere we went. My husband says he has scored goals in every archaeological site in Ireland: Tara, Newgrange, the Hill of Slane, the lot. His school should have gone to Birr: the maze would have done for them and their football.

Where we went was decided by either religion or history. Not all history, of course: no Big Houses where we might knock over priceless vases or climb on furniture. The site of the Battle of the Boyne was perfect because the amount of damage we could do to an open field was limited. As we saw it, there were plenty of open fields a stone's throw from Ballymahon where we could have eaten our banana sandwiches and Aztec bars just as easily. We liked Dublin because there was more to see and a better chance of losing someone so the bus got delayed and Sister got frantic and the culprit got her head handed to her when eventually she popped it, all smiles, round the dark bus door.

The worst thing about the tour was the inevitable essay the next day, titled 'Our School Tour'. You had to leave out all the fun stuff and concentrate on what Sister called 'the educational side'. Who won the Battle of the Boyne? What was the name of Joseph Mary Plunkett's fiancée? Where was Michael Collins shot? (Josie said the answer to this was 'in his head', because she'd seen the bullet hole in his cap in the museum.)

I know that now a lot of schools go on tours to foreign parts. In Sermione, a small town by Italy's Lake Garda, my mother-in-law recently encountered a school group of eleven-year-olds from Enniskillen singing 'I'll Tell Me Ma When I Get Home' down a hill. That's all very well, but who then will kick a ball through Tara's invisible halls or through the open goal of the lavabo at Mellifont? Who will buy the sticks of rock? And who will keep our national ghosts company with an annual update of Young Irelanders, jostling through the turnstiles, delighted with their day?

AT THE RANCH HOUSE

Leo Cullen

I had cause, recently, to spend a few days on the Dingle peninsula. On my drive there it occurred to me that it would be my first time in that area since my wife and I celebrated our honeymoon with a week there all of thirty years ago.

I spent my few days – visited the Magharees of the roaring waters; crossed the Conor Pass; viewed the Blaskets through the rain – now you see them, now you don't. Revisited all the scenes we had enjoyed.

Then I spent a night in a B&B in safe little Dingle, but woke up in the early hours in a state of shock. I sent a text message home to my wife: 'I just can't believe it's been thirty years since last we were here. Nothing in life has changed.'

The sudden realisation of time's passage, without any indication of change, had startled me.

Then on my way home I stopped at Inch Strand and walked the length of that pensive two-mile stretch, that sand dune outcrop to forgetfulness. I was looking across at the massed reeks of mountain on the far peninsula of Iveragh. We had crossed over there too, thirty years ago. We had spent the final night of our honeymoon in the home of a character by the name of Mick Murphy of Ballinskelligs, known far and wide as 'The Cowboy' for the hats he wore. I had enjoyed Mick's company and droll, sometimes wise sayings in the wild days of my unattached youth. And on that final day of our honeymoon, I had been paying him a courtesy call, seeking his blessing.

It was then, looking over at McGillacuddy's ageless Reeks from Inch Strand, it suddenly dawned on me: some things had changed. Mick Murphy was dead these ten years gone.

Mick had kept an open house. The 'Ranch House', as it was known. A pious altar boy and verger of the local church into his forties, he had, on reaching fifty, with the death of his mother, converted and become a hippie. Everybody stayed with Mick: rucksack-carrying continentals, Donnycarney ballad singers, UCD dropouts, American hippies ...

They were there, a sampling of that floating population, when we arrived on that honeymoon night of ours thirty years ago with our offering of tender lamb cutlets bought in Cahirciveen and then burned on the pan to a cinder by Mick 'The Cowboy' Murphy.

'I likes things well cooked,' he said.

Mick kept, as he called it himself, a 'graffiti room'. He liked the modern sound of the word 'graffiti'. There, fellows and lassies — anarchists, philosophers, transcendental meditators — scrawled their world-shattering slogans on the four yellow-painted walls. Mick liked to pour scorn on these sayings and yet proudly wanted to show me the additions since last I had been.

'Powerful, Mick,' I said. 'They would affect you.'

'What's powerful about them? No effect on me, man dear,' Mick answered and puffed on his Afton cigarette.

Nothing ever affected Mick. Nothing was powerful enough or over-cooked enough — anarchist slogans, cider or marijuana — for the Cowboy. He preferred, he said, his Afton cigarettes. Everybody laughed when he said that. And everybody continued to embroider the walls of Mick's 'graffiti room' with the spirit of that Idealist Age.

That night on which we stayed, there were recitations around the table. Sedition, as always, was in the air. We had Kahlil Gibran's *The Prophet*, the thoughts of Black Panther, Eldridge Cleaver, manifestations from Karl Marx. Then up rose the Cowboy and rendered, with a flourish, 'The Ballad of Sam Magee'.

My wife and I found us a bed, leaving him at the kitchen table. The others had already left; he sat on, cupping his cigarettes, staring into empty space. The Vincent van Gogh of the 'Ranch House'. It was his nightly practice; he would follow it with a visit to the 'graffiti room' to, as he said, 'see would he be affected'. The others had gone down the beach to have psychedelic experiences, or to listen into the cockle-shell depths of their own individual oceans away south of Ballinskelligs Bay. They would return later and anoint him all night with their metaphysics.

Next morning, taking our leave of Mick, I asked him how the night had gone, how it had affected him.

'No effect, man,' he said. 'No effect man dear, just some vague suicidal tendencies towards morning.'

May you rest in peace, Mick Murphy, man dear. May the thirty years of change that have passed by us rest in peace, with their ups and downs, their delights, their shocks, their vague suicidal tendencies towards morning.

THE JAMES KELLY STORY

Sam McAughtry

James Kelly, born in 1910 in Macken Street, North Belfast, went out to Australia in 1927 on an assisted passage scheme under which he was contracted to work for a set term of years. He was put to work on a farm in Queensland owned by a man who treated him very badly. The lad sent distress messages back to Belfast for money to buy back his rights and allow him to go out on his own, but there wasn't much money about the place at that time. That's when the story came to my attention because we were blood related to James Kelly.

It's complicated: my maternal grandmother married Billy Condit, and put together a family of Condits – three girls and four boys. Billy Condit died in his thirties. Charlotte married the lodger, John Kelly. The issue of that marriage brought James and other Kellys into the family circle, only it wasn't a very symmetrical circle, more like an oblate spheroid, because the Kellys were Catholics, and we weren't. This meant that, especially after an outbreak of sectarian trouble in 1935, the Kellys were drawn deeper into the Catholic part of Belfast and visits were very rare. But before that happened, the serious plight of young James out there, far away, where a letter took six weeks to reach him, did bring us into things.

I remember as a boy of about eight, in 1930, my aunt Lizzie Emerson, one of the Kellys, in our house, wringing her hands and crying sore at the plight of James away out there in Australia suffering hardship. One thing she said I've never forgotten: 'The oul farmer's not even feeding him right,' Aunt Lizzie said. 'He makes him eat whole melons out of the crop in the field before meal breaks so that he'll be too full to eat meat. He spends half the time starving.'

The purse came off the mantelpiece for James. I don't suppose it would have been more than a shilling. That was a time when my father's ship was laid up and there was only the brother Jack working as a message boy, bringing in a wage of five shillings. I was carrying two heavy pails of milk around doors after school hours for an old milkman called Barclay. He gave me three pence a day for it. Those were days when tradesmen came around the streets offering to paint the windows and sills for two pence a house, and men who'd fought in the 1914–18 war were singing for their suppers in the streets. Every now and again I used to think about James Kelly and thank God I wasn't that badly off. Melon's all right in its place, but you'll not fight many three inute rounds on that alone. We were getting the good ham bones and pork knees, ling fish like leather and the best of tripe, of which we were never short.

There was another whip around for James, I recall, and then there was silence. For seventy years. If you can imagine that an e-mail breaks silence, that's what happened in late April last. I got one from my publisher telling me that a Mary Downes from Queensland, Australia had come across my name on the internet and wanted to get in touch with me. Her maiden name was Kelly.

The computer has been red hot ever since. She's looking up her family tree and she simply can't get enough of me and my recollections, and I can't get enough of her because she's a retired lady, the loving daughter of James Kelly, and he came out of his troubles all right. He was required to find twelve pounds to get out of the obligation of the free passage from Belfast and the bond to Mister Skinflint and he walked off the farm and worked and worked until he got it. I have just received over the magical internet a picture of the bold James taken on his wedding day in 1939, and didn't he do well? He's actually wearing the kind of wedding clothes that in those days we thought were only for film stars or the Lord Mayor of Belfast — claw hammer coat, silken bowtie, a bride dressed for *Vogue* magazine and the two of them looking as if they wore a rig like that every weekend. Jessie French was her name and they were married in Queensland.

He died in 1990, and left behind him a lovely family, including Mary, who is leaving no stone unturned in tracing his Irish relations. We are something to each other, Mary and I, and it's great. But isn't that a lovely touch to finish on: a Kelly, married away out there, in a place called Innisfail?

FOR THE LOVE OF MIKE

Clodagh O'Donoghue

I must have had a romantic turn of mind from an early age. Although I don't remember it, I have been told that my first official crush was on RTÉ broadcaster Mike Murphy. Apparently I met him at the age of three or four, at his father's garage in Harold's Cross, when I was out for a walk with my granddad. He was on the telly and he had shaken hands with me; that was enough. I don't know how long my romance with Mike lasted, but certainly it was over by the time I started school. I know that for a fact because I can remember that a picture of my new love was pasted inside my schoolbag – a mini briefcase that clicked open to reveal the jet-black, slicked-back hair and steely gaze of Jack Lord who played Steve Garrett in *Hawaii Five-0*. I can't recall much about this second affair either, but I do remember that I only ever saw half an episode because my bedtime came midway through. I don't know if the early 1970s boasted a distinct lack of teenage soap stars and boy band material that a four-year-old girl had to turn to this older, more rugged specimen of manhood to have a crush on – but Jack Lord was what did it for me in Low Babies.

When I was seven or thereabouts, my roving romantic eye fixed on another Steve – Steve Austin, the Six Million Dollar Man, so named because that is how much it cost the FBI (or was it the CIA?) to give him two bionic legs, one bionic arm and a bionic eye after he suffered terrible injuries in a disastrous space mission. I thought Steve Austin was only gorgeous and I laughed unreasonably loud and long at any little quips he cared to make.

My crushes tended to focus more on the characters than the actors. I knew, of course, that Steve Austin was played by Lee Majors, and even though celebrity gossip was not what it is now, you would have had to be living on Mars not to know that Lee Majors was married – in real life, like – to Farrah Fawcett from *Charlie's Angels*. Now, knowing *that* presented a problem because, although I was naïve, I was not stupid. And even my vivid and romantically inclined imagination could not quite run to imagining that Lee would leave his tanned, toned, buxom beauty for a slightly plump, painfully shy seven-year-old in Ballinteer. So I concentrated instead on pretending to be this incredibly wise-beyond-my-years, strangely enthralling girl that Steve Austin would meet as he battled sundry evil threats to US security. Or, later, I pretended to be Jamie Sommers, the Bionic Woman – two bionic legs, one bionic arm and a bionic ear. I could truly understand and sympathise with the problems of being bionic. And Steve would be very drawn to me because we had so much in common.

After the Six Million Dollar Man, there was – in no particular order – the Invisible Man, the Gemini Man (who else remembers him?), Spiderman, Superman, but not, for some reason, Batman – and so it went on. By eight or nine, it was the turn of the Hardy Boys. My first choice was the younger brother – Joe, if memory serves. He was the lighter-hearted, more humorous, upbeat one in the pairing, and he was played by Shaun Cassidy who, I'm nearly sure, was also a singer. Joe was a great flirt and regularly struck up a jokey, sparky relationship with some well-matched, wise-cracking girl he met in the natural course of his mystery-solving endeavours. The more serious relationships were saved for his older brother, Frank, who tended to fall for the more trou-bled, more complicated female. In due time, the frivolity and carefree attitude of Joe Hardy wore thin and – frailty, thy name is woman – I sought solace in the arms of the more mature brother, Frank. Having fantasised about days spent laughing with Shaun Cassidy, I switched to dreaming about deep chats with the always somewhat pained Parker Stevenson.

I moved on from the Hardys to an older, much cooler crime-solving duo. With most women my age, you can say, so, who did you like, Starsky or Hutch? With me, of course, the answer was *both*: first Hutch, then Starsky. And then back to Hutch again. Saturday evening was bath night in our house. When we had all been washed and I was in my pink, quilted dressing gown with a headful of foam rollers to create a headful of ringlets for mass the next morning, we all sat down to watch Dave Starsky (the funny one) and Ken Hutchinson (the soulful one) do their thing. As the series went on, the storylines got darker and they spent more of their time hunting criminals in dodgy go-go bars and strip joints, so its appeal as a family entertainment waned. Eventually, it was abandoned altogether in our house and *The Two Ronnies* became the mainstay of our Saturday night viewing shortly after. You will be glad to hear I didn't fancy either Ronnie!

And so, from Rory in *Wanderly Wagon* to Buck Rogers in *The 25th Century,* I managed to be in love constantly throughout the entire 1970s and fairly well into the 1980s. Happily, my tendency to fall in love so frequently and indiscriminately did not endure into later life and, in fact, I married my first boyfriend. But although he has no ex-boyfriends to feel threatened by, he has a long line of crime-fighting, mystery-solving, space-travelling, high-flying, cape-wearing, bionic, supersonic, iconic types to live up to – not to mention Mike Murphy.

WINDOW SEATS

Enda Coyle-Greene

After he had scraped the block,
swept the floor and shut the shop,
he counted out the takings
in the company of Radio 3.
He knew all about Sibelius, Beethoven,
Bach, Puccini, Verdi and especially
Wagner: he didn't have much time
for Mahler.

Once, I saw him naked
to the waist, trouser braces tailing
George Webb shoes, standing
stirring at a vat of molten wax
fat for the soap factory
in Dun Laoghaire. It was very late.
We should have been at home
by then, the car safely bedded

in the suburbs, the tea's debris
still on the table, television's fables
black and white
behind a snow-blind screen.
She fussed around in lilac checks

and Paris high-heeled shoes; undressed,
a light bulb swept across the blue
in her black hair, his
sweat-greased, pig pink head.

We waited, drawing on the torn-off sheets
of off-white paper
used for swaddling steaks
and mince; the hearts
years later, he would make me mark
the price on
with a slippy pencil
after I had weighed them.

Outside, the Corporation truck sucked up
abandoned apples, pulpy
cabbage leaves, the still sea-reeking ice
the dealers left behind them;
agonised grey shouting gulls
culled fish-less heads.

*

On the shoe shop's propped up wall
two fire-grates breasted the weather in the street.

He always parked the car there; he didn't walk,
he lurched, between the gutter and my school bag

and Burke's pub opposite, on the corner of the lane;
brownly invisible, I drank red lemonade,

he sank a pint, before he let our money slide
down the cool tight throat

of the bank's night safe.

*

Don't call me uncle, doll, his youngest brother said:
it made him feel as old as the old man
I imagined him to be; then, like Frank Sinatra,

he would flick his cigarette away between stiff fingers
way before the tip, as if there were plenty more
there, where that had come from.

*

Saloon, put me in mind of flouncy ladies
slinging whiskey back in stubby tumblers;
I never noticed that they'd left an *O* out
when they'd written it
in glass on Knox's door
below the woman's face turned sideways.

I looked through her onto Moore Street.
Darkness coloured in the light
behind her head, swelled the time
I counted in the split ends peeled apart
to see if I was loved, not loved.
Half-moon rinds

of fingernails I'd sent in spittled orbit
landed nowhere, as the door behind me
opened up enough to let a laugh escape
the smoky steam, and someone else's air
of beauty passed me
on the stairs.

*

I could see the stars stretched over Henry Street,
slung between cold chimneys. I could see

the moon hung out above the rooftops.
I could see her take the plums she'd bought, hard

cash handed over. I could see that they were soft
and not the ones she thought she'd chosen,

I could see that they were taken from behind
the hand-marked sign.

I could see her skim the mirror of the windows'
thin reflections. I could see

what she could never see: the stars
stretched out in darkness, dying

in her eyes.

*

Thirst slaked, the beardy man embraced
his brown-bagged strangled bottle; folded
at the neck, the knees, heeling over
on the street, he spread out
on a sheet of pee. He'd made his bed.

She told us not to look. Trying hard, we didn't
step on lines. One, two, three, we jumped
the grass the cracks spat up; gaping
at his black-mawed flies, we straddled
cellar gratings I was sure would open wide

and swallow us.

*

The lights went out
in one by one rectangle;
purple fly machines whined.

She carried crisp new
shopping bags that rustled

loud as money,
he balanced books and papers,
struggled with the keys
that rang like gaolers'

on the ring he'd hooked
around the padlock.
Stubborn, in the car

we sat behind them,
fighting
over window seats.

WALK, DON'T WALK

Kate E. Foley

The lights are flashing and there she goes again in her little singsong voice ... 'Maaamm – "Waalk: Don't waalk; Waalk; Don't waalk."'

That was the chant of my then three-year-old to the rhythm of her buggy wheels as we set out on our daily walk down Third across Eighty-sixth Street, from Lexington to Park, Madison to Fifth, and then to our oasis of playgrounds in Central Park. This was uptown Manhattan and early spring mornings could sometimes be a pleasure with bright blue skies, warm sunshine, cherry blossoms and that quiet lull for a few short hours, when all those busy trendy yuppies had long been swallowed up by the network of subways snaking deep below us. It was then that we, the mums and kids, older residents and their beloved dogs, jovial doormen and janitors, came into our own. The mailmen too, having dispatched thousands of pieces of mail, were now following that hypnotic aroma of freshly baked blueberry muffins and bagels, steaming coffee and hot chocolate wafting from the café doorways, abandoning their postal trolleys for a few precious snatched moments of sustenance and typical New York banter.

But, if this was the somewhat tranquil scene after the morning rush hour, then there was an entirely different one in the evening. Indeed, if Central Park meant playtime and leisurely strolls in the morning, it certainly meant something different for me and that whole merry band of joggers, runners and walkers who took over, darting from block to block, avenue to avenue, before the evening shadows caught us unawares. With our colourful display of designer t-shirts, trainers, headbands and caps, this was no catwalk; this was serious business and we women were on a mission. As April blossomed into May 'Walk; Don't walk' took on a whole different meaning.

With the New York Women's Mini Marathon on the horizon, swift action had to be taken and after a few quick warm up sessions at the New York Road Runners Club, off we flew like migrating swallows around Central Park reservoir for as long as we could last the pace. The reservoir was then and still is a Mecca for the serious and not so serious runners, joggers and walkers and with a track of one and a half miles, it certainly was the ideal training ground – four times around and you had a mini marathon! The air was always cool and fresh from the evaporation of the water and if you managed to lift your head up now and again you could catch a quick eyeful of the Manhattan skyline.

But this was back in 1985 and participation of women in running events was still only gaining momentum. Much praise and gratitude was due then to the late Fred Lebow who was a champion of runners. He was the founder of the famous New York Road Runners Club and many major races, including the New York City Marathon. He was also a dedicated advocate of equality for women in running and worked tirelessly during his lifetime to ensure that women were no longer marginalised. Fred, along with champion pioneers of running Nina Kuscsik and Kathrine Switzer, co-ordinated and staged the world's first ever Women's Mini Marathon in New York on 3 June 1972. In fact, the sponsors initially wanted him to launch a women's full marathon but Fred felt that a six-mile race would be more suitable as a launch race. Strangely enough it was named the mini after the fashionable miniskirt of the time. A lot has happened in women's running events since then and 1984 saw the staging of the first ever women's Olympic Marathon in Los Angeles.

And here we were at last, on Marathon day, after months of dedicated training, this brave bunch of amateurs in the presence of legends, including the first ever Women's Olympic Marathon winner Joan Benoit and silver medallist Grete Waitz. Central Park was a frenzy of activity with its unique atmosphere of celebration, hand clapping, warm-up exercises and music. The fact that the starting point was close to the famous eatery Tavern on the Green was proving a bit of a distraction to me personally, as were the ascending balloons, to which I seriously contemplated anchoring myself, in true Mary Poppins style. Reality struck as I suddenly felt myself being propelled forward to the point of no return.

Some four miles on, I spotted my wildly excited coterie of supporters. I waved to my bewildered daughter as she watched her equally bewildered mother being swept past in a kaleidoscope of puffy red faces, flying pigtails and flailing arms and legs. All the time I was wondering if I would ever see Tavern on the Green again, or her for that matter. Promptly dispelling such negative thoughts, I strode onwards, now lacking some of my earlier grace, and made a last valiant effort to reach the finishing line. Spurred on by the euphoric cheering crowds, I made it. I had survived, received my medal and the ever-telling photo that clocked my finishing time. And no, I didn't break any records.

Next morning the buggy took its rightful place alongside the postal trolleys, and blueberry muffins never tasted so good!

THE SNATCH

Leo Cullen

For one important year and a bit I was a porter with CIÉ at Westland Row station. I worked off a roster that contained a variety of tasks. These included:

(a) Sweeping the carriages, under the stewardship of a superintendent named Jim whose great hate was the Knock excursion train, of which he complained there was 'no mankier rolling-stock'.

(b) Polishing the ashtrays and other metal fixtures with a gang of great cleaner ladies, notably Vera, who gave Jim lip and who one day when Jim asked her what position of authority did she see written on his cap replied, eejit.

(c) Cleaning the tracks. You were requisitioned a bucket and tongs for that task.

(d) Sorting the mail into separate buggies for early departure to the pier at Dún Laoghaire. Sometimes tasty morsels peeped temptingly through holes in mail bags – it was the days when Limerick cooked ham and smoked wild salmon were sent to England.

All these jobs had their own importance, but the most important job of all was the 'snatch'.

The route west from Westland Row ran along a single gauge line. The snatch was a security system to ensure that only one train ran on a given stretch of line at a given time. It would not do to be racing westward if an opposing train was also on the track. The consequences just did not bear considering and those train drivers relied on the man standing in the engine alongside them, the porter, who was charged with the snatch. It was a foolproof method of security but only if properly executed. Once you made that snatch as you sped through your small country station, for instance Kilcock, you had right of way to the next station, Enfield, on the line. The train that had last come down in the opposite direction had left it there. On *your* way up, *you* returned it for the *next* train down and so on. Without the snatch in your possession you did not have authority to travel on.

There were two types of snatch. The hoop: the station-master stood on his platform and held it and as you flashed by you picked it up by running your outstretched arm through it. Or the staff: a cumbersome device which you picked up by lowering a set of iron jaws from the side of the train and which grasped a stiff canvas paten, known as the staff, left on another set of jaws attached to a pole at the outskirts of the station. On the staff was engraved the name of the station. You conducted this hazardous manoeuvre at fifty or sixty miles an hour, your body out the window to the waist, water streaming from your eyes and the wary gaze of the driver upon you. Believe it or not, I found this second method easier.

The Iron Horses had engines of two types, one British, one American, the Bobo and the Coco. You raced your Bobo or your Coco, your gleaming brown and orange chariot, across Royal Meath and on to Queen Maeve's Connaught. Bob the driver was a stickler for time-keeping, a grave-faced man whose face was automatically drawn to clocks wherever he went. You never engaged drivers in conversation anyway, the legend being they were notoriously grumpy. Bob certainly was so. His only moment of levity was when he gave two hoots of the horn at a small cottage west of Lucan. It was a greeting to his two spin-ster sisters with whom he lived. I learned later it was also an alarm clock, to wake them up lest they sleep all day long in his absence. His only other moment was when he muttered 'bull's eye' each time you scooped up the hoop so he could gallop onward, westward bound.

Arriving into Athlone, you always got a little thrill as the train slowed like time itself slowing and the Shannon flipped slowly past like an upside down sky and you felt that you too had been somewhat respon-sible for arriving punctually to pick up the nuns and the soldiers and take them on to Roscommon.

But a day arrived when the passengers were kept waiting: Bob was the driver, I was the snatch man and Vera was the cleaner whose job was to doze in a carriage until journey's end, whereupon she was to spring into action, rendering our train spotless for the home journey. At Kilcock as we approached, faster than usual, I saw the station-master stand commandingly on his platform, hoop held high. I saw the flash of face and ample tummy as we whizzed past. My arm was crooked for the pick-up but I picked up only fresh air. I missed the hoop.

Bob's normally impassive face turned to thunder. Immediately he took his foot off the dead man's clutch, and eventually somewhere on that stretch between Kilcock and Enfield the train squealed to a slow halt. After an age the station-master appeared along the track, carrying the hoop. I received nasty looks, passengers put their heads out the windows, the train hissed, the country smelled of hay. Then we slowly chugged away, and the prime heifers of the Midlands returned again to their grazing.

In Athlone, where, as laid down by regulation, Bob, Vera and I took our cup of tea in the staff canteen, the nuns looked in at us. 'What are they looking at,' Bob complained. 'You,' said Vera. 'They are readin' the time. You have a big round face on you like a clock.'

And so it dawned on me: Bob the clock-face. Bob, the hooped snatch. His face had grown to resemble the timepieces he was always gazing at, to resemble the hoop of that snatch; with its 'bull's eye' centre through which the trainloads of passengers that were his care had to be safely guided.

MARIONA

Cathy Power Hernandez

If you want to visit someone in the Mariona prison, outside the Salvadoran capital, you better be there early on Thursday or Sunday morning. The more hardy women are there at midnight the night before, but a six o'clock start in the queue should guarantee you a visit that day.

There is a women's queue and a men's queue and guess which one is shorter and moves faster. He was in within the hour; five hours later I got to see our Rafael.

Meanwhile, I stood in the sun, between the prison wall and the traffic, like an eejit, with no headgear and no sun cream and no bottle of water and considered how far from home I was but how well I could relate to this whole business. Women looking after their men is a universal thing and whether it be visiting Mountjoy or Mariona, the Mater or the Bon Secours, the same chat and the same sentiments are there.

How he was the last time, how he might be today, what he needs, what he thinks he needs, what you know he needs, how you are without him, when will he be home, will he ever, will we ever be the same again. Women doing their best to make their man happy, self-sacrificing, self-effacing, inventive, resourceful, brave and loyal. And they are bringing with them fine cooked meals, maybe better than they eat themselves at home. They are looking after their men.

On visiting days a whole market materialises along the busy, dusty road running alongside the prison wall. Everything a prisoner could want and cannot buy inside is for sale, and as everywhere else in El Salvador, the entrepreneurial spirit is alive and well so the range of services is amazing. You can have your hair cut, washed and blow dried while you queue. You can have a manicure. You can leave your bag to be minded. Prison regulations dictate that men cannot enter wearing black, so if you have the misfortune to have travelled a long distance and arrive in your black jeans, you can peel them off in a makeshift, curtained booth and rent a pair of denims for the couple of hours.

Chicken and chips, bought earlier at KFC by the vendor, is sold while still lukewarm. You can buy milky coffee, homemade cheeses, breads, biscuits, paper dinner plates of meat, two veg, salad and rice, toilet paper, soap, shampoo, clothing, shoes, brushes, combs, razors and all from stalls of which there will be no trace tomorrow and not until the next visiting day.

When it eventually opens at 9.30 a.m. there is an Ahhh from the crowd and the shuffle forward begins, as the erratic, momentary openings of the gate become the focus of attention. Once inside, the first searches begin. There is the bag search, the body search and the food search all inside the front gate.

The bags are emptied and everything examined and not put back, leaving you scrambling to gather your belongings and move along. You are physically frisked, prodded and poked. Long-handled knives and spoons are used to trawl the bottom of pots of warm rice and veg, forks are used to prong meat and fowl. It is horrifying to see the same utensils used for all if you have tried to avoid botulism in your own offering. But there's the choice. Let them search what you have or don't bring anything in.

Once inside the front gate and through the first search, there is a steep climb for about a kilometre to the next hurdle: the showing of identification. More searching of body and bags and body again and handing over of photo ID and being looked at twice and then a third time in comparison to the photo and it is so hot that you think you will fall down and die and disappear into a little pool of sweat on the ground and the weight of the rice, meat and salad meal is killing you and so are your feet and still you are in a queue to see your man.

When you get to see him then, it is all worth it. It puts you in a good mood and prepares you for the reverse process, which takes about half the time but still involves queuing to get your ID back, to be searched, to be scrutinised, to be exhausted. If it is a Thursday you have two days to recover before the whole thing starts over again. If it's Sunday you have three days. Greater love than this has no man.

YOKO ONO SAYS YES

Deirdre Mulrooney

1989. After two years of French and English at University College
Dublin, it was on the number 10 bus, swinging around Baggot Street,
that the 'there's got to be more to life' epiphany hit – time to avail of the
'year out' option.

Intrepidly, browsing Eason's international magazine section shelves,
an A3-sized magazine called *Paris Passion* leaped out at me, saying, 'Come
do an internship in Paris.' Who was I to say no? 22 Rue Yves Toudic,
Paris 75009. I wrote it down.

No sooner was I comfortably ensconced in my teeny Chambre de
Bonne on the swish Avenue de la Grande Armée than I consulted my
Rough Guide for the aforementioned Rue Yves Toudic. Well, when I say
comfortably, it was a little wider than myself – my room consisted of a
single bed and one plug-in electric cooking ring on which I cooked
porridge for *le petit dejeuner, le dejeuner, et le tea!*

Map in hand, out of my Chambre de Bonne I marched, down the six
flights of stairs, up past the Arc de Triomphe, down the Champs Elysées
and all the way to Place de la République. It was my first foray in Paris.
Before the end of the day, I was in the *Paris Passion* magazine offices
saying, 'Hi, I saw your advertisement for interns, when can I start?'

I was assigned to the culture editor, who in turn assigned me to the
Classical Music and Opera listings. 'Great,' I enthused. I knew nothing
about classical music and opera, but thought it best not to mention that.

For my first assignment, the rather glamorous culture editor (I heard
she went out with John McEnroe afterwards) asked me to deliver an

RSVP to a gallery on Rue de Seine et Buci. Couldn't they have faxed it? 'No problem!' I responded cheerfully and set off on my mission like Indiana Jones.

Beloved Rough Guide in hand, I found the narrow Rue de Seine et Buci. Confidently, I counted down the numéros to find the one I was looking for. But it wasn't there. How could that be? I paced up and down the rue, trying to figure out the logic of its street numbers. Finally, I decided to bang on the boarded-up entrance of a derelict-looking building where in a causal universe, the gallery should logically be.

Time passed. Eventually a door where there was no door creaked open. Within, a little man whispered, 'Shh, Yoko Ono and John Cage are in here.' John who? The little man led me into a small, brightly lit space with television cameras, a white ladder against a white wall, and yes, Yoko Ono standing there in all her understated glory with short hair and big bug-eyed glasses. It was unmistakably her.

I found myself squashed up beside a gentle-looking, tall man who smiled at me benevolently, before moving over so I could lean on the wall beside him. That was John Cage, I discovered later. Yoko nodded at me and returned her gaze to the camera. I watched on incredulously as she climbed the stepladder, reached up, took hold of a magnifying glass that was dangling on a piece of string from the ceiling, peered through it at something on the ceiling, and then tried to climb down the ladder again. She took a moment before pronouncing delightedly to the camera: 'It says yes!' Miming out climbing actions, she elaborated, 'You see, life's like that, you're climbing, climbing, climbing, climbing – and the answer is YES!'

As soon as Yoko concluded her strange display, I handed over the RSVP and ran out of there as fast as my legs could carry me. Weirdos!, I thought.

Back in the safety of *Paris Passion*'s open-plan office, I sidled in front of my computer screen and returned to compiling my listings. A while later I mumbled in a throw-away manner, 'Oh yeah, Yoko Ono and some guy called Cage were there recording stuff for TV.' As if back where I came from – Joyce's land of the yes, yes, yes – this was the sort of thing that happened every day.

A BLOW-IN'S WEDDING

John Wakeman

Nine years ago my wife Hilary was appointed rector of a Church of Ireland parish in west Cork. I came with her and so did our daughter, Rosie. In the spring of 1996, the smell of wild garlic in the air, we moved into a big Victorian rectory and began to take stock of how life had changed.

Our last home had been in the middle of Norwich, a busy city on the east coast of England. Hilary had been vicar of a parish in downtown Norwich and I had just finished a geriatric degree at the local university. This was a different world, a world made of rock, wildly beautiful, and silent except for the wind and the birds and maybe a cow somewhere keening for a stolen calf.

And the people were just as different. The anonymity of English life was stripped away from us. Everyone knew who you were and everyone wanted to know more. This shameless curiosity alarmed us at first, but gradually we came to realise that the curiosity wasn't idle. A close community was making room for us, and needed to know exactly where to fit us in.

A couple of weeks after we arrived, we went to a traditional session in the Courtyard bar in Schull, our nearest big village. The place was packed. Late in the evening, an enormous young man in boots edged his way in and peered around him through the smoke. His eyes lit on Rosie's face as a compass needle fixes on true north. This was Richie, then a fisherman. A year later they were married. That is when we really began to learn about the people of west Cork and about kindness.

Very little rain fell that spring. With the wedding near, our well began to dry up. We hoarded water like money, but it was useless. In the end, only mud was running out of the taps, or air. The wedding reception was to be at the rectory, but how could we cater for 150 guests? You couldn't even flush the lavatory.

I went to the local pub in Drinagh, where I had never been before, and asked the unknown man at the counter if he could rent us a water tank for the wedding. He gave me a hard look. 'I could not,' he said. Then he smiled and added, 'I could lend you one, of course.'

The problem was that his tanks held only 300 gallons, and he reckoned that wouldn't be enough for a wedding at the rectory. How did he know I was from the rectory? It's west Cork. His mate joined in and they discussed the problem as if it were their own. Then a young farmer who was waiting for service spoke up. 'Peter has that big milk tanker,' he said. 'Wouldn't he want to wash that out, and fill it with clean water and tractor it over to the rectory?'

'Ah, he would of course.'

Would he? I didn't even know who Peter was. Why would he? And that was only one of such many acts of kindness, incomprehensible to the likes of us, accustomed to a society where you got what you paid for, or less. We were lent chairs and tables and glasses, and given a churchful of arum lilies. An electrician spent half an unpaid day rigging up lights in the old stone outbuilding that was to house the bar, as well as outside above the rectory's big yard. That's where the reception had to be. There wasn't room indoors.

But then a new problem loomed. Serious rain was forecast at last, and it was forecast for midsummer's day, the summer solstice, the wedding day.

The morning dawned grey. The house emptied as friends and visiting family headed down to the church along the road. Rosie emerged perfected from her room and my brother-in-law chauffeured us to the church in his beribboned Volvo. Inside it was packed, and there were three priests robed at the altar – Hilary, the parish priest of Schull and Richie's Uncle Connie, a missionary priest home from Nigeria for the occasion.

After a tear-jerking certainty of the I do's, we straggled out of the church and into a spatter of rain. Liam the fiddler began the wedding tunes and we all tramped behind him along the road and up the long avenue to the rectory. By the time we got there, the rain had stopped and the sun came out. It stayed out all day, for the imitation champagne, the speeches, the food, the music, the dancing and the joy.

And who had sent the rain away? The Infant of Prague — several families had put a little statue of the Infant under a bush facing south. That will always guarantee fine weather, or so many people in west Cork believe. And it did, didn't it?

THE FORCE THAT THROUGH THE GREEN FUSE DRIVES THE FLOWER

Mary O'Donnell

When my daughter was very small I quietly pledged that I was never going to be one of the women who spends her time chauffeuring children from one fixture to another. No, *I* was never going to be part of the permanently dashing crew of driving women whose days are defined by getting their progeny from A to B or even X, with a batch of buns thrown in for voracious kids to scoff after a camogie match. This, as far as I was concerned, was the surest route to a life of permanent distraction which would result in the death of my most cherished beliefs.

But ideology and what we call 'the *rale* world' have always been uneasy bedfellows and the less said about the driving, the better. However, next September my daughter goes into secondary school and I realised recently that there's one routine I will genuinely miss when that time comes. For the past eight years I have turned up, like most of the other parents, at three o'clock on the school road in Straffan. I have sat waiting in the car, tuned into the radio arts programme, sometimes muttering to myself if I disagreed with the reviewers. On other occasions I have been reading as I waited, or sometimes there's time for a quick chat with another waiting parent.

Often, though, I'm more likely to sit enjoying the sight of two things: the heavy chestnut and beech trees that overhang the road, and the lines of children heading down towards the village. There is nothing more reassuring to the adult mind than mature trees in any season, and, beneath them, half-shaded, groups of young people liberated from school, tramping steadily down the road. That sounds very idyllic, and I know that all children carry their own burdens of worries, often invisible to adult eyes. But for those few minutes as I wait, it's a chance to consider the notion that some things are going along very properly and are in tune with the process of growth.

Trees are budding and leafing, even as horrendous events are taking place on our technologically networked planet. I am reminded of Dylan Thomas's poem that begins 'The force that through the green fuse drives the flower/Drives my green age; that blasts the roots of trees/Is my destroyer.' Sitting in the car, I am aware of sap rising up, and of the murmuring energy that goes on and on, regardless of moods and discontents. In the silence of growth, a voice is speaking and the godly is awake. The shafts of light and shade, the spattering of spring buds, the sienna leaves of autumn and the pure skeletal quality of these trees in winter have been absorbed into the panels of my seeing.

Beneath the trees, the children come, moving steadily towards the cars where the parents wait. When my child first began school, the memory of the tragedy at Dunblane primary school in Scotland was still fresh in the heads of most of us. Mental images of lambs and wolves abounded, or birds of prey, of falcons striking down the fledglings that had not yet had a chance to spread their wings. Now in the final year of primary school, I see the force in the green fuse that Dylan Thomas spoke of, driving through her and through all the children.

They have changed in eight years. Some were quivering infants in their first year, and the teacher was a goddess dispensing kindness and wisdom in equal measure. 'Mrs Toolan knows *everything!*' I was once defiantly informed by my five-year-old. Handwriting has changed from huge, leaden, effort-filled carvings to the capable dimensions of the kid-in-a-hurry and all notes are scribbled in text. Language is changing and will change even more. The children's bodies have stretched. The boys have prominent noses and jaws and make a fists-clenched, triumphal *Yesssss!* sound to any news or achievement. The girls are tackling the joint subjects of fashion and mobile phones with doctoral studiousness. Hair is a vital means of self-expression for both. But mostly, they have formed friendships, and move and think in groups. They are a collective of younger humans drawn magnetically to one another's lives.

As I sit in the car I see her coming into view, the tallest of the girls, the familiar furry-edged blue coat, the long hair, watch the steady tramp of trainered feet as they come towards *us*, the *waiters*. It's a strange thing to realise how we women will wait for our daughters probably for the rest of our lives. What else would we do, except wait for their growth? What else would we do but observe that green fuse bursting up through them, even as we sense the next line of the poem: 'And I am dumb to tell the crooked rose/My youth is bent by the same wintry fever.'

The waiting is a guardianship. When my three o'clock beat on the school road ends in June, I will never again experience its privilege in quite the same way.

JULY

TWO AMERICAN ACTS

Vona Groarke

Act I: Our Trees

We never owned a tree in Ireland, but now in North Carolina, we find ourselves with twenty-three of them scattered round our lot. Look at an aerial photograph of any block in even this suburban neighbourhood, and it can be difficult to see the houses for the trees.

All this sunlight suits our trees: they dress for it as if for the chicest parties; preen themselves for all its play, its elegant conversation, its light touch. They make a light show of our house, raking the floor with shadow and the walls with the imprint of their leaves that we sift through raised fingertips, and let lie on our skin.

We bought a book that tells us we have a persimmon, an almond and a clutch of oaks. Walking the dog one evening, I admired a flurry of white blossoms at the end of the road, only to discover as I neared home that the tree was on our front lawn.

So, we spent every Saturday last fall sweeping up leaves and dead-wood that came down in even half-hearted winds; what of it? We wake to birdsong. We have cardinals throwing darts of red against our back door. We have northern flickers, a brown-headed nuthatch, blue jays by the dozen. Best of all is the woodpecker in the back yard. When I'm putting out the clothes on the line, he's always up there, drilling his quick, persistent heartbeat into another sky-high day. It is, I think, the most cheerful sound that I've ever heard.

For Christmas, I gave my husband a bird feeder to hang on a low branch of the willow tree. We spend hours watching what happens there, spectating, as though it were Fifth Avenue or Grand Central Station. Some of these birds have come farther even than us to settle in sunshine in North Carolina, to make light of our day.

Act II: New York

Have you ever found a place to just sit in New York City? I did recently, on the steps of the public library, where a group of iron tables and chairs had been set out, presumably for time-killers like me.

My mother was a local; she spent the first twelve years of her life there, before sailing home with her family to Galway aboard the *Scythia*. She had very vivid memories: watermelon being sold on the sidewalks and the way it dissolved on your tongue on the hot days; sledding in Central Park; her mother taking her downtown to where Rudolph Valentino's cortege was due to pass, and all the women crying and wailing behind black lace veils.

Because it was her city first, I've always felt as though it could be mine. Her stories made it real for me so that even the first time I went there myself, it felt like a hand-me-down winter coat that still smelled of somebody else.

But a city like this doesn't rest on the second-hand. It has to be constantly on the move, doing itself up, putting on glad rags, trying on novelty and playfulness for size.

I could easily imagine my mother racing up the steps of the public library. The fact that she had never told me about any real occasion when she did so gave me the freedom to put her there, any way I wanted, pigtails and rib tights, freckles and cotton skirts. It was up to me. Just as it was up to every person I saw on Fifth Avenue last month to remember what they chose of that fine day.

I saw women walking dogs in fur coats that matched their own. I saw working people, busy people with somewhere to get to; I saw time-killers like myself. I saw a fight over a yellow cab. I saw the whole unlikely business of a city in thrall to itself, New York being New York, pulling itself here and there, passionately and frantically and deftly and earnestly.

I sat until my feet were cold. Then I took myself and my suitcase off to Grand Central Station to catch a bus to catch a plane to a place that is the opposite of this. To where I live now, to where someday, my children might tell their children of our misplaced living here and then, wherever. What they keep of it in the telling is entirely up to them, but it's likely too that some hot day, some small, blue-eyed boy or girl will be handed a slice of watermelon, and will make of that moment a whole chain of memories that links these cities, these stories, these slight lives.

FORMAL

Conor O'Callaghan

The weekend shuttle to the mall at King of Prussia, every hour on the hour from Main Lot past the light-rail line and gratis on the college. We disembark one evening into Seniors, trussed up for their end-of-year formal. We're just arriving back and they're waiting to depart – bare arms, shifts, rented tuxedoes, roses – like revenants of a garden party between the wars.

We separate, we drift between them, elvers scattered by the slightest current. We're ancient, alien, transparent, retiring further from the same young night they're still graduating towards, its consent of age, its coming. They can't see us and we, much as we want to, can't make them. The driver bounces the embers of his Marlboro into magnolia petals, yawns 'All aboard' in a mock-southern accent. The bus slips off down Lancaster in the direction of the interstate, leaving the parking lot deserted but for us, and even we (what's new?) are scarcely here.

THE IRISH IN THE WILD WEST

Myles Dungan

The American West produced a number of larger-than-life characters, not as many as Hollywood would have us believe, but some who were as big as the big sky they boast about so much in that part of the world. One was an Irishwoman who could have starred in *The Good, the Bad and the Ugly* all on her own – except for the good bit!

If Mary Gleeson had been a prize-fighter – and God knows, she regularly acted like one – she would have been a super-heavyweight. Though she was only five foot four inches tall, she weighed in at 200 pounds for a considerable part of her adult life – that's over fourteen stone. She was a brothel keeper, born in Ireland in 1845, who made a fortune out of the skin trade in Missoula, Montana between her arrival there in 1888, with her totally hen-pecked husband, John Edgar Gleim, and her death in 1914.

Mary Gleeson Gleim's notoriety doesn't come so much from the business that brought her a large fortune as from her violent and erratic personal behaviour. For example, in January 1892, she was charged with assaulting two Roman Catholic priests. In her defence she claimed that she had spoken to the clerics in Latin and had been frustrated by their inability to reply in the vernacular language of their own Church. The court was unsympathetic. She was found guilty and fined $50. Two weeks later she was in trouble again for breaking a bottle over a fellow citizen's head. On this occasion an intemperate rant about the legal profession earned her two counts of contempt of court.

But in 1894 she went too far even for her. She was accused of the attempted murder of a business rival, C.P. Burns. He had already felt her wrath when, after testifying against her in a property dispute, she whipped him in the street. Then, in the early hours of 12 February 1894, his home was levelled by an explosion that Burns, by some miracle, managed to survive. Two men were arrested for causing the explosion and Gleim was accused of having conspired with them to kill Burns. She was taken into custody but was quickly bailed on the grounds that her 'considerable girth' made it difficult for her to flee the jurisdiction without detection.

When some of her own prostitutes testified that they had overheard Gleim plotting with the two men who had caused the explosion, and later, when one of her co-accused turned state's evidence against her, not even a nineteenth-century Johnny Cochran could save her. Mary Gleeson Gleim was sentenced to jail for fourteen years. However, what her expensive lawyers did win for her was a retrial on the basis of subsequent technical arguments in the Montana Supreme Court. When the new trial began it was discovered, astonishingly, that most of the prosecution witnesses were no longer in Missoula.

While awaiting her retrial, Gleim entertained herself by assaulting one of her West Front Street tenants and almost beating her to death (that cost her $550 in fines and costs). Then, in an example of the kind of good fortune that always favours the virtuous, the State of Montana case against her finally collapsed when C.P. Burns obliged her by dying of a heart attack. The attempted murder case against her was dropped in May 1896.

Relieved at such a let-off, did she mend her ways in the future? Not in the slightest. In February 1897, she was accused of entering the house of one C.A. Clayton, along with two men, and bludgeoning him on the head, face and shoulders. She pleaded self-defence. She was found 'not guilty' by her Missoula jury.

Gleim died of influenza in 1914. She left nearly $150,000 in her will. Legend has it (which almost certainly means it's untrue) she left instructions that her tombstone face the railroad 'so her boys could wave goodbye to her'. From this we must assume that despite her record for personal violence, she had a good grasp of customer relations.

SOME THOUGHTS ON THE PURSUIT OF HAPPINESS FROM A MID-LIFE VANTAGE POINT

Sue Norton

I remember when we were teenagers and thought we were so 'deep'. We would say things like 'I don't expect to be happy all the time; I just want to be content.' We would say this as though there were some sort of sage difference between the two. And there was one, I suppose, but it certainly isn't the kind of difference that a sixteen-year-old can apprehend.

I did manage to dupe myself for a long while, though. During difficulty, confounding or just plain tedious times in early adulthood, I would lament the elusiveness of happiness, but persist in my quest for this allegedly more achievable state of mind, *contentment*. My desires were typical of other Reagan-era young women in that what I wanted most was a cool job and a warm boyfriend. And my own apartment. And great clothes. If only these things could be acquired, well ... while we were all too sophisticated to imagine that some delirious state of happiness would set in, surely contentment would present itself. This is what we thought.

And, to be sure, sometimes contentment arrived as though on a breeze from an unknown direction. It would swoosh into a room freshly cleaned or after a meal prepared for friends. It would flit around in the air after a satisfying conversation or the submission of a carefully composed graduate school term paper. Here contentment would be again, sitting on top of a large pile of just raked leaves or a small mountain of shovelled snow, ready to be jumped in. But it would blow away, scatter away, melt away again by morning, to be replaced once more by perpetual yearning.

But did I see a pattern? No, I did not. Did it twig with me, with any of us that our yield of contentment was in direct proportion to our investment of energies? Not even a little bit. When would we earn enough for that new car? When would those shoes arrive in a size eight? When would we meet our husbands? Would we ever have kids?

Like the through-and-through Americans that we were, we expected to have to pursue happiness, but we also expected it to pursue us a little too.

Eventually, enough aspirations were fulfilled (cars, homes, husbands, kids) to lay bare the lack of connection between conventional 'success' and an abiding state of satisfaction, happiness or contentment, call it what you will. For on any one ordinary day, so many things can disrupt bliss. Traffic jams, for instance. Bills. Paperwork. Smog. Teenagers. Illegal dumping. Death. What has become clear, at least to me, is that while lengthy stretches of contentment are rare in this life, short bursts of reward can be rapidly recurring and reliably repeatable. They result from jobs well done, relationships well nourished, projects lovingly tended, the inadvertently revealed admiration of our children, and yes, from raked leaves and shovelled snow.

So if I have learned anything by now, by these, my middle years, it is that a lifetime of happiness is a possibility at best, but a lifetime of reward is anybody's for the effort.

HOSPITALISATION

Fiona Poole

The intern stepped into the cubicle carrying several files. He exuded calm.

'How are you, Fiona?'

Opening a file, he thumbed through to page three. It doesn't take three pages to say 'No problems. All clear.' There must be a problem.

'I'd like you to see Mr O'Neill, the consultant. Can you wait?'

'Yes. But I have a meeting at 6.30 p.m.'

'He'll be here at 4.30.'

Dazed, I sat on a bench in the corridor. Sister spoke gently to me, suggesting I go for a coffee. I was touched that in a hectic schedule she had time to notice and comfort me.

It was a beautiful July afternoon. I sat outside, wondering how and what I would tell family. Children pulled on parents' sleeves, pointing to the crying adult. They looked away in embarrassment and walked on. Clickety clack. Clickety clack went the heels on the concrete path. A hand rested on my head.

'You've had bad news about a relative. I'll pray.'

Clickety clack faded into the distance.

Mr O'Neill shook hands. 'It is malignant,' he said. 'Come in on Monday, surgery on Wednesday.'

I had Thursday, Friday, Saturday and Sunday to build up a reservoir of worry, concern, fear, dread and stress. The hospital telephoned on Friday. 'Check in this afternoon.'

'What?' Stroppy as ever. 'I'm not due in till Monday.'

'Well, we have a bed free now.'

'Can I think about it?'

'No, we have an emergency call this weekend. We may have no free beds on Monday.'

'In that case, OK.'

More pressure, a suitcase to pack and a lunch date to keep.

A young doctor filled in my details and casually remarked, 'That's fine, Fiona. You'll go to theatre on Wednesday.'

I came to a jolt.

I'd be in that bed, in that ward, not immobile but immobilised, imprisoned, till Wednesday — Friday to Wednesday.

'Oh no, doctor.' Patiently, I explained that as I checked in on Friday, I should now have surgery on Monday.

'No, no, Fiona, Wednesday.'

That was the last straw. Turning my face to the wall, the floodgates opened. I sobbed uncontrollably as the enormity of the situation over-whelmed me. The stress of the past weeks had caught up with me. Fear stared me in the face. Suddenly, I realised that after all, I was human and vulnerable.

'Telephone call for you, Fiona.'

'What is wrong?' said the shocked sister.

'Nothing.'

Childishly, I refused tea and comfort. Back to that bed, face to the wall, more sobs.

'Will you tell me what is wrong?' said the young intern.

'I can't stay here till Monday. I'll go mad. To get well physically I must be well mentally. I'll pay to have my bed kept for me. I'm going home in the morning. I'll return on Monday.'

Face back to that wall, more sobbing.

'Surgery on Monday, Fiona,' I heard.

The black cloud lifted. 'Thank you.'

I had been listened to, I had been heard. My distress had been regis-tered. Another lesson learned. Care, support, concern and humanity had prevailed in an exhausting, stressful workplace.

Good news, I am alive, healthy, stroppy as ever, and enjoying this glorious summer day, many years later.

FIGURE

Liz Carty

Just after my mother had her first stroke I met an old friend of hers at the hospital. Mom's friend had married young and gone to live on the other side of the county and they'd lost touch – they hadn't seen each other since they were girls at national school together sixty years earlier. Yet now, by chance, they lay side by side in their hospital beds, wakened by sickness and old age. And while my mother dozed, her friend told me that, in their youth, my mother had been a wonderful dancer. 'She was a fine figure of a girl,' the woman told me. 'The finest girl in the seven parishes.'

I looked at my mother, with one side of her face distorted, her once-strong body lopsided from the stroke, a hand hanging uselessly down by her side, the other pillowing one white, wrinkled cheek, and I smiled a little at the woman's exaggerated praise.

I'd only seen Mam dancing once, at a cousin's wedding when the bride's father, with far too much to drink, was insisting that I, a gawky fifteen-year-old, should dance with him and she stood up and offered him her hand instead. Watching them, she with her back ramrod straight as he guided her round the floor with the cautious, thoughtful steps of the very drunk, I thought that they looked like a pair of clockwork soldiers.

Years later, I learned that her upright, arrogant stance was because she wore a heavy steel corset, the legacy of a car accident years earlier which she had barely survived and seldom mentioned.

She survived her stroke as well and lived for another fifteen years. Independent and alone, she clung to none of her children. We were expected to make our own lives, as she had made hers, without self-pity or fear of what the world might hold. She came to see me the week before she died, her back finally bent into submission by the rigors of old age. She hadn't been in my home for over a year. I think she came to say goodbye.

The following night, she died in her sleep. Clearing out her house after her death, I found a photograph of her that I never knew existed – it was taken, according to the date on the back, on her twenty-first birthday. She was wearing a white dress patterned with roses with her dark hair falling about her shoulders. She had the same gentle, dark-eyed smile that I remembered, and the same familiar, erect stance, softened by the gracefulness of youth. Shortly after that photograph was taken she'd left her job to care for her younger brother and widowed father. During the Second World War, when her younger brother married and brought a new bride into the house, she'd gone to England and worked, during the height of the Blitz, in an aircraft factory in Birmingham. After the war she returned home and married my father, and fifteen years later found herself widowed with a young family to bring up alone. She had borne eight children, of whom only four survived.

She was nearly forty when I was born, and during my teenage years, I, who associated 'fine figures' with the flawless beauty of film stars or the muscular grace of athletes or the cold, elegant splendour of statues of famous men on marble plinths in the great cities of the world, saw Mam, with her greying hair, slightly stooped shoulders, her heavy-rimmed glasses, as just another ordinary middle-aged woman who happened to be my mother.

Now I remember her best in old age – stooped and weakened, unsteady on her feet, her hair an uncompromising grey, her face grown thin and lined. But her smile still as bright as the day she turned twenty-one.

She was a fine figure of a woman, my mother – the finest in the seven parishes.

TURNING FORTY

Vona Groarke

The birthday card verses say it all.

> '40's not old, so don't feel blue. You're not over the hill, you've just improved your view.'

> 'Don't worry about turning 40. You'll get used to it. Of course, by then, you'll be 50.'

> 'There's life after 40 — there may not be vision, teeth or much hair, but there is life.'

It's no joke. One day, you're trying to choose between Barbie and Cindy, saving up for your Sparkle Annual and laughing away good-oh at those girls in Mallory Towers. The next, you're trying to get double sheets dry on a wet day and worrying about the tooth that needs pulling or whether you can get away with that shade of flamingo red.

One day someone tells you that you don't look twenty-two; the next, you have to admit to yourself you no longer look thirty-eight. You cling to 'still in my thirties' for as long as you possibly can, but then even this toy's taken off you and you're left to stand in a remote corner, where the natives glower and wear jumpers under suits. It's not fair. It's not reasonable. It's a terrible mistake.

Recently I showed a class the film *The Dead*. 'John Huston made it,' I prelim, 'and Angelica Huston's the star.' Nothing. Like feeling Lenin's body for a pulse. 'Watch for Colm Meany, too — you might know him from *Star Trek*.' I'm floundering. I'm going down. I've turned into Mr Coonihan who started his Religion class by playing 'What's It All About, Alfie?', asking did we know the words?

I'm the fogey who still thinks ELO are pretty cool, who laughs at Dick Emery reruns, who remembers when Elvis died, who'd still watch *Love Story* and find it kind of sad. As in *sad* sad, not *tragic* sad, as I know my kids would say.

As if someone has held up a huge cue card, shop assistants have begun addressing me as 'madam'. I want to tell them, 'Listen you, I'm not a madam, I'm a *chick*.' Time was, if someone said 'good girl' to me, I'd give them a filthy look – now I'd want to give them a tenner and lavish gratitude.

I'm not sure how it happened, but I'm now officially a cliché. I fumble with the video timer; I spell out text words like 'for' and 'to' instead of using numbers in their place; I have vests in the hot press. I yawn after midnight. I have health insurance. I finish conversations with 'goodbye'.

Am I only a granny step away from a tight perm and checking the schedules for anything with Nelson Eddie and Jeanette McDonald to kill the afternoon?

My sister tells me her forties were the best decade so far. She worried less, she says, she was more settled in herself. And Kitty Casey, who's ninety-three, tells me I'm only a child. Of course, to anyone over forty, I probably still seem young. Young-ish. It's just that there's more and more of the other crowd around, who want to address me as 'Mrs' and wince at my CDs.

I'm glad to be alive and grateful for my health, and I know that turning forty would seem a privilege to some, but still, it hurts to have to give up claim to something I've owned for forty years. Of course, I never rightly owned it: I had a leasehold on my youth, and for all my older friends' assurance that I haven't been evicted, I know the rent has gone way up, well past what I can afford.

So, I'll never wear pigtails again. What of it? My hair's been short for twenty years. And I never had the legs for a mini-skirt. Maybe I was just growing into myself, maybe my sister is right. What I'll gain will turn out to be something greater than whatever it is I've lost. If not, there's always the chance that things will swing back my way: that those white ankle boots in the wardrobe will be all the rage again, or that ELO remix will be No. 1, and I'll know all the words.

LÁ D'ÁR SAOL

Cyril Kelly

There are days that lie in wait for us. As if they had been prowling around in the shadowlands of the future, plotting an opportune moment, the most propitious place, to catch us unawares. I was ambushed recently by just such a day. In Dingle, *An Daingean*, whatever. One of those days that the West can fling in your face. Dark, windswept, rain lashed. A scavenging day that seems to pick the flesh from the very bone.

We were wandering aimlessly around the town, the missus and myself. When *Hey!* A roar from the other side of Main Street. So the *lá breás* are back. '*Lá breá*' is the good-natured sobriquet which locals have for youngsters who come to Corca Dhuibhne every summer learning Irish. Across the road, a ginger head that I hadn't seen for, oh, it must have been thirty years. Mick! That *meangadh gáire* hadn't changed, nor the shy roguery of the eyes. And the wild geaits of him; it had always set him at odds with the urban habitat when we hung around among the same crowd in Dublin. Of course, now nothing would do him but to take us out to Baile Riabhaidh, five miles outside the town, out to meet the *bean a' tí*.

And there's one of the things that intrigues me about women. They seem to have instant rapport, one with the other. After ten minutes in each other's company, their communication is like collaboration; word, gesture, empathy of expression. There is something exclusive, even sensuous about it. Whereas men are often awkward, angular together.

Eventually, with the two women chatting away, Mick suggested that himself and myself might go out, see if we could catch a few mackerel. From the window, he indicated his fishing boat, a twenty footer, prancing and snapping at its mooring in the middle of the choppy bay. Before I got time to argue, I was being togged out, oilskins, wellingtons, lifejacket.

Suddenly it was all action. Driving down the *bóithirín* to a remote spot, dragging the oars and boat from under a clump of fuchsia, Mick steadying her for me, the land-lubber, to clamber on board. Hopping in, he dropped the thole pins into place, settled the oars and began to row. Long, powerful strokes, a man in his element, plashing the prow through waves, heading out to the fishing boat that was moored a hundred yards off shore. Many years ago, not long after he left Dublin, in fact – as I listened, story became metaphor – Mick had driven tractor and trailer out into Dingle Bay to the farthest ebb of a neap tide. Solid with concrete, a tyre was dropped as anchor that day and it hadn't stirred since.

Nosing the fishing boat out of the bay, out between Beenbane Head to the east and Reenbeg to the west, Mick pointed to various landmarks – ring forts, promontory forts, ogham stones. Buffeted by gusts and squalling rain, his roaring commentary was a mixture of folklore and history; famine works, Lord Ventry, the War of Independence.

When we hit the open sea, Mick cut the engine and produced the spools. As the boat rode the heavy swells with ease, we dropped the weighted lures over the gunwale, paying out the line slowly. But the only bite we got from full fathoms five below was the tug of memories. Like a swarm of feeding sprat, craic and craziness from our early twenties kept shoaling to the surface. Every now and again, the quickening swells would smack the boat broadside on, shunting us towards the rocks, dwarfing us under The Bull promontory, that black slab of cliff towering hundreds of feet into the air. Seemingly the wind from the northeast can rouse the waves to treachery. Frequently Mick had to start the engine and head for the open sea once more. And the tiller of memory also whacked and turned, and turned again. Before the mackerel eventually began to bite, we had recalled the death of parents, the birth of children, the advance of another generation.

Heading back in, I was the helmsman. Busy gutting fish, Mick was tossing entrails into the air. Gulls screeched and swooped above us. A daring few perched on the gunwale. And suddenly, there before us was

Fungi. For an exhilarating twenty minutes he capered and cavorted fore and aft, lolling, racing, laughing, lunging.

Driving up to the house once more, both of us drenched to the skin, Mick outlined the enormous changes that had taken place in Corca Dhuibhne since the time he'd left Dublin thirty years ago. Less poverty and more affluence, undoubtedly. But the land and the language were slowly being abandoned. As he spoke I hardly recognised the committed, passionate man beside me; *fite fúite* in his own locality, caught in the warp and weft of progress and decay.

Pulling up at the house, lines from 'The Rhyming Weaver' came to me:

> *The savage loves his native shore*
> *Though rude the soil and chill the air*
> *Well then may Erin's sons adore*
> *Their isle which nature formed so fair.*

WHEN THE DUST SETTLES

Joe Kearney

With time, everything returns to dust, and recently I watched, from the comfort of my living room, as a satellite came safely to rest on the dry floor of the Utah desert. The cargo it contained was truly wondrous, a handful of stardust from the very outer edges of our universe; a fistful of the very stuff we are made from. Dust to dust. But the good news was a mere sound bite; it was followed by the usual litany of sorrows and disaster. I was, however, intrigued by the small satellite that contained the dust. Following its long seven-year journey and fiery re-entry into the Earth's atmosphere, it resembled some long-defunct piece of farm machinery. A vessel that might have been part of a milking machine from the 1960s, for example; something that would have been overtaken by polished stainless steel and finally dumped between the rusted shafts of an old hay rake, where docks and nettles would soften its battered shape and cushion its rest. The TV footage of the night-time landing was composed of grainy infrared images, and I remembered another time when I watched a similar scene.

20 July 1969, in the Crown public house in Cricklewood, London, through a haze of roll-up smoke I watched the crew of *Apollo 11* walk on the moon. With the jerky movement of puppetry, they made history for us on that lunar Sea of Tranquillity. As spectators, we shared much in common with astronauts Neil Armstrong and 'Buzz' Aldrin – we, too, were kitted out in a form of 'moon boots'. The exception was, however, ours kept us more firmly secured to the surface of England

than we would have wished. Our construction hob-nails were slathered in the muck of the London trenches and that, conjoined with lumpen gravity, ensured that we remained earthbound and did not seek to soar beyond our situation.

We looked for our Sea of Tranquillity at the bottom of pint glasses of Watney's Red Barrel, and because we sometimes found it, that was, presumably, why we kept returning to its insipid depths.

On that day in the Crown, I had worry beads of a sort in my shirt pocket. I was, at that time, a drifter, a piece of dust at the whim of fate, capable of being easily blown off course. A couple of days previously, a blue envelope had found me. It contained three lined sheets of Basildon Bond notepaper. The handwriting was unmistakable; my mother's. The heavy-handed script, taught to her by the Mercy nuns, had been pressed into the paper by her blue Biro so hard it seemed like Braille when I fingered the letter in my pocket. It was written with love but you had to find the sentiment between the lines; that's the sort of family we were.

> It was a good year for the early spuds but Tobin's bull had broken into the garden and trampled the carrot and cabbage bed. Young Alice, down the road, had gone to Australia to take up nursing. The family were worried about when they might see her again.

We never voiced our own wishes and desires, but instead chose to express them, obliquely, through the lives of others.

The envelope was one of a packet of twenty-four that she would have bought at Kerwicks newsagents. I calculated that by the time they were used up we would be into a new year and Christmas would have passed. Would I be home? In my pocket rattled just one entrance fee to the Sea of Tranquillity, and unless the winds of fortune blew more favourably upon this particular dust mote, home would be as far removed as Australia or the moon.

I took the letter out again. On the TV screen we were long past the moment where Armstrong had told us all about 'small steps' and 'giant leaps'.

As I refolded the notepaper, I noticed that stuck to the back of the third sheet was a solitary breadcrumb. When my mother had written, the passion of her enterprise against the unyielding surface of the worn oilcloth had forced an overlooked crumb to adhere to the letter. I picked it off, this small particle of home, and tasted it. It was hard and stale but it was the closest I had been to the kitchen table in a long time and I stared wide-eyed at the grey flickering images until I was certain that I could command the tears to remain unshed.

There were men on the moon. We were stardust and I was but one slight speck in the whole universe. However, I know now what I did not know then – that dust eventually settles.

GOLD WALLPAPER

Enda Wyley

The night was ours —
young art students clambering up cathedral hills,
not afraid to force a window open, creak a door
inwards, brush cobwebs like a gasp of cold air
from our cheeks.

We were finding old houses
to make paintings in — you, a corner of shadows
to place your easel near, while I spent evenings
sketching the way starlight fell through cracked
glass and how the bone moon creaked.

Over ancient wooden floors,
ice-blue marble mantelpieces, the dusty mattresses
with the dent of those long gone still there,
the yellow light crept, a ghost across our canvases.
Old houses forgotten by all but us.

On and on we'd wander
up avenues swirling their yew tree spells,
scraping our knees and notebooks on the forbidden
chipped sills, our pencils and brushes scraping for life
while the rest of the city slept.

Until in one crumbling mansion,
your fingers touched mine and we stripped back
from the thick walls fat with damp, seventies swirls,
sixties floral patterns, the formal fifties lines —
and found gold.

Gold wallpaper lanterns and flowers trailing
delicate stems and light up to the shattered cherubs,
the intricate cornices, the tinkling, blackened chandeliers.
So beautiful we could not paint that night —
held hands and stared and stared.

Even now in the hush of our own home,
in the dark of our middle years, when your back
turns from mine in sleep, your mouth muttering dreams
I cannot know, I reach for your skin
and want to peel back time —

gold paper falling onto me from you.

ARDMORE 2005

Leo Cullen

I am told that nowadays it is vacant, that swallows dive through the broken windows of the laundry room. But again in my memory I am back at the hotel on the cliffside, looking across the expanse of sea to Mine Head. The district of Ring and Helvick is around the corner from the headland. Though I have never been over there, I know that; the patrons at the hotel long ago told me so. The men of Anglo-Irish descent, and the merchant sons of Cork and solicitors of Carrick-on-Suir, the ones who holidayed here and spent much time gazing out to sea from the barroom window, they told me, old salts. I am back, and walk the corridors and bedrooms, look on the sea through the windows that fog over some days and bear a permanent glaze from the salt spray. I am back in 1966, the year England won the World Cup, the summer I took the Leaving Cert, when I worked here in the hotel. For three pounds a week I was potboy and general dogsbody, and then when the barmaid Miss Merry ran away home to Mallow out of homesickness, I was put behind the bar, smartened up and my weekly pay was raised by two pounds to five. Miss C., the manageress, was the lady who smartened me. In the same way, she kept her female staff shipshape. She wore corsets, glasses with film-star frames, smoked Craven A cigarettes and was a diabetic. She jabbed her insulin-filled hypodermic through her corsets and into her rump, unblinking, while at the same time telling her staff to eat less, to take care of their shapes, or they would grow into fat lumps. I think she may have been the reason for the homesickness of Miss Merry, who liked a few glasses of Pale in the afternoon.

I am now again in the gardens. They are overgrown; I am told they have been neglected for some time. Then they were tea gardens. Through the gardens I walk; Frank and I are taking the bottles to be dumped. I don't remember who once tended those pleasure gardens with a scent of rose, of fuschia and flock; I push my wheelbarrow of empties along the mazy pathway that leads to the cliffs.

And here is Frank, who owned the hotel – who educated me, callow at eighteen, too young to know my Medoc from my Margaux. Who plucked me from the heart of the buttermilk countryside and landed me in sophisticated Ardmore. Who introduced me to the wines of Bordeaux, the wines of Burgundy and of High Germany. There were no New Age wines, no wines out of anywhere else. From Frank – leather-soled shoes, tweed suit, white shirt, tweed tie – I learned all about wine.

You had to be good on wine in Ardmore in 1966 – the Claude Cockburns, the William Trevors, the Molly Keanes dined here in the evenings; the Fleischmanns, the Dwyers of Montenotte, the remnants of the East India Company who settled here, and whose names are now fading off the limestone headstones in the cemetery behind St Declan's Tower; the Beresford-Poers; the Jameson-Chaplins, the Fitzgeralds, the Sir John Keanes. You didn't give them red with fish, you gave them German hock. You let St Emilion breathe: Beaujolais you popped and poured fresh. Ardmore, where G & T was grace before meals.

You had to know your wines, but then, when all the goodness had been drained from the bottles, you had to know how to dispose of the empties. On the cliff that drops below St Declan's Well, where thousands came on Pattern Day, Frank gave me lessons on disposal.

You must break them. Frank would let a bottle fly with venom, clenching the briar pipe between his teeth. Smash them against the far cliff. And while seagulls dodged out of shot, he would go: smash. Now you try. My throw would fall short and the bottle would fall into the ocean and float down there in the swell. Again he would show me: It's in the swing of the arm. Frank had thrown the discus at school and now was my athletics coach. And I watched his braces strain beneath his tweeds with his exertions.

How many empty bottles bearing the labels of Courvoisier and Chablis and Cork Dry Gin, how many squat bottles, tall bottles, square bottles, did I allow to sail into the seven seas from the breaker's yard of Ardmore in 1966?

Oftentimes I think back on Ardmore and my first employer, Frank, the testy wine expert; my first staff officer, martinet Miss C of the hypodermic jabs; my first work colleagues, the housemaids, waitresses, the local boy Gerald who took over as potboy when I was promoted and who ran around tables and beds after the girls until one day Frank clop-clopped along on his leather soles and caught him; the chef who came home from England each summer and carried on outrageously camp but yet did a steady line with the elderly head waitress, his summer belle, Nan. And some nights we were all seen in Redbarn ballroom outside Youghal: Watney's Red Barrel Ale, Nan and Chef dancing to an old-time waltz.

Again in my memory, I said at the outset. It is because each time I see a bottle bobbing on a tarry sea, off the coasts of the Atlantic, the Irish Sea, the North Sea or East Australia, Ardmore comes back to me. The bottles that sail in on the tide and ebb out again. The bubbles of my mind, bobbing, bobbing on the vastness of the ocean, disconnected messages attempting to come together, out of my own origins, out of the foreshore on which they were launched, attempting to make one coherent statement.

BLASTED STONES

Margaret Hawkins

No, I didn't like the Gaeltacht. That's what I told the oral Irish examiner, wondering at the same time if I hadn't, in one fell sentence, ruined
my chances of a good mark in the Leaving Cert forever.

Cén fáth?

The words dropped from the examiner's lips as I knew they would,
but deciding that there was no way back now, I told him honestly that
all I'd seen there were stones – walls and fields and ditches full of them.

It was the dozens of new bungalows situated in the middle of those
tiny, rocky fields, though, that hadn't made sense to me.

They looked out of place, inappropriate.

Where I came from in County Wicklow, new bungalows were then
few and far between and usually built on better, rock-free land.

'It doesn't make sense,' I said, digging more of a hole for myself. 'You
can't make a living out of land like that.'

When it came to people making a living in their own area, my
teenage eyes somehow hadn't seen past the stones to the thriving fishing
port of Ros a' Mhíl, nor to the many small industries that had sprouted
up along the roadside between Spiddal and Inveran.

I hadn't taken account, either, of the crop of tourists that stopped at
the shop opposite Coláiste Lurgan in that hot summer of 1976 and
asked in funny accents if they were on the right road for Connemara.

For years after I couldn't understand my dislike of the place until, visiting it a long time later, I decided that the secret was probably in the stones.

Stones meant hardship for Wicklow farmers anxious to plough land in the progressive 1960s.

Stones were for blasting sky-high so that the cow could give way to the plough, like had happened on our farm near Tinahely.

It was Lar Clare who did the job. Lar was a bachelor in his fifties and he drove his red Ford 500 van the length and breadth of counties Wicklow and Carlow 'blowing the stones'.

In the summer of 1964 he arrived in our townland of Rosnastraw, a couple of miles off the main Aughrim to Carnew road where some of the fields were 'alive with them'.

You'd have said it too. If you'd stood on the Winny Hill gate you'd have seen the big blue rocks peeping up, tip of the iceberg fashion in the Stony Field, the Little Field and what was then known as the Far Bog.

We children watched as Lar and his young assistant, Pat, removed the equipment from the van.

Jackhammer, compressor, hand tools, fuse wire and finally the sticks of gelignite that looked for all the world like outsized 'peggy's leg'.

Watching them from the yard, our teeth later rattled as the jackhammer burrowed into the stones.

Eventually we saw Lar hurry back toward the upturned horse's cart at the far side of the field, leaving Pat to light the last of the fuses.

The first one, of course, much longer than the last so that he had time to get away before the charges were detonated.

'Run!' Lar shouted, and then we saw Pat exit the field as if the devil was after him.

The first of the blasts shook the ground underneath us. From the haggard came the sudden scrawk of hens and, several fields away, the rapid roar of cattle taken by surprise.

When we were allowed to climb the gate again, a different landscape lay before us.

Great brown craters had appeared in the Stony Field and bits of rock were scattered all over the place.

Bits that would keep many hands busy for many months to come, not to mention the horse and drag that would shift the bigger stones to stand sentry in the ditches.

Stone blasting was a common occurrence in the locality over the next few years, but eventually Lar Clare went into well-earned retirement as reclamation grants came to an end and the outbreak of the Troubles in the North called a halt to anyone being allowed to carry explosives along country roads.

The negative associations of the stones were probably forgotten until I visited the Gaeltacht, a place that remained happily alive with them.

Did I get a good mark in the exam? Well, better than I'd expected, but sometimes I can't help wondering if that examiner hadn't come from a farm himself. If he hadn't, at one time, witnessed the blasting of stones to make way for progress.

Or listened to a collective sigh from his parents, who hoped that from now on farming might be easier.

AN CÉILÍ

Catherine Foley

Is cuimhin liom na céilithe ins an Rinn. Rachaimís ann gach oíche i rith an tsamhraidh. Rachainn-se ann le mo dheirfiúracha cé go mbíodh saghas leisce orm go minic. Bhí mé cúthaileach ag an am toisc nach raibh aithne agam ar mhórán buachaillí agus bhraith mé go raibh brú orm aithne a chur orthu.

Agus mar sin, le hosna mhór an déagóra, chuir mé iachaill orm féin dul ann. Bhíodh déagóirí eile an pharóiste in éineacht le scoláirí óga an choláiste ag triail ar na céilithe céanna, ins an Rinn i gColáiste na Rinne i gCo Phort Láirge ins na seachtóidí.

Fad is a bhíodh an ghriain ag dul faoi is ea a thosódh muintir óg an cheantair ag triail i dtreo an halla bhig sin. Bhaileoimis gach oíche i rith mí Iúil agus mí Lúnasa, an spéir lasta lasmuigh le dathanna geala na haimsire mheirbhe – oráiste, dearg, buí, corcra agus dúghorm, idir eagla agus sceitimíní orainn. Ní chaithfimís ach eadaí éadroma mar seó faisean dáiríre a bhí ann chomh maith.

Is cuimhin liom an rúille búille ag doras an halla, buachaillí dána ag iarraidh éalú ó fhear na dticéad agus sleamhnú isteach uaidh. Chuaigh an chuid eile againn isteach go réidh mar nach raibh ag teastáil uainn ach mealladh lách an cheoil chun sinn a mhealladh.

Istigh, bhíodh an áit dubh le daoine, na soilse ar lasadh ar phócaí áirithe, na ceoltóirí thuas ar an ardán ag seinnt – ag féachaint amach thar chinn na rinceoirí ag smaoineamh ar rudaí eile a bhí i bhfad uainn, saghas mearbhaill ina gcuid súile agus fear an tí, máisitir fíochmhar an chéilí ag sceamhail agus ag coiméad súil ghéar ar na himeachtaí a bhíodh ar siúl ins na cuinní ar fad – pleidhchíocht le *stink bombs*, lasáin, sceanna agus caitheamh tabac le toitíní b'fhéidir.

Bhí linn nuair a thosnódh an cor seisear déag – bhímís ag súil go bhfaighfea cuireadh dul amach ag rince. Bhí an t-ádh leat dá n-iarrfaí ort dul amach mar bheadh ról lárnach agat ansan i meadaracht cumhachtach na hoíche agus i rithim traidisiúnta na dtreabhanna a chuaigh i bhfad siar, cosa an halla ag mairseáil timpeall i gciorcail mhór sular thosaigh an rince i gceart.

Ansin, bhí deis againn céimeanna a úsáid agus splancanna a bhaint as an urlár – ár lámha timpeall a chéile, ár gcosa ag léimt, ár méaranna ardaithe agus ceangailte lena chéile ag déanamh slabhra mhór. Tharla an buaic pointe nuair a stadadh an cheoil don bhuille coise. Bhí gach buille le cloisteáil i bhfad síos an bóithrín, agus leanfaimís le buille láimhe agus rachaimís ar aghaidh arís, gafa i gciorcail mhóir an cheoil. Dom, dom, dom dom, dom dom dom dom, agus an slabhra ina shlabhra arís. Bhí draíocht ag baint leis an chéile agus a bhí a fhios againn go rabhamar páirteach i miorúilt éigin ag an bpointe sin.

Casadh ar dheis, casadh ar chlé, a béiceadh fear an tí. Seacht gcéim ar dheis, seacht gcéim ar chlé, a leanfadh sé.

Leanadh na hordaithe ar feadh na hoíche, sinn á dtreorú ag fear an tí, sinn á ngríosadh, a ghuth mar a bheadh bun torann taobh thiar den cheol.

Fallaí Luimní. Ionsaí na hInnse, na sluaite againn ag gluaiseacht le chéile agus fear an tí ag lúirigh, agus ag déanamh corr ionsaí ar na rinnceoirí a bhí ag pléidhchiocht ag bun an halla. 'Amach *squirt*', a bheiceadh sé ag fáil greim cluaise ar an duine ba chiontaí agus thairringeodh sé amach as an halla é, ag tabhairt cic deas sa tóin dó agus é ag dul thar tairseach an dorais do.

Sa bhaile an lá dár gcionn, is cuimhin liom m'aintíní ag caint liom. 'Ní thiocfaidh sé síos an simne chugat,' a dearfadh aintín amháin agus í ina suí ag ól tae in aice leis an tine, ar chuairt chugainn. 'O, sea,' a d'aontódh m'aintin eile léi agus í ag baint sásaimh as a toitín. 'Is cuimhin liomsa nuair a bhí mise óg go mbíodh an-chuid spóirt againn ag na céilithe. Is cuimhin liom na hoicheanta a chaitheamar ag rince agus ansan an spórt a bhí againn ag dul abhaile ina dhiaidh sin. O, bhí an-chuid cairde againn,' a leanadh sí.

'Caithfidh tú dul,' a dhearfaidís liom agus oíche i ndiaidh oíche, sheasfainn-se go minic ag taobh an halla ag fulaingt – ag fáil bháis, ar drioslu, an bláth ag seasamh ag an bhfalla ag fanacht ar an ghrá nó ar fhuascailt ó fhulaingt an náire – blianta ciapaithe an déagóra.

Is cuimhin liom go raibh speis agam i mbuachaill amháin. Bhí sé fionn agus bhí sé fiáin. Tháinig sé ón chathair. Ni raibh mé in ann caint leis, gan amhras, ach bhí mo dheirfiúir an-mhór leis mar nach raibh inti ag an am ach páiste agus bheidís ag deanamh spóirt le chéile. 'Tar amach ag rinnce,' a dhéarfadh sí leis, ag déanamh ghrinn. 'Táim tuirseach,' a dhéarfadh sé ag iarraidh fáil réidh léi ach tharraingeodh sí amach ar an urlár é. Sheasfainnse go balbh in aice leo, at stánadh ar an urlár. Ní dhéarfainnse focal.

Ag deireadh an tsamhraidh, bhíodh ceolchoirm. Sheas fear an tí ag an barr an, agus 'An Croppy Bocht' a rá aige. 'Sinte ar thaobh an tsléibhe, chonaic mé an Croppy Bocht,' a duirt sé. 'Bhí an drúcht go trom ar a éadan, bhí piléar trína ucht. Bhí sé i bhfad óna chairde, i bhfad óna theach is a mhnaoi, is é ina aonar fágtha, ar an bhfear fuar fliuch ina luí.' Stad na buachaillí ag pléidhchíocht, stad na cailíní ag cogarnaíl. Sheasamar go léir ag éisteacht lena ghuth.

Chuaigh mé ar ais go dtí halla an chéilí i gColáiste na Rinne cupla bliain ó shin agus d'fhéach mé isteach. Bhí na páistí óga istigh ann ag imeacht timpeall, ag baint spóirt asan oíche, as an gceol. Bhí siad lúcháireach, ach ní raibh me in ann páirt a ghlacadh. Bhí mé ró-mhór. Bhí mé ró-shean. Bhí mé ró-fhada uathu, ró-chleachtadhtha ar an domhan mór. Bhí rud éigin caillte agam agus rith sé liom go raibh an t-ádh liom gur cuireadh iachaill orm – m'aintíní ach go háirithe – dul go dti na céilithe oíche i ndiaidh oíche, fiú má bhí me i mo sheasamh ag an taobh line go minic.

LOVE ALL

Pat Boran

In the Portlaoise of the 1970s, where I grew up, there were two tennis clubs. One was owned and run by the ESB as their staff social club. It was just at the then outer limits of the town and was open to the general public, the young lads of whom, like myself, gravitated to the pool tables in the clubhouse, happy to watch their sisters and friends knock a handful of yellow tennis balls from the local tennis ball factory back and forth, desultorily, until the sun went down. The other tennis club, the Portlaoise Lawn Tennis Club, was a very different affair.

The Portlaoise Lawn Tennis Club was situated behind a small Protestant parish hall more or less in the centre of the town. The fact that it was right across from the wonderfully named Dead Wall, which, being the biggest wall I'd seen for at least the first fifteen years of my life, gave it a kind of central authority. But if the Dead Wall had been built to hold up and back the weight of the thirty-foot railway embankment that runs through the town, the small lawn tennis club across the road from it was proof that gentler, more fragile activities could occupy the hearts and minds of the populace of our Midland town.

In truth, I don't think I ever actually played what might be called a game of tennis, either in one of those two clubs back then, or since. Despite the fact that my mother had often done so in her time, and later both of my sisters regularly went out on summer evenings, tennis racquets in hand, to play at one of the tarmac courts that would later appear in the grounds of the Presentation Convent, tennis remained for me a strange, if strangely fascinating, game.

It was true that unlike any other game I could think of or saw anywhere around me, tennis alone broke the gender divide, which was a divide worth breaking, as far as I was concerned, and couples could often be seen playing together, even in Portlaoise. And it was even true that the championships at Wimbledon, and maybe even at other tournaments, had a category called Mixed Doubles, which was exactly that – as if, despite its apparent tameness and a dress code that gave it an *olde worlde* feel, tennis was at the same time somehow, discreetly, revolutionary.

Yet the truth was that, in my age group at least, tennis was a girls' game, a game that us boys could watch, or pretend *not* to watch, but about which we were, as in so many other respects, in the dark. Surely there was more than meets the eye to a game in which the word 'love', not to mention the word 'match', was used over and over.

But boys simply did not play tennis. By which I suppose I mean Catholic boys. Where Gaelic footballers, soccer or rugby players of my acquaintance seemed intent on mucking up their kit as quickly as possible after the initial throw-in or kick-off, tennis players at the end of a match would come off the court in the same virginal whites as they'd gone out. It seemed to go against what games were all about, a kind of rough and tumble, a kind of letting go and giving in and going wild.

As it turned out, it took just a small incident one summer's night, in the late 1970s, to change my mind about tennis, and to see it less as some affected pastime of the gods, stopping to sip their ambrosia, and more as just another, if more stylised, version of a great cosmic game.

Having spent the afternoon after school at a friend's house (where the main activities had been drinking Coca-Cola and pillow-fighting in his elder brother's bedroom), this particular summer's evening I took a shortcut back home up Railway Street, which meant I had to pass along by the side of the Dead Wall (looming up over me like a cliff face), and of course by the Portlaoise Lawn Tennis Club. And as it happened, whatever evening of the week it was, a Friday perhaps, a tennis club social was in full swing: some local tournament had concluded earlier in the day, and now disco music and the glow of flashing, coloured lights was spilling out of the high windows of the small building.

It was then I noticed that the parked car beside which I was idly standing, half listening, half thinking of nothing at all, was moving from side to side and up and down. And, just as others in my class had claimed, though I hadn't believed them, when I stepped back, startled, and glanced over again, through the steamed-up windscreen I could just about make out two shapes, two figures, one female, one male, and both dressed in white, their arms wrapped tight around each other, for all the world like two angels struggling to be human again.

LIFE, DEATH AND FOOTBALL

Catherine Brophy

Ireland had got to the World Cup for the very first time and the TV, the radio and the newspapers were making an unmerciful fuss. Big deal, I thought. It's a game, lads, it's only a game. However, it was an international competition and Ireland was playing, so I kept an eye on it. Then came the day that Ireland played Romania in Genoa. I was all set to watch the match when my mother became very seriously ill.

She'd taken several turns in the past year, but this one looked the most serious yet. The life seemed to drain from her. She couldn't eat, she couldn't drink and she could barely speak. We called the doctor and he immediately ordered an ambulance to take her to hospital.

I sat by her side, waiting and watching. Every breath looked like it might be her last. Outside the sun shone and the road was deserted because everyone was watching the match. I waited and waited, no sign of the ambulance. My mother looked haggard and grey, her eyes were closed and she seemed to be barely breathing. I was afraid she would die before the ambulance arrived. A neighbour came in and insisted that I take a break while she sat with my mother.

I made coffee and turned on the TV to see what was happening to the match. Extra time had just finished and the score was Romania nil, Ireland nil. Well, at least we hadn't been beaten. They were standing around on the pitch waiting for the penalty shootout. Jack Charlton prowled about, clutching his cap behind his back. Packie Bonner pulled on his gloves and stretched. I began to feel nervous.

Packie's first up in goal. He blesses himself. Hagi places the ball on the spot. He kicks, boom, one nil. Yeah, well … even I knew that Hagi was good.

Lung, the Romanian goalie, replaces Packie. He looks experienced and crafty. Kevin Sheedy comes up and boom. Yes, yes, you little jewel. One all.

Packie returns. He's looking better this time. Lupu places the ball, he kicks … two-one … oh well, that's to be expected.

Lung looks meaner this time, but Ray Houghton looks good, he looks springy. Yes, yes, yes! You're a jewel and a diamond, Ray. Two all.

By now, I swear, Packie has grown a couple of inches but Kotariu looks dangerous. And he is. Three-two.

Lung too has grown and looks positively vicious. Tony Cascarino is up next. Tony has Italian blood, and he is in Italy, I can hardly look. He kicks. You darlin', you pet. Three-three. Yes, yes, yes! I can hardly breathe.

Packie looks edgy but determined. Timofete comes to the spot. He looks as cool as all get out. He runs, he kicks … Oh my god, oh my god, Packie's saved! Packie's saved. Oh Packie, I love you, I love you. The crowd's delirious, I'm delirious. I'm trying not to scream too loud and upset my poor sick mother upstairs. Besides, we all have to settle down once again and bite our nails. It's the last Irish kick and it's David O'Leary.

Lung takes his place in the goalmouth. He looks like Mephistopheles. He seems to take up all the space. Oh please God, please God. David places the ball, cool as you like. He runs up, he kicks and he scores, he scores, he scores. Oh David, I love you. The crowd is dancing and screaming. I am dancing and screaming. I dash up the stairs two at a time.

'We won, we won, we won.'

My mother opens her eyes. She is looking bleary and puzzled.

'We beat Romania, Ma, we're into the quarter-finals!'

'Ireland won?'

'Yes, yes, yes, we won!'

'I never thought I'd see the day.' She smiles and she sits up in the bed.

The colour has come back to her cheeks and she can't keep the grin off her face.

'I think I'd like a cup of tea,' she says, 'and maybe a bit of toast.'

Two days later, when I went to bring her home from hospital, the doctor told me that patients were leaping out of bed, fully recovered, with 'olé, olé, olé' on their lips.

The following Saturday I found myself watching the Ireland–Italy match and explaining the offside rule to a visiting American. Now, finally, I understood what Bill Shankley meant when he said, 'Some people think that football is a matter of life and death, but it's not, it's far more important than that.'

SEA OF TRANQUILLITY

Patrick Chapman

He came home from the party.
In his pocket was the satin star
He'd plucked from decorations.

He woke his daughter, not yet four years old.
He took her, drowsing, out into the road.

He pointed at the sky: the gap
Between Orion's shoulder blades.

'You see that space above the clouds?
I got a great long ladder, laid
The top rung on the moon,
And caught this star that now I give to you.'

IN SUBURBIA

Eamon Delaney

I recently finished writing a novel, which dealt with the subject of suburbia and city life. The idea was of a group of young people who come to live in the city after growing up in the suburbs of Dublin, and what a completely different experience that metropolis is. They are anxious to experience the 'real' world, a release away from conformities and parents, like the characters in New York movies or Isherwood's Berlin novels. It mirrors what has been my own experience, of growing up in Blackrock, County Dublin and moving later into the Baggot Street area of the south inner city, a once-bohemian demimonde, in which I have perhaps dwelled in for far too long.

My own experience, indeed, is in four parts – high street Dún Laoghaire, leafy suburban Blackrock, followed by the dramatic contrast of a windswept beach in Connemara and, finally, the metropolitan venture into Georgian Dublin. I am hardly unique in this, as many Irish people – many people – experience the profound difference of moving from one very different locale to another, especially that of coming 'from the country' into the 'big smoke'.

The experience of the suburbs is increasingly common, given that almost everyone is slightly suburban now. Even country villages grow to resemble suburban parts of large towns and cities. But for us, in the early 1980s, it was a particular type of living that did not seem quintessentially Irish. Typically Irish was small town, or country cottage or inner city. The housing estates of south County Dublin suggested something less than this, something underdeveloped and new. It suggested shopping malls, traffic roundabouts and tennis racquets. It was a type of living that was more the UK or US, an atmosphere reinforced by our voracious consumption of rock music and TV from those same places. And yet, here's the strange thing – these areas are, in many ways, the creation of country people.

In my novel, I have it that three of the four characters have country or non-Dublin parents and this was exactly as it was when I was growing up. Both my parents were from the country and it was the same with others around us. The McInerneys from Clare built our estate. The one next to it was done by builders from Cavan. This was the prosperous 1960s, when people were moving en masse to southside Dublin, developing whole green spaces, just like what is happening in other parts of Dublin now. It was a great migration, similar to what you see in other formative cultures, such as the US. Around Stillorgan and Clonkeen Road, you would still see the country origins in the car registrations at the weekend when the relatives came to visit, or in the names of the houses – Errigal, Leenane, Sneem, named after rural places now departed.

And you could see that some of the old transplanted residents had difficulty with the transition, marching around in their wellingtons at the weekend, frustrated that they had no more than a hedgerow and dahlias to cultivate. For me, however, it was a liberation.

High street Dún Laoghaire was a cramped world, and also an older one in which we had few friends. I was a teenager now and suburban Blackrock opened up a whole new world – a world of housing estates, gangs, girls, bonfires and parties in garages, playing records and swapping magazines. It also coincided with the punk rock boom of the late 1970s that I embraced thoroughly. Punk and the suburbs seemed to go hand in hand. Even the band's names echoed it – the Suburban Kids, the Suburban Studs and the song titles, 'Sound of the Suburbs' by The Members, or 'Treasure on the Wasteland' by Irish band, The Atrix. We used to travel into the city to see these bands at McGonagle's or the Dandelion Market and then go back home and try to form our own bands. The paradox of punk, or alternative culture, is that it criticises the suburbs for being allegedly 'bourgeois' and 'boring', while secretly, I believe, loving it. Aside from anything else, it means you've got a world to react against and try to reshape. It is where kids grow up to be teenagers, and for me, and for millions like me, it is where we very much came of age.

WHERE DID YOU SAY
SLOVENIA WAS?

Theo Dorgan

One of the more absurd consequences of the Cold War, an American
rhetorical invention, was the shrinking of old Europe to more or less the
Atlantic fringe countries and Germany. Everything east of the Iron
Curtain vanished into the steel grey penumbra of communist Eastern
Europe, a kind of virtual unreality where great cities, whole cultures,
entire literatures dropped off the map. National boundaries became
notional things, as if they signified no more than administrative divi-
sions in the Soviet Empire. We imagined, many of us, if we thought
about it at all, that life in Prague could be little different from life in
Budapest, or Ljubliana, or Warsaw. As if distinction could be so easily
erased. As if we could so easily escape from ourselves.

It was Tom McCarthy's idea that as part of Cork 2005 a team of
Cork poets should translate a poet each from the new accession countries. Between the time Tom conceived of this translation series and Pat
Cotter, the inspired manager of the project, handed out assignments, I
was out of the country. By the time I got home there was only Slovenia
left. What I knew of Slovenia then – its culture, its history and its literature – could have been written on the back of an average-sized rejection slip. Still, I was intrigued. It was only one of the former Yugoslav
Federation countries that had avoided the murderous civil wars that
followed the break-up of the Federation. Trieste, I knew from the life of

James Joyce, was a Slovenian city that had somehow ended up annexed by Italy.

With the help of the newly appointed ambassador, I armed myself with anthologies and journals containing recent poetry in translation. I made 'Slovenia plus poetry' the default search term in Google on my laptop. I was looking, as one should, for a kindred spirit, someone who had a quality to her poetry that I responded to on an intuitive level. I was looking for poems so different from those I write myself that I could write them out in another kind of English, in another voice. I found Barbara Korun, and how I found her tells a certain kind of story all by itself. I was sitting at my desk, late at night, reading a poem called 'Wolf', in a fairly clumsy translation to be sure, but nevertheless one that disclosed the hypnotic power of the original. 'Ah,' I was thinking, 'this is the one.' Just then, my companion knocked and came in, a magazine in her hand. 'Here,' she said, 'I think this is the one you'll go for.' The page folded over so that the lamplight fell on 'Wolf'.

I neither read nor speak Slovene. I would become deeply indebted, therefore, to Ana Jelnikar, who supplied me with line-by-line literal versions of the poems and with minutely detailed, illuminating scholarly notes – I was able to cross over into the territory of Barbara Korun's poems by means of a strong, well-engineered bridge. The poems in their final English versions would come out of these bridge translations, and even more out of the extraordinary e-mail conversations that flowed through the long nights between Barbara Korun and myself. Barbara's English is good. Not enough for her to be her own translator, but good enough for her to spot where I was going wrong, missing an emphasis, creating the wrong kind of atmosphere.

In the end, as she said herself, she got a master class in English, I got a fool's pardon for my temerity and errors and we both learned a great deal about poetry.

In the central square of Ljubliana I was shown a monument of a ragged vagabond, a burly, bearded fellow in a great cloak. Even the erudite Ms Korun cannot explain how he fetched up there in the long ago, this wandering Irish Druid. Not a monk, mind you, a Druid. I've been thinking of him all this time, of his long journey on foot to the heart of old Europe. A long time he's been waiting for us to come find him.

A FORGOTTEN TREASURE

Henry Hudson

Recent proposals regarding the development of Dublin's Poolbeg peninsula brings thoughts of the Pigeon House, a treasure trove of history and culture that stands at the tip of the peninsula near the mouth of Dublin Bay.

The history of Pigeon House began in 1717, when Dublin Corporation built a new south wall on the River Liffey. Of timber pile construction, it extended seawards a distance of 7,938 feet, to where a wooden block house cum store was constructed. A man called John Pidgeon was appointed as watchman, and to supplement his income he sold 'refreshments' to seafarers as they waited for longboats to take them upriver into the city. Locals also sampled his hospitality, and soon the place became known as Pidgeon's House, and later still as Pigeon House.

In 1735, a road was constructed from Ringsend out to Pigeon House, and in 1795 the Corporation for Preserving and Improving the Port of Dublin built a hotel and harbour on the site. Pigeon House then became the main landing point for ships travelling between Britain and Ireland. However, in 1798, fearing a French invasion and/or a native rebellion, the British military took over the area. A large fort was constructed, with the hotel serving as officers' quarters. Napper Tandy was landed as a prisoner at Pigeon House in 1799 and Robert Emmet planned to capture the fort as part of his rebellion in 1803. Forty years later, Daniel O'Connell called a rally at Clontarf in support of his efforts to repeal the Act of Union, but the threat of shelling from Pigeon House forced the pacifist O'Connell to abandon the meeting. When Charles Dickens visited the fort in 1865 he wrote, 'The open jaws of the guns grinned down the road with an air of menace.'

Pigeon House remained in military hands for almost 100 years and there is evidence of this in the area to this day. The site was returned to Dublin Corporation in 1896 for the development of a municipal sewage works, but Pigeon House was meant for greater things.

The Electricity Lighting Act of 1882 required local authorities to supply electricity to the public, so in 1892 Dublin Corporation's Electric Lighting Committee opened a power station at Fleet Street, in the heart of the city. However, demand soon outstripped supply and a site for a bigger station was needed. Pigeon House was suggested, but it was miles from the city and no one had supplied electricity over such a distance before.

Then, John Hammond, an English electrical engineer, came up with a brilliant and innovative solution. He proposed generating three-phase current at high voltage in Pigeon House and feeding it directly to Fleet Street. It would then be distributed to sub-stations around the city, where it would be reduced to low voltage for supply to consumers. This ground-breaking system became the model for almost every other distribution system now in use in the world. The station came on line in July 1903 with a capacity of 3,000 kw. Although its red-bricked turbine hall and boiler house are now derelict, they are nonetheless fine examples of early-twentieth-century industrial architecture, while the hotel building is regarded as an architectural gem of its time.

Putting its social, military, industrial and architectural merits aside, Pigeon House holds an even greater claim to fame. James Joyce immortalised the place in his novel *Ulysses*, in his short story collection *Dubliners* and also in *A Portrait of the Artist as a Young Man*. Joyce was indebted to Timothy Harrington, the man who laid the foundation stone of the station, because as Lord Mayor of Dublin he gave Joyce an invaluable letter of introduction before the author went into exile. Likewise, the Aelous episode of *Ulysses* also immortalises Councillor J.P. Nanetti, who was both business manager of the *Freeman's Journal* and also a member of the committee charged with the construction of the station. The names of Harrington and Nanetti are inscribed on the foundation stone of the Pigeon House that now stands outside the adjoining Poolbeg Station.

If all goes to plan, the Poolbeg peninsula will soon be transformed. How will the embattled Pigeon House fare in this new landscape? One also wonders what future generations will say when they visit the area only to find offices and apartments, a sewage works and an incinerator but little trace of the Pigeon House, a place that any other country would have long since preserved as a national treasure.

AUGUST

A SEA-SIDE DAY

Vona Groarke

It has its own inbuilt ritual. You can vary it according to family tradition or personal need, but some elements are constant. You know how it goes.

You wait on for the weather forecast after the news the night before. It's promised good. You put the togs out to air on the back of the kitchen chairs. You hope to god they weren't wrong and you won't find yourself tomorrow battling slantwise rain over a deserted beach to get back to the car.

Next morning, you get the picnic ready. Tea made in the big flask, the milk added because last year you brought it in a separate bottle and it poured like porridge from the neck. Ham sandwiches, bananas, salt and vinegar crisps that won't object too much if they have a bit of added sand later on the beach.

Hats, sun cream, bath towels, lilo, buckets, spades, windbreaks, rain-coats (just in case), jumpers for when it gets chilly later on, books and magazines, the beach tennis set, lunch in the cooler box and don't forget the tea and the huge plaid rug.

You'll forget something anyway, but that's OK, as long as it's not lunch. If you're really serious about it, you'll bring chairs with pygmy legs and fold-out tables and a portable barbeque from which the smell of toasting rashers will drive the other punters home and leave more beach for you.

The kids tumble out from cars parked bumper to bumper alongside the prom. They're off like buckshot, leaving you to carry all the gear and to elbow a spare wedge of sand to claim for the afternoon. You can spot them over on the rocks, searching for crabs and starfish and the brightest-coloured shells.

Later, they'll come back to you to recruit your help for the sand castle. They want you to fix the water so it doesn't disappear when they pour it in the moat. If you can't, they'll bury you in sand and stick a triumphant seaweed flag due north of your belly button.

A day on the beach is nearly always the same as every other day on the beach. It's as if time stalls and loops in on itself. The weather scarcely matters. I bring my kids to Spiddal beach, where I spent so many Augusts in my youth. They do exactly the same thing I once did, climbing on the self-same rocks, writing their names on sand that once held the impression of my own. We play ring-a-rosey down at the water's edge, just as I did with my own father. They pick out the Aran Islands, beg for ice cream, scream at jellyfish.

A beach day is a couple of hours at a slant to your real life. There are few enough activities that essentially don't change at all, regardless of how old you are or what you look like or how well you are when you take part in them. It's as if you lift a stone in a rock pool and underneath it is your life, perfectly preserved just as it was the last time you were here. There you are in the bright pink togs your Auntie Anna sent you from the States. And there's your mother, sunbathing. And your dad lifting a baby jellyfish to pretend to throw at you. It's all there exactly saved because the beach hasn't changed at all and the water is just as cold and the rocks as warm and the same sun lies around your ankles like an old cat and drains your vision so the two children waving at you from the water's edge could just as easily be yourself and your brother, backed into sunlight with the crystal sea behind, hoping for some company so you can go on in.

This evening, you will drag everything back up to the car. The rug will be heavy with sand, even after you shake it out over the road so a shower of fine particles falls over the windscreen of a passing car. The children will heft themselves onto the back seat, too tired even to complain about the leather's heat and the way it sticks to the back of their necks and behind their knees. Your daughter's fist will close around a pure-white conch she found in the rock pool. Your son has a swatch of the kind of seaweed that a book he borrowed swears will foretell the weather every day.

Tonight, your sheets will be sand-strewn and on edge. Tomorrow, if the weather holds, you'll do it all again.

THE FAIR

Gerald Dawe

It was like this.

It seemed to be every summer, late on, when the fair took over the football ground across the road from the house I grew up in. When the football season had ended, of course, and before the reseeding of the pitch, battered and mauled in the rain-soaked, windy months of use.

From my bedroom window, atop a mid-terrace of seven red-bricked houses, I could see across the walls and turnstile to the Ferris wheel and stalls and hear as plain as day the slightly eerie, strained music and watch the people traipse into the old football grounds to try their luck – pot-shots, throwing discs, buying candy floss, riding a miniature Dodgem car, spinning wheels of fortune. Chancing their arm. Mothers and fathers and kids; young couples; groups of boys and girls wandering about the place in the gathering dusk sometime in the summer of the late 1950s and 60s. A travelling fair. I didn't know how long that stand had lasted. Did it happen there every year before the war – the Second World War?

The part of Belfast of which I speak had escaped the Blitz of 1941, but nearby had not been so lucky. Had the families and crew who worked that fair been doing so for years, decades, generations? I suspect so. Whatever happened to them is another mystery. By the early 1970s, when I had gone, the fair hadn't appeared for some time, but I can still see it clearly, and the groups of people squeezing in through the door into the grounds in a kind of Fellini-esque evening light. The background night is lit up with street lamps and the amber strobes of the descending city, not too far in the distance, and the mechanical chains and pulleys and noise of the fair, with its repetitive music and the shouts and cries of kids and people strolling or showing off or trying their hand at winning garish prizes that everyone knew didn't amount to much but who cared anyway.

It was all a bit of fun that came around once every year when you were least expecting it. It was the trucks pulling up and even parking on the pavements and the fair being put up like a child's toy set, like a toy train or a farm with animals and tractors and pens. The Ferris wheel spinning away above and over everyone, lit up it must have been, unless I'm only imagining it all, and a horse or two or a donkey and cart and plastic mementoes like BLESS THIS HOUSE or TO THE MOTHER I LOVE. The sound of all the different stalls and the people milling about and shouting in an excited way for things, knowing each other.

I could see them closing up when the night was over, and in the morning, before anyone came, there was a watchman in a trailer or a caravan wandering on his own through the deserted fair as if he was lost somehow, but was really checking on things, going about his business, whatever that was. In the surprising brightness of the day, everything looked very matter of fact, mechanical, ordinary, much more different from the night before, when you'd imagined it was a bit dangerous. But there he was, one of the men walking through the fair in broad daylight as if he was just walking in his workplace, looking after something with a hammer or a monkey wrench in his hand and for all I know he could have been whistling. The sky was mostly cloudless and the sounds were of the everyday, like a bus taking the corner at Alexander Park Avenue, a ship clearing the docks a couple of miles away or the sound of a transistor radio in someone's back garden or kitchen porch, and all the fair's gadgets and tents and entertainments were standing there in the old football ground, silent and still until other people appeared and started to clean the place for the evening time. I think it was always night they opened, but needless to say I could be wrong, all wrong.

Maybe the fair only stayed for a week or two. Maybe it was in August before school started back and there was not a Ferris wheel, not really, just an imitation one to attract punters, but no one actually sat in it and spun around looking over the north of the city to the lough and the rising hills. But there was a man, he I can still see in the morning light walking through the fair, knowing what's what by the looks of him, and the way he looked at things looking maybe for something wrong or checking, double checking, seeing about something that maybe broke the night before. He I definitely saw from my window at the top of the house overlooking more or less the football ground and the fair in the summer sometime ages ago.

THE FLIGHT OF THE EARLS

Éamonn Ó hUallacháin

One of my favourite places in Rome is San Pietro in Montorio on the Janiculum Hill, not too far from the other St Peter's. It is here, in front of the main altar, that the Earls of Tír Eoghain and Tír Chonaill, the Great Hugh O'Neill and Ruairí O'Donnell, lie buried. This is where their epic journey, known forever in Irish history as the 'Flight of the Earls', finally ended. A simple stone marks the grave of O'Neill and states, in Latin, that 'here lie the bones of the Leader Hugh O'Neill'.

The journey began in Slane, a little under 400 years ago, in 1607. While he was in Slane, word came to O'Neill from a Drogheda businessman named John Bath that a Breton ship had arrived into Lough Swilly and would soon sail for the continent. Hugh travelled quickly northwards on horseback, covering up to fifty miles a day. On Wednesday he passed Tullyhogue, where twelve years previously the crowds had proclaimed him 'The O'Neill' and leader of Tyrone. But no crowds greeted him this time, and even the stone on which the O'Neills were enthroned for centuries, the Leac na Rí, lay broken, smashed into pieces by Lord Mountjoy. On the Friday, at dawn, he arrived in Rathmullan on Lough Swilly, where the ship lay at anchor. O'Donnell and his people were already there, loading the sixty tons of provisions which they were taking with them. At mid-day the party of ninety-nine set sail for Corunna in the north of Spain. The group consisted of O'Neill, his wife, Catherine McGuinness, some of their children, Ruairí O'Donnell, his brother, Cafarr, their wives and children, and others from the leading Ulster families.

They sailed down the west coast of Ireland and stayed further from the land than they would have liked, fearing the English ships. The weather conditions on the twenty-one-day voyage were sometimes awful. At one stage, they trailed a gold cross in the sea, which contained a relic of the true cross, in an attempt to calm the sea. Eventually they decided that it was too dangerous to make for Spain and landed instead in France, not far from Le Havre. As a gesture of goodwill to the local governor, they presented him with two falcons that had landed on their ship during the storms. King Philip of Spain asked them not to go to Spain, but to remain in Spanish Flanders instead. They stayed in Louvain, which had strong Irish connections, and were well treated there. One of those they met was O'Neill's son, Enrí, a colonel in the Spanish Army at nineteen, who he hadn't seen for seven years.

At the end of February they were advised to go to Rome, and thirty-six of the group set off on horseback; six of the women went in a carriage. It was an amazing trek at that time of the year. They crossed the Vosges Mountains and the Alps in frost and snow. On St Patrick's Day, their first day in the Alps, while crossing a raging river over a small bridge, known to the locals as 'the Devil's Bridge', one of the horses slipped in the icy conditions and fell into the torrent below. It was the horse that carried their money, about £50,000 in today's values. Though they searched for days, the money was never found. They went through the St Gotthard Pass, 7,000 feet above sea level, and stopped in the old traveller's hospice there, which is still in use.

Finally, 235 days after leaving Slane, they arrived in Rome. They went along the Tiber, into St Peter's Square, unyoked the horses, tied them there and went into the Basilica. The Pope received them with great respect at his palace on the Quirinale, where the President of Italy resides today.

Events soon began to turn against them, however. In July, due to the oppressive heat in the city, some of the younger members of the group went to Ostia, on the sea, fifteen miles from Rome. They stayed two days and lay out overnight in the moonlight. Almost immediately they were struck by a fever, probably malaria, which was common there until Mussolini drained the Pontine marshes. Despite being attended by the Pope's physician, O'Donnell died and was buried in St Pietro in Montorio. He was just thirty-three years old. One by one, the Ostia group died in rapid succession. When Hugh's son, the heir to Tyrone, died aged twenty-four, it was a mortal blow to the whole group's morale.

O'Neill continued with his efforts to get help from the Pope and Spain, but to no avail. He grew increasingly disheartened and died in 1616, aged sixty-six, a very broken and dispirited man. He too was buried in St Peter's on the Golden Mountain.

Some years ago I was amazed to see Romans still putting flowers on Julius Caesar's final resting place in the Forum, after more than 2,000 years. Last year, a couple of us from O'Neill's own territory of the Fews in South Armagh took some fuchsia from there to Rome, and put them on the Irish chieftain's grave, so that it might be known that our Caesar too has not been forgotten, among his own people, even after hundreds of years.

COROT AND COLLECTORS

Niamh Ann Kelly

On Parnell Square, in the Dublin City Gallery the Hugh Lane, there is a small painting by the French artist Jean-Baptiste-Camille Corot called *Woman Meditating*. The seated young woman is painted in muted tones, the whole canvas made up of olive greens and earthy browns. She gazes just past where I stand looking at her, with her hands clasped lightly around her knee, as though she may be rocking her body slightly. Her gaze has the intensity of someone utterly lost in thought, or meditation, as the title suggests. Her eyebrows are slightly raised, her lips barely pursed, her facial expression serious. The tonal quality of the painting conveys the contemplative mood of the work as much as her posture.

It is an unusually stark portrait – there are no clues to its context, though it seems logical to assume that these are not the woman's usual clothes. Perhaps she is dressed in this medieval-style costume for a play or a ceremony of some sort. Her hair is tied up in a deep red band to complete the period look, with small drop earrings, only one of which I can see.

There is a sister painting to this one in America's Cleveland Museum of Art – a more staged and larger work, depicting a woman in a similar costume resting her head on her hand as she sits in a clearing in a forested area. It shares a sense of contemplation with this painting in Dublin as the woman gazes downcast, past her feet. But somehow, while the *Woman Meditating* at the Hugh Lane may have been more of a study than a finished allegory of some sort, it seems to me more immediate and more revealing of Corot's sensitivity to exploring human emotion through portraiture – a subject he is not usually associated with. Without any specific context provided, the *Woman Meditating* in Dublin appears quite solitary, so I am left to focus on her, without distraction, as an individual, and to share with her a quiet moment of thoughtfulness.

So how did this painting come to be in Dublin? It was not part of Hugh Lane's own collection, but was presented to the city's gallery when it first opened to the public in 1907 by a group called the 'Ladies of Ireland'. Harcourt Street was the first location of the gallery and I found a reference to these women in a review text written that year, in which the group are referred to as the 'Irishwomen's Picture League', and the unusual qualities of the painting are noted. At that time the painting was known as *Woman Resting*.

Who were these women who had the foresight to acquire an atypical work by Corot, and further, had the spirit to present it to the city of Dublin on the occasion of the first exhibition of what was to grow and expand into one of Europe's finest municipal collections of modern art?

I am perpetually in awe of the philanthropic aspect of art collecting when the imperative of individuals transfers into the public arena for the benefit of so many. Some years ago, I had the pleasure of meeting the late Gordon Lambert on a few occasions in relation to research I was doing on his pivotal contribution to the development of the collection at the Irish Museum of Modern Art. Like talking or listening to Patrick J. Murphy, or reading about Chester Beatty, Hugh Lane, Sir and Lady Beit or John Hunt, to name a few, Gordon Lambert took my breath away with the sincerity of his passion for art. Without the intervention of such individuals, the public and municipal art collections of Ireland today would be sorry exhibitions indeed.

Women in this area are somewhat less recognised than their male counterparts, but at the Dublin City Gallery the Hugh Lane, this exquisite Corot painting is on display because of just such a group of women. Even earlier, in 1905, another key painting in the gallery's collection, *Blush Roses* by Henri Fantin-Latour, was presented by Lady Ardilaun. Born Olivia Herbert, she was a keen art, design and garden enthusiast and her more famous husband was Sir Arthur Edward Guinness. The rose, Souvenir de St Anne, was named after the couple's garden in Clontarf in Dublin. So I imagine that this luscious Fantin-Latour painting, with its delicately described pink rose petals, meant a lot to Lady Ardilaun.

And it was another woman, the artist Sarah Purser, who we can thank for the current location of the gallery in Charlemont House at the north end of Parnell Square. Purser was also responsible for founding the Society of the Friends of the National Collections of Ireland, an organisation that continues to contribute hugely to our public collections today. The behind-the-scenes role of collectors is, unfortunately, often underestimated in the histories of art – the most evident clue to their activity is to be found on the provenance of works as it usually appears on the labels beside their display.

As I return to gaze at Corot's *Woman Meditating*, I can't help but wonder about the journey of this small painting from Corot's studio to inner city Dublin; how it came to be, finally, in my line of vision.

A SENSE OF HOME

Mary Folan

'Look out for the two ugly guys in the white van!' he said. 'Hmm, surprise me,' I muttered as I dashed across town to Blackhall Place. It was my D-Day, delivery day – more to the point, the delivery of the designer shelving unit, that extravagant piece of furniture I'd bought on a whim months previously when the frustration of ever getting the keys to my first home manifested itself in a mania for buying things I *definitely* couldn't afford. On that sunny Saturday morning, the delivery men in the white van, a father and son team, Stephen and Darragh, of course turned out to be handsome, fun and curious, giving me an excuse to be giddy and relieving the slog and tedium of turning house into home.

Finding a home of my own began the previous August in my pal Marguerite's Ford car. I was what you could call a more discerning first-time buyer, since I had delayed it for so long. I didn't dare tell Marguerite that I hadn't a clue where I wanted to live but would *know* when I found it. Instead, with notebook and pen in hand, we toured the neighbour-hoods of Dublin city – Harold's Cross, the Coombe, Meath Street, Dunore Avenue, Rialto, the South Circular, Crumlin, finishing up in Stoneybatter at dusk. Little did I know that evening, while staring into the window of an estate agent in Manor Street, that I had come home.

Seven months later I was a proud denizen of one of Dublin's oldest and most vibrant neighbourhoods – Stoneybatter. Well, almost – I set up home at the junction of Stoneybatter and Blackhall Place, in a build-ing which once housed a clothing factory and more recently, a pharma-ceutical depot.

Up to then, that indefinable thing, 'a sense of home', had sort of eluded me since childhood. I had felt it as a teenager, stretched out on the big rock behind the family home in Spiddal, holding host to the cormorants on sunny afternoons. Or swanning around the medieval city of Galway, a place that always allows me to be myself. Or when I lived in Triana in Seville, a neighbourhood populated in previous generations by sailors and gypsies and exuding a carefree, spontaneous feeling of being part of something vital and vibrant. Was it instinct or just serendipity, then, that in such an historic and colourful part of my own capital city, I would find home, again?

Dealing with the cut and thrust of setting up home didn't come as instinctively. People kept telling me they found moving house a stressful life event. I thought smugly, 'They were just disorganised.' After all, with six weeks to go, the architect, Peter and I had snagged-listed to our hearts' content, until the affable foreman showed signs of losing his temper. I had washed and ironed everything in sight, boxed and labelled all my treasures, and with military precision had begun the process of moving in. Why, then, with ten days to go, were things suddenly out of sync – with the plumbing, that is. Noises similar to Air Force One taking off in water tank; water gushing from spout underneath sink; light bulb going 'bing' in bathroom – water in light bulb, yet not enough in toilet cistern. Was this a nightmare or the never-ending snag list, all over again?

Thanks to the three Cs – coffee, Coca-Cola and Carmina Burana – I finally set up home. Yes, when things got really tough, Carl Orff's insistent rhythms and raunchy lyrics never failed to rouse me as I dragged my tired body on to the next 'to do' list.

These days, to put me in a calmer mood, I stand under the canopy of the majestic oak overhanging the pavement from the Law Society's front lawn, a stone's throw from my new home. After all, it spent 300 years a-growing, and is now 300 years a-living, so maybe it has some wisdom to impart.

My father has this endearing habit of always greeting me with a welcome and a sunny smile, no matter what the circumstances of my arrival at his home in Spiddal. Now when he, a fanatical follower of Galway football and hurling, comes up to Dublin to cheer on the Tribesmen in Croke Park, it will give me great pleasure to say, '*Fáilte abhaile, a Shéamais, go Baile na gCloch!*'

ONE FOR SORROW

John F. Deane

That glorious painter, van Gogh, has always been difficult to understand. Even his parents could not figure out their remarkable, intractable son. Although Vincent was the eldest of the children born to Anna and Theodorus, he was not the first child. One year before, to the very day, a son was born and named Vincent Willem van Gogh. Our painter was also named Vincent Willem. The stillborn Vincent Willem was buried near the church door with the name clearly written on the gravestone. Every Sunday of his childhood, the young painter had to pass this gravestone. Not a good beginning; without a doubt, this would be one of the black feelings van Gogh carried with him all his life. I know that the existence, or non-existence, of a child born in such circumstances just before your own birth and given the same name you carry around for life issues in a strong feeling of guilt, as if, somehow, you have usurped another's place in life, as if you were the cause both of that child's stillbirth and your mother's grieving over that non-life. There was no gravestone already bearing my name; indeed, the stillbirth was scarcely ever mentioned, yet always, always something niggled me.

Over the wall into the pine grove, we dumped potato peels and chicken bones, eggshells, fish heads and tails. I often stood in that grove, in the fragrance of escallonia; this was locus for daydreaming, for a boy's rich imaginings and absences. I was young then, and now I have come back, like a thief, to stand in the heavy greatcoat of adulthood, to listen to the rain drip through thinning foliage, and to touch, again, the unlife that passed this way before me, that survived a while where I have been, on sea-nourishment, rehearsing limb-movements, imbibing knowledge of the gravity without. I think of that life, stillborn, and given, I believe, my name. I think of my mother, the bleak stone hospital, chickweed growing in the walls, and she, in the grim ward, moaning, the sweat and tearing, her two hands holding to the bed bars; and then the wet head showing, its small plastering of hair, all orifices on the world shut tight in full refusal. Was there pain? A baptism? Would they have given him my name?

Now I stand here in the pine grove, where he never stood, holding his space and hesitation between not-flesh and flesh, know how his birth song began as requiem, false notes played on flawed instruments in the ongoing cacophony. I stand alone, and in the sudden vivid brightness of imagination I am in the past and see her, our mother, coming to the brightly painted back door of the house, I see her stand in a patch of sunlight and stare straight into my eyes, until I turn away, confused, though that was half a century ago and she has found her lost, unmentioned son again. And how am I to cope with it? How can I deal with such a memory, or non-memory? I think of her again, mother and sadness growing old together, something that swelled between her and light, between her and me, and I speak, *John, John*, aloud into dark spaces between the trees; there is a little consolation, even a little bravery, in saying the name, my name, his name, out loud into the living world.

A solitary magpie watches from the branch of a tree, his high-gloss tail feathers twitching, meaning *trespass*, and he scolds me loudly, and lifts away into the trees. I scuff the layered pine needle falls, reveal a tiny vegetal riot, grub and maggot in bloated white until tears come, and prayers, guilt that I have climbed these trees, my hands graced with resin, and known the joy of breeze and sky, the breath of necessary being, and I ask forgiveness for existing, that I forgive myself and her, she me, I him, for being there and not there – and someone, something, passes, in a white gown, silently through the day-dusk, the tree-gloom, the decay, leaving me breathless, though purged, a gentle sadness at the condition of the world remaining in me, like a blessing.

Vincent van Gogh wished to fill the world with light, with sunflowers. And the flowers he painted are alert with gold and yellow, yet they droop, as if they were already aware of the going down of the sun that would force their lives into the misery of darkness. In one of his last paintings, *Wheat Field with Crows*, the sky is a broken and angry blue and the dirt path is in turmoil, the track curving away into the field and disappearing off the sides of the canvas. In Auvers, some twenty miles from Paris, he worked with extraordinary inspiration and fever, completing sixty paintings in two months. This is not the work of a madman — his style is free and conscious, he is aware of what he is doing. One day he picked up his easel and headed out into the day to paint. He had a revolver in his pocket and put that to his head and pulled the trigger. It appears to have been a sudden impulse rather than a premeditated act. Perhaps it was in atonement to his brother, the other Vincent Willem van Gogh who had ridden all his life on the painter's shoulders. The black crows. The magpie. One for sorrow.

BLAEBERRY SUNDAY

Pádraig McGinn

Whether you approach Castleblayney from east or west, you'll know you are near the town when you see Conabury Hill. It is a steep, drumlin hill, crowned by a mane of old beech trees, visible for miles in every direction. From this hill you can see the spire of Annyalla Church four miles to the west, Sliabh Gullion in Armagh thirteen miles to the east and Mullyash Mountain four miles to the north. And whenever we mitched from school, we always hid on Conabury Hill because from there we had a commanding view of the two national schools and could time our arrival home to coincide with those who had attended school that day.

It was one of those days when I was mitching that I met Mick, an old bachelor who was walking his dog on the hill, and he told me about Blaeberry Sunday on Mullyash Mountain.

'Did ye ever climb Mullyash for blaeberries?' he asked. And when I answered that I'd never heard of blaeberries, he said that some people called them bilberries and others whortleberries. I had never heard of either, so he took it upon himself to enlighten me.

'The first Sunday in August was Blaeberry Sunday,' he began. 'People for miles around climbed Mullyash to eat blaeberries or to gather them for jam. There'd be fiddlers there and melodeon players and young people dancing sets and lancers at the crossroads below, in the evening. Some people would bring new potatoes and eggs and boil them, and have a picnic. Many a boy and girl met their future wife or husband there. It was a great place to meet a woman. The custom went back to ancient times. 'Twas a pity it died out.'

I asked him why it died out if it was such great fun and the people enjoyed it so much.

'The clergy and the Gaelic League,' he spat out. 'The people danced foreign dances, sets and lancers and barn dances, and the league didn't like that. But it was the clergy that gave it the knockout. The bishop declared that crossroads dancing was a sin. And the bishop himself often appeared at the open air dances, a big ash plant in his hand and stopped the dancing. It was amazing the power he had. Nobody would go against him.

'There was another reason too why the clergy were against the clebration of Blaeberry Sunday. It was originally a feast in honour of the pagan god, Lugh. His name is remembered in the month of Lughnasa and in Lughaidh, the Irish for Louth. It was time to kill off the last traces of pagan culture in the new Ireland.'

Although I was only ten or eleven at the time, I wondered if Mick's bitterness at the ending of Blaeberry Sunday on Mullyash was related to the fact that he never got a wife. I kept my unspoken question to myself. I resolved to climb Mullyash as soon as I was old enough and taste the blaeberries. They say that the way to hell is paved with good intentions and it was sixty years later before I made my way, last August, to Mullyash in search of blaeberries. Alas, the blaeberries, like the ancient customs, were long gone and a forest of spruce trees covered the land where lovers once danced and shared wild berries.

FROM CLARE TO BURGUNDY

Margaret Hackett

It is early in the morning.

The train is crashing through the night before entering Montbard station.

It only stops for three minutes, time enough for a few dark shadows to come aboard. Next stop is Paris, the train's final destination, and for me, the last stage before leaving France.

The early mist is slowly lifting. A timid sun reveals the outlines of isolated farmhouses. I try to read but I cannot concentrate. The silent landscape flashes by.

The taxi had arrived early, she had set the alarm clock, but I was already dressed when she knocked gently at the bedroom door. I had told her not to get up, it was too early, but as always, she had prepared breakfast and she was fidgeting about. The discreet horn of the taxi reminded us it was time to part. A sudden sadness and an immense guilt at leaving her to her loneliness engulfed me and we were both masking our emotions behind the conventional words.

'Look after yourself, will you.'

'Kiss the children for me.'

'I will ring as soon as I arrive.'

'My best wishes to Tony.'

'I'll be back soon.'

I took her in my arms, held her close, and as the taxi was leaving, I waved at her.

I so much look forward to these precious visits to my elderly mother, who resides in Burgundy among the vineyards, in the charming village of Meursault. This is where I was born, where I spent my childhood, my teenage years. For the little girl I was growing up there, and for the mature woman I became, the structures of life have remained unchanged. Values and traditions have also remained. Computers, e-mail addresses, modern machinery, fax machines have taken their place quietly behind doors. No Sunday openings, no twenty-four-hour shopping, no Chinese take-away, no McDonald's. The small shopkeepers on the square have the support of the local population. The large shopping centre a few miles away is a threat, of course, but the locals know the small traders on the village square will close doors if not supported. The social pattern of the village will be no more, as it is the case in some of the neighbouring villages.

While I am there, I sometimes get up at dawn and leave the house furtively. I walk through the vineyards up the hill, inhale the morning scents and look at the sunrise in the valley beneath. As I return to the village square, I pay a visit to the baker, who welcomes me with a broad smile through the steamed window. His floury T-shirt and pale face give him an early morning ghostly appearance. '*Ah, Vous etes de Meursault pour quelques jours!*' ('So you are back for a few days!') he asks while wrapping up the warm croissants.

What does Europe mean for these people? Well, Europe has not happened overnight. Europe has always been; it is like a street with neighbours living more or less in harmony with each other. France has always been at the crossroad. The notion of being European is a different matter, however; the people of Burgundy are very proud of their heritage and perhaps feel that this heritage is somehow threatened by the powers in place in Brussels.

As far as I am concerned, I can certainly say that I am a European: I feel at ease in both cultures, even though I may have now become a tourist in France and I am still a foreigner in Ireland after all these years.

The train is now approaching Paris, going through the vast cereal plains of La Beauce. The sun has now fully risen and illuminates the fields and paints them with bright green and yellow in its morning splendour.

A glance at my watch indicates it is now mid-morning. As I am sipping a coffee, I imagine my mother's frail silhouette going in and out of the shops in the square, chatting with the shopkeepers, greeting her neighbours, telling everyone how she enjoyed her daughter's visit, and perhaps she is slightly pleased that her daily routine has returned to normality.

The aircraft is now approaching Shannon Airport; we are flying above the hills of Clare, over the familiar dark bogland we love to roam, and below the majestic Shannon glistens in the pale sun. I am returning to mystic Ireland, my adoptive land, to the dear friends and loved ones I yearn to see. I am home.

THE END OF HISTORY

Ronan O'Flaherty

In 1649 the bubonic plague came to Galway. The wealthy left the city and fled to the countryside. The poor stayed and died in droves.

One might expect that the horrors of this holocaust would dominate the writings of the period, that its gluttonous consumption of human life would not fail to be recorded by all contemporary chroniclers. However, for one scholar, Dubhaltach MacFirbhisigh, the plague was just one more disruption for a man who was very busy indeed. At this time, MacFirbhisigh was in the middle of compiling his *Great Book of Irish Genealogy* and he was ill-pleased to be disturbed, even by a plague of biblical proportions. He makes no direct mention of the event in his writings, but simply apologises for any shortcomings in the text, remarking, 'I ask him who can to improve it, till God give us another time more tranquil than this to rewrite it.'

Dubhaltach MacFirbhisigh, alternatively known as Dualdus Firbissius, or as he occasionally styled himself for English speakers, Dudley Ferbisie, was born sometime around 1600, in Lackan, County Sligo. He was a classically trained Gaelic scholar whose family had served for generations as professional historians and poets to the Ó Dubhda chieftains of County Sligo. Virtually nothing is known about his early life, although he seems to have received his education in Galway, where he acquired a working knowledge of English, Latin and Greek.

Ireland in the seventeenth century was not an easy place to live if you were a Gaelic scholar. The power of the Gaelic aristocracy had been broken following the Nine Years' War, and although the peace was generous, the Gaelic princes found it hard to stomach life as ordinary landlords and held hopes of leading a continental army back to overthrow the English. When they left, four years later, to seek that army, the Attorney General of the day, Sir John Davies, gleefully wrote, 'We are glad to see the day wherein the countenance and majesty of the law and civil government hath banished Tyrone out of Ireland, which the best army in Europe and the expense of two millions of sterling pounds did not bring to pass.'

Gaelic Ireland was leaderless. A brief resurgence under the Confederacy of Kilkenny was crushed by the New Model Army of the Beast Cromwell. The Lord Protector landed at Dublin in 1649, the same year that the plague swarmed off a ship on the other side of the country. War and pestilence followed in the wake of each, and Ireland would never be the same again.

Through all this, MacFirbhisigh wrote doggedly on. He makes no reference to contemporary events; perhaps, like many others, he felt he could not afford the luxury of commentary. Gaelic Ireland, its traditions, laws and history, was slipping away. The Gaelic scholars knew this and set themselves the task of preserving what they could for future generations. Histories were compiled, old manuscripts were transcribed, genealogies recorded.

There is a flurry of activity around this time, and as the tide finally ebbed away, small pockets of traditions, laws, histories, myths and genealogies were saved, clinging like seaweed to rocks on the foreshore. There was no time for idle commentaries on the state of the nation – an entire race was disappearing from the face of the earth.

Over a period of perhaps thirty years, MacFirbhisigh worked tirelessly. The historian Nollaig Ó Muraíle has commented 'that an astonishingly large proportion of the manuscripts we still possess passed through the hands of this one scholar, and it may be by that very fact that they have actually survived.' Sometime around 1664, MacFirbhisigh seems to have won the patronage of Sir James Ware, the noted historian and Auditor General of Ireland, for whom he provided translations of extracts of the various Irish annals. However, when Ware died in December 1666, MacFirbhisigh was forced to the highways again. The following year finds him in Gort, where he addressed a praise-poem to a local dignitary, Sir Dermot O'Shaughnessy, with whom he may have found refuge for a while. He then turns up in Antrim, possibly seeking the patronage of the Marquess of Antrim, Randal MacDonnell. After that, he seems to have decided to go home. He was now around seventy years old, and tired. He packed his few belongings, leaving up to twenty important manuscripts in the care of learned friends in Antrim, and went back to Sligo.

There, in 1671, Dubhaltach MacFirbhisigh was stabbed to death by a local landlord, one Thomas Crofton, in a tavern near the present-day village of Skreen. The cause of the altercation is unknown.

His great work, the *Leabhar Mór na nGenealach*, has recently been published for the first time. There are five volumes, and some 3,000 pages of genealogies, histories, king lists and commentaries. This is a time capsule. Find a copy, and as you turn the pages, spare a thought for Dubhaltach MacFirbhisigh, who wrote all this down 300 years ago, at what was for him and for many others the End of History.

SEPTEMBER

COME SEPTEMBER

Dympna Murray Fennell

They say August is a wicked month. For anyone who has ever faced back to school in September, the last week of August is particularly hard. True, the 'back to school' notices have been in the shops for weeks; as with Christmas, the pressure to buy starts earlier each year. However, the 'holiday mode' can tide you over until the last week, when it's 'count-down' to the first day of term!

Students think they are the only unfortunates at this stage of the year, but a lot of teachers have similar feelings of dread and depression. Arms anticipate the aches from hauling bags of copybooks, eyes already feel the strain of spanning 360 degrees, antennae must switch to full alert after the long break.

At second level, the return of the masses is usually staggered, to ease the transition for the new first years – or maybe for the staff! The staff room has had a facelift – that strawberry pink paint won't help flushed faces when exchanges at staff meetings become overheated. Thank heavens there is new crockery, though you know there will never be enough cups, or even seats, to go around at break time. On Day I, however, nearly everyone is determined to be positive and pleasant. Stories and snapshots circulate around the room. Adventurous folks have gone whitewater rafting in Africa or trekking in Nepal; you catch snippets of gossip from race week in Galway, or Writers' Week in Listowel, or that exciting summer school – was it the Donegal one? In a quiet corner, others are sharing their experiences, the stresses of looking after the grandchildren, the goings-on of the new neighbours, how the varicose job turned out … maybe being back in school is not so stressful after all.

The bell shrills to start the day, and the term, and the new school year. Students throng into classrooms that have been scrubbed and painted over the summer, all traces of last year's graffiti gone. Does M.T. still love T.M.? Or has that too been erased during the holidays?

The new first years try to look at home in their new school and new uniforms. Already a kind of pecking order is emerging. Sarah and friends know all about the system from older sisters who have been here – Kate's aunt is a friend of the French teacher, Anne's mother is on the staff (though maybe it's better not to advertise this fact). Girls who knew each other in primary school flock together, or avoid each other, depending on past experiences. Youngsters who know nobody gravitate towards each other. In years to come, many a story will be shared about first impressions on this milestone day in September.

Older students observe the newcomers with a kind of superiority tinged with sympathy. They get on with the business of counting the days to mid-term break. Serious folk are already planning study timetables and time management schemes. Stories circulate about the achievements of last year's class, who got what, points-wise. Newspaper listings of college courses and points are analysed by those who will face the final hurdle in nine months' time. But most people are looking back at the summer that was, who went where and with whom – all the happiness and heartbreak of the teenage world distilled in sharing and reminiscing.

First days, first week back, it is as if the long break has never been. As September slips along, new resolutions begin to slip – just a little! Graffiti reappears on locker doors; school uniforms lose their crispness, skirts are hitched up well above regulation length while tie knots loosen and sag; study timetables are scaled down or put on hold until after mid-term. September sunshine floods into classrooms, teachers revert to wearing summer clothes, and student resentment of school uniforms surfaces again. Rumours abound that the traditional half-day in mid-September for Junior Cert results has been forbidden by the Minister. Media people are on the look-out for dire behaviour in celebrating the said results. The equinox passes almost unnoticed, September having launched yet another school year, fades into the limbo of history.

THE TEARS OF ALL-IRELAND SUNDAY

Joe Kearney

We must have seemed an odd pairing on that Sunday afternoon. Myself, the fledgling hippy, and the man in the blue suit huddled against a telephone pole in Dollis Hill Park, north London. I had drifted into the tired acres of beaten grass and gaunt shrubbery with a melancholic indifference that can only be provoked by empty pockets. The park was cheating autumn on that September day in 1967 by delivering a display of hot, sunny defiance.

I observed the man in the blue suit, saw him press a small transistor radio against the tall pole and would have sauntered past him had my ears not been arrested by a familiar voice, an unmistakable singsong-chant ebbing and flowing from the tinny speaker. The man in the blue suit was using the telephone pole as a conduit to enhance his radio reception. Its own aerial, even fully extended, was as useless at this distance as a hayfork with a broken tine.

The voice on the radio was the voice of my childhood Sundays, from a place I thought I'd lost and a self I thought had vanished forever.

I gestured to the man in the blue suit. Was it OK if I joined him to listen? He shrugged an indifferent 'suit yourself'.

I was aware that he was appraising my appearance; saw him take in the tie-dyed, beaded and long-haired creature that was as contrasted to his white drip-dry nylon shirted-self as could be imagined.

The national anthem followed the county anthems. Emotion within me built in incremental steps. The hair stood on my arms and on the back of my neck. The water level built up behind the fragility of the dam. I defied the overspill with sheer willpower and self-control for as long as I could. That was until Michael O'Hehir extended a welcome to all those listening in Boston, New York, Chicago ... London. The Croke Park roar reached us in waves like a phantom sea in a shell held to the ear of memory. It was then that the tears found the line of least resistance and coursed down my embarrassed cheeks.

The man in the blue suit observed all.

'It's times like this that you'd miss the auld place,' he said, offering me a cigarette from the fresh packet of Major.

The softness of his lilt hinted at his origins.

'You're from Cork?' I asked.

His eyes crinkled with mischief. He trotted out his icebreaker, his party piece: 'Cork me hole!' he shouted. 'I'm from Mallow.'

Seeing my reaction, he crumpled under the power of his own wit and was overtaken by a spasm that was part laughter, part cough until the tears that sprung to his own eyes matched mine.

'What county man are you, yourself?' he enquired. I hesitated before replying, for I had grown up in a divided household where the waspish black-and-amber jostled with the banner of the red-and-white-blooded bandage. I could assume either allegiance. However, on this afternoon, county loyalty was unimportant. What was important was the reawakening of memories of previous All-Ireland Sundays and all that they meant – the end of summer and the return to school, pencils in their wooden case, pointed and sharp, schoolbooks that would leak knowledge from the wallpapered protection of their covers. Copybooks with pictures of round towers, also pointed and sharp, as sharp as the attention we promised to pay to our teachers, as sharp as the bittersweet blackberries of the hedgerow. As sharp as the crack of tar bubbles when they burst beneath bicycle tyres in potholed country lanes, as sharp as the memories flowing down the tarred pole and out of the radio.

When finally the 'hip, hips' were counted out, we shook hands and parted. Back home, soda bread was being cut for tea, ash plants were being picked up, wellingtons pulled on and cows gathered for milking.

We left the park and returned not to the small fields of our origins, but to the bed-sits of Cricklewood and Kilburn.

I will remember the man in the blue suit today as I do on all other All-Ireland Sundays when I renew my vow. When Micheál Ó Muircheartaigh welcomes those listening in Sydney, New York, Brazil, London, and when the roar goes up, I will not cry; this year I promise I will not cry.

ALTERNATE LIVES

Joe Kane

Took your time, there was no rush,
young sapling in the photograph, 1887.
Bending and swaying with the northwesterly.
Today, stiff and broken-limbed,
rot set in your heart. Now,
the last to wake up in spring,
first to sleep in autumn. Your doom
held in the trough of some future storm,
bringing you to ground to complete the cycle.
Good only for the kitchen range.

But you could've been a contender:
Taken down in your prime
waxed and left to dry slowly
rimmed and dressed,
ready for the workshop:
the right hands would have found
the fruit within, dense, flexible, responsive,
spoke-shaved to its final shape,
sanded for the hand of a virtuoso.
The first puck of the sliotar would have told all.

THE HURLERS' SEAT

Cathy Power Hernandez

I recently heard Seamus Heaney read his poem about a garden seat, and as his poetry always does, it touched me. Especially because I have a project in progress, involving the seat that stood outside the house where I was born: 23 Gardiner Place, Dublin.

My parents were from Kilkenny, and so was the culture of that household. It was called Kilkenny House although by rights it should have been called Kilkenny Hurling House and it sat in the middle of the capital like a Kilkenny embassy, a little bit of that county's soil in a foreign place.

The seat never rested in a leafy bower or shady nook, it was naked and exposed there on the steps of that Georgian house. It was where we sat in the evening sun to watch the world go by, in the time between clearing up after middle-of-the-day dinners and before the lodgers came home for tea.

On that seat we chatted to neighbours and watched the goings-on of the street. It was where a million moves on the hurling field were discussed and argued over and where the wood became shiny from use by hurlers' and former hurlers' backsides.

In Kilkenny House, the day of a hurling All-Ireland, no matter who was playing, was bigger than Christmas, back when going to an All-Ireland final was not something done after breakfast and before your evening meal.

People travelled the day before or came on trains and buses that began their journeys in the middle of the night. Working men who had gone to make their living in England would come home for the All-Ireland. Arriving a few days beforehand, they would be welcomed into the house like family, invited down to the basement kitchen to chat and drink tea or large bottles of stout and small whiskeys at all hours of the day and night. This was their annual holiday, so they were going to make it a good one.

Regulars would know to book their bed well in advance for that first weekend in September. As a small child, I would be stationed, weather permitting, outside on that seat on the Saturday evening to tell people that we had no room and to redirect them to neighbouring houses. But no matter how many we had staying in the house, it was a dead cert that my father, having spent the evening in Tommy Moore's of Cathedral Street or Club na nGael in North Great George's Street, would come home with some poor auld divil that hadn't a bed, and sure, you couldn't leave him out. And it was many the morning of a match that we found someone stretched out on that seat having failed to find a bed elsewhere.

By lunchtime, the house would be full of huge countrymen eating plates of ham, spuds and mushy peas, followed by jelly and cream and cups of tea to fortify them. And amid it all there was the hunt for tickets, the swapping and bartering, buying and selling, the begging and pleading. If you had a spare ticket it was the place to come to sell it or swap it or even give it away, but which or whether, to find a good home for it before the throw-in.

This was before the public address in Croke Park started calling the people 'patrons' and telling them not to enter the 'playing area'. We used to call it the pitch and we had many ecstatic moments swarming onto it to watch trophies being lifted in the Hogan Stand by men in black and amber. Then we would gallop back to sit on that same seat and watch the huge stream of supporters moving down Gardiner Place on their way home again, many stopping for a quick post-mortem of the game before heading for pints and more food at the Castle Hotel or Barry's.

A year or so after my father's death in 1965, we moved to Phibsboro, leaving a lot behind us. But my mother took the seat, and so it has rested, at last in a garden, for nearly forty years. My mother died last year and it is from her house that I am about to take it now, to Kilkenny from where, for all I know, my grandparents brought it when they moved to Dublin at the start of the last century. All going well, and with some repairs and a coat of paint, it will be a resting place for hurlers' backsides for another hundred years or so.

EXISTENTIALIST DOG

Leo Cullen

The dog walks freely towards the turnstiles. Freely, he lives in the small streets behind the stadium and falls in step with the pair of feet he thinks he recognises but ultimately doesn't. The feet go through the stiles; he follows. Black and white dog, small, but it doesn't matter what size or colour, because he is just a dog like any other, curious. He walks between legs, now there are more and more legs. He sniffs the ground, free dog, he sniffs the steps leading up to the terrace. He doesn't sniff anything he knows – things that smell something like him. Small boy drops packet of crisps before him. Can dog believe his eyes? He doesn't have to; dog is not interested in belief, only freedom. He munches crisps, he licks crisps, he licks the bag until it is see-through cellophane. Then he ambles along. He looks up at all the faces. Nobody has any time for dog. Everybody hurries, everybody walking in the same direction. Dog follows. Sniffs the virgin concrete. Everybody sits, he sits too for a moment. Does he consider why everybody is seated and talking, all talking, about the same thing? Dog doesn't consider. Only thing dog ever does consider is Mr Buckley, the butcher who lives down his street. Butcher Buckley isn't here. Or at least he hasn't spotted Butcher Buckley. Or smelled Butcher Buckley, who he can smell a dog mile away.

Dog considers the field below him. Big spaces, running spaces, are things a dog, a free dog like he, does consider. If his path goes by that way at some stage, he might just pop into that field.

Everybody sits down; dog sits down. Then everybody stands up; dog stands up. It gets noisy. They are shouting all around him. Swelled chests and tonsils. First one big shout accompanied by waving of cloths. Then another big shout, accompanied by waving of other cloths. Dog doesn't consider colour. He doesn't differentiate red and white from maroon and white, doesn't bother. He doesn't consider that they are all shouting at him, all waving their cloths at him. Only Butcher Buckley shouts, only Butcher Buckley waves his cloth, at him.

Dog grows bored. Ambles down towards where he came from. Now there is nobody down there. He squints out at the street he knows. Nothing out there on which a dog like he, an athletic dog like he, might achieve his potential. He licks another crisp bag. He licks melted chocolate and ice cream. He licks a burst peach but he doesn't like peach. He licks his lips and returns to the fray. This time through a new entrance, through a tunnel! Dog likes tunnels. He catches a glimpse of the field. Men in there, with sticks! Dog likes to run after men with sticks. Then he can't help doing just that, because he is in there too.

He runs right across the field. Noisy on that side also. Runs right across the field again. Who to follow? This one with socks down around his ankles? This one with the ball? Now he hasn't got it any more! Confusion for dog? Dogs don't get confused. Dogs run, stop and sniff.

Dog likes to lie and scratch his back on grass. He does just that. On his back, he scratches his paws against the sky. The noise up there is like black thunder. Dog doesn't think that. Dog feels it. Who cares what a dog thinks. He licks a burst bottle. Now he stands in the very centre of the field. A man with his hand out to him, a whistle in his mouth. The man is not Butcher Buckley. Dog knows that much. But still he runs away from him. Now dog runs not across the field because across the field leads to nowhere, as he knows, but right along the length of the field. Dog runs into a net. Man with wide stick tries to jump on him. Dog escapes. Oh, great roar goes up when dog does that:

'Goalie, you can't even block a shaggin' dog!'

Come to think of it, everybody now is trying to block him: 'Here dog. Dog, dog. Get off the goddamned field, dog.'

Does dog hear things properly? Do the massive roars and laughs, and even screams, he hears on the stands happen to coincide with each time somebody makes a lunge for him and misses? Man in white coat lunges; dog sidesteps. 'Run, funny dog, run!' The stands erupt with gleeful laughter. Is dog enjoying it? – Dog running so fast his ears lift in the wind? – No, dog is just there, just playing the game of his life. Life is a dog's game.

MY FIRST THEATRE

Michael Harding

For me there are two very special places in Paris. One is the dark vaulted majesty of Notre Dame. And the other is the ghostly, creaking, haunted interior of the Bouffe du Nord, a theatre just behind the Gare du Nord. But I have never been quite sure what the difference is between a theatre and a church, and I often wonder is there any difference at all.

I remember once saying mass in Notre Dame in Paris. It was a weekday and I was permitted to celebrate the Sacred Mysteries on a side altar. The sacristan unlocked the gates of the enclosed alcove, I entered, and then he locked me in.

I did not realise that people were watching me through the bars of the grill, or that to enact the Eucharistic Rite was as exotic to Japanese tourists as a Samurai ritual might be to the children of Belmullet.

But when I elevated the Consecrated Bread in the air above my head, in what I thought was a private moment between me and the Almighty, I was stunned by the sound of what I took to be a flock of pigeons flapping their wings. I turned round and was blinded by a battery of cameras discharging their flashes, as dozens of tourists captured the experience to bring back to Japan.

It was a moment of perfect refuge.

The ancient stones of the great cathedral.

The silver chalice.

The isolation of public ritual.

Many years later, I found myself very far removed from the grandeur of a Catholic cathedral. I was tinkering with Buddhism, and I ended up trying to meditate in a coal shed, a small stone building behind the house. It was a space lying there, empty of coal, and waiting for something to happen.

I cleaned it out. Put in a new wooden floor and ceiling. Broke out a space in the wall for a window.

For a year or two, the coal shed became my prayer hut.

My refuge.

My little Tibet.

My spider's cathedral.

And when I was six, I used to steal upstairs to where the Child of Prague stood on a dressing table with his arms outstretched. He stood on a lace mat. Either side of him were little silver jewellery boxes. One was necklaces and bracelets and the other was full of powder for making up a face.

I had all I required to impress the Almighty in a ritual of gobbledygook that closely resembled the local parish priest mumbling his mass in Latin.

My first hocus pocus, abracadabra world. The invisible made visible in the performance of a ritual.

My first theatre.

MAYBE IT'S THE HORSE CHESTNUTS

Grace Wynne-Jones

I am not a great fan of most advertisements. It seems to me they often offer things that can't be bought, such as love and youth and happiness. But there was a time when I cherished certain ads as much or more than any pop song by The Monkees. And if they came on the telly or I saw them in a magazine, I would love them again because they once spoke powerfully to my teenage heart.

The one for Badedas bath oil has an enormous place in my affections. It often featured a woman wearing nothing but a large towel staring out the window at a most attractive man and a horse. 'Things happen after a Badedas bath,' the accompanying words explained seductively. 'Perhaps it's something to do with the horse chestnuts.'

This seemed entirely reasonable to my sixteen-year-old self. Love was a strange and mysterious business and horse chestnuts might indeed have something to do with it. The thought of a total stranger suddenly appearing on the lawn was wonderful. I preferred him to the Milk Tray man, who didn't have the same poetry about him, though he bravely scaled walls and had possibly once been in the army. I often hung around in the bathroom for a while after my Badedas bath. I'm sure I didn't really expect to see a man and a horse on the lawn, but I liked the idea of them. The idea of them made me happy.

The Martini ad had an entirely different and ebullient atmosphere. The people in it seemed happy because they were drinking Martini and there was no mention of horse chestnuts. 'Try a taste of Martini,' the song went. 'The most beautiful drink in the world.' Sometimes the gorgeous men and women drank their Martinis in a hot air balloon that soared above a stunning landscape.

Speed seemed to be a factor in these advertisements. The Martini people were going somewhere. I don't recall the details of all their adventures, but I think there may also have been horses and speedboats. The Martini ads spoke to me of freedom and adventure – of distant places and a more jolly, party-like form of romance. I didn't particularly like the taste of Martini itself, but that was a mere technicality. Martini wasn't a drink, it was a whole way of life.

You wouldn't think the Electricity Supply Board could compete with the allure of Martini, but it did, and Dusty Springfield definitely helped. The ad was about a young man returning to his home in the countryside at Christmas. His dad was driving him and Dusty was singing, 'I think I'm going back to the things I learned so well in my youth … I think I'm returning to those days when I was young enough to know the truth.'

The young man looked out the window at the familiar landmarks, and at home you saw his mum beaming and baking food. There was a lot of electricity around in the form of lights and the oven, but there was also a strong sense of homecoming and love. The ad somehow managed to be both worldly and innocent.

By the time I fell in love with the ESB ad, I had left home myself and had lived in big cities. I knew what it was like to return to small country roads after getting off an airplane. This was totally different to the world the Martini people inhabited. This was coming back and appreciating what had once seemed ordinary and almost too familiar. This was about the habits and needs of the heart … and the importance of electricity, which was already pretty much accepted. If the ad had been about aftershave, the whole tone would have been different. It would have seemed manipulative somehow – but electricity was fine. Electricity was just there anyway.

Of course there are some great ads around today, including the classic ones for Ferrero Rocher. I love the idea that a box of chocolates can turn any gathering into an ambassador's party. It is wonderful, ridiculous and extremely clever. I also enjoy the charged sexual chemistry between the Maxwell House man and woman, but the Badedas Bath Oil one is still my favourite. It could be the man, or it could be the horse …

Or maybe it's the horse chestnuts …

SWIMMING THE CHANNEL

Mae Leonard

I made up my mind to swim the English Channel when I was eight years old. I had just learned to swim and all the grown-ups said that I was good enough to, so I said, Yes, I AM going to swim the channel, and I was very affronted when everyone laughed. The fact that I had nearly drowned the previous year didn't have a profound effect on me. I WOULD, I declared, swim the channel – maybe next year. Yes. I'd show them. Put the smile on the other side of their faces. But somewhere in between school and life happenings, I forgot all about my decision until I was sixteen. There was this boy in the swimming club who told me of his ambition to swim across Lake Windermere. He wasn't exactly the best of swimmers and I was a swimming champion by then – but a sprinter, not a long-distance swimmer. This guy had the stamina and determination that I lacked, and, well, I fancied him. *I'm going to swim the channel*, I told him – *someday*. He laughed at me and went off and swam across Lake Windermere. I had to do better than that – I WOULD swim the English Channel.

I made tentative enquiries through the Channel Swimming Association and was told that the end of the summer is the best time to attempt a crossing. How wide is it? About twenty-four miles from the White Cliffs of Dover to Cap Gris-Nez in France. Twenty-four miles, but that's depending on weather conditions, tides and shipping traffic. You could end up doing thirty to forty miles. Thirty to forty miles? I'm a sprinter, for goodness sake! One hundred metres maximum. Instead of a one-minute swim, I'd be in the water for something like sixteen hours, or even a lot more. Cold water. Icy water – sixty degrees, in fact. And no, you're not allowed to wear a wetsuit or even a second swimsuit – rules decree that you must have the same equipment as the first channel swimmer, Matthew Webb. He did it in 1875, crossing in approximately twenty-two hours. They say that he sipped warm brandy all the way. And that's another thing you need – sustenance every thirty minutes.

Gertrude Ederle, an American, was the first woman to swim the English Channel – she did it in 1926. She swam from France in a sea so rough that steamship crossings had been cancelled and she was buffeted by waves so badly that she became seasick.

In order to protect herself from the cold water, she coated her body with layers of lard and petroleum jelly to insulate herself. She made it to Dover in fourteen and a half hours. A world record, although since then it has been done in a lot less. There are several attempts every year, of which forty or so are successful. Would I be successful?

Training and preparation takes something like three years of gruelling swimming in sea water, winter and summer. Most channel swimmers now use front crawl, although changing strokes from time to time can break up the monotony. You need to be fed to keep up your energy. Although you may halt for food or a drink, you are not allowed to touch your accompanying boat. Yes, you have to have a boat with you and that costs in the region of €2,000. Those boats can be hired in Dover with your support crew aboard to dispense hot drinks and food and a pilot who will plot the course during the swim. Usually you swim no more than ten to twenty metres away from the boat, and every thirty minutes or so to be fed from an extended pole and informed on conditions and expected time of arrival. The more you stop, the slower your overall time will be and you have to be careful, as the English Channel is one of the busiest shipping lanes in the world. You could be mowed down by a super tanker.

You have to be aware of neap tides, the phases of the moon and, of course, the weather. I sat down to consider the possibilities. I had no money. I had a Leaving Cert to prepare for and suddenly there was this other boy – not a swimmer, but a hunk of hurler – who had become the focus of my attention. I couldn't possibly go out on a date with my hair drenched and eyes swollen from long training in the icy river. Yes, I had to get my priorities right. And I did – I married him. So I never did get to swim the channel.

FULL TILT

Gail Seekamp

Belfast to Bantry is a long way — over 300 miles. Many years ago, I faced the same distance on another route, from Middlesboro in England's industrial north-east to sunny, seductive Brighton on the south coast.

I was aged eighteen, and off to Sussex University. Eager to trade a bed-sit and hotel job for the 'thrills' of college. And to kick-start the fun, I had decided to travel down on my Honda 250.

She was aged but reliable, with golden bodywork and a gutsy engine. A metal pony — of sorts. On leaving Ireland in my mid-teens, I'd had to sell a beloved horse, and my stepfather bought me a Honda 250 to soften the blow. She had barely managed twenty-five miles per hour, even with a tail wind. But as I graduated to more powerful machines, I grew intoxicated.

I sat my 'biker' driving test a week before the big trip, and failed — to my horror. The motorway was out, so I had to plot a route on smaller roads. I bought a trunk for my clothes, books and records and sent them by British Rail. That still left the record player, with a large external speaker, my horse's saddle and various bags.

Late in September, the day finally arrived. I ate a solitary breakfast, lashed my belongings to the carrier and passenger seat and coasted off, brimming with elation and nerves.

You can picture the sight of me. A taut, young face; dirty wax jacket and trousers; the stereo making a crazy *Easy Rider* back rest, padded by towels and anchored by nasty nylon rope. Perched on top, stirrups and all, sat the saddle.

It was, despite the horsey statement, a highly 'unstable' structure. At lower speeds, the bike wobbled madly. On the outskirts of one Yorkshire town, I braked too sharply at the lights. The whole edifice rocked, and I tumbled onto the pavement in slow motion. A group of passing lads hauled me upright. 'Ist thou injured, lass?' one asked solicitously. I muttered thanks and left, mortified.

This journey had a bad feeling to it. I had ridden from Middlesboro to County Wexford once, in a glorious sweep across the Pennine Mountains. I'd gotten drenched in a rainstorm, had chased a rainbow and survived several scrapes. I'd even sat up all night on the ferry, buzzing with excitement and chat. This long trek south was different; an interminable stretch of grey, lonely road, punctuated by suburbs, shops and filling stations. My arms ached from holding the bike upright in jagging gusts of wind. I felt I was swallowing each mile, and getting physically sick in the process.

My top speed was fifty-five mph. At that rate, I wouldn't reach Brighton until the small hours.

Night was falling as I stopped at a petrol station north of London. The rope was now slack from the slipping and stretching. As I fumbled with it, a couple in their fifties approached. The husband vigorously reanchored the stereo, and his wife extracted information – as some mothers can. Where was I was I off to? All the way to Brighton? Tonight? 'Oh yes,' I replied airily.

They exchanged glances. As I pulled back onto the dual carriageway, they followed. Discreetly. Not for one mile or two, but for several. Then they overtook and signalled me onto the hard shoulder. Listlessly, I obeyed.

'Come home with us,' the woman ordered. 'You can stay in our son's room tonight, and head off first thing tomorrow. He's gone off to college, too.'

So I did. They treated me to dinner, a cosy bed and a flask of tea and sandwiches in the morning. Even a pair of their son's socks.

I never wrote to thank them, of course; such is the thoughtlessness of youth. But I often recall how they rescued that wayward eighteen-year-old girl, and I am so grateful. My own child is now a fearless six. She loves racing on her pink bike – 'Faster, faster!' – and turning tight corners. I still have a Honda 250, this one concealed in her grandfather's garage. Out of sight, out of mind!

LANDSCAPES

Denise Blake

We drove past Ailsa Craig, a single molar tooth
standing in the North Channel as we ferried our son
with all his belongings, to Freshers' week in university,
and I thought, 'imagine the pain in having that removed.'

Once it was Ben Bulben, with all its shifting shapes,
embleming our travels to and from his school.
It used to crouch, a snow-coated lion ready to pounce,
or lay down, a brown flecked hound by the hearthside.

On Aidan's last night at home, I heard the sound of him
pouring kettle-boiled water into his sink for shaving.
I asked the pillow, When? And How?
as his growing up speed-reeled through me.

We don't have the Scottish landscape rooted in us
and we can't predict what is around any corner.
In order to come back, he needs to go away –
have we given him all he needs for his journey?

This morning, that final bob of his navy beanie hat
as he was swallowed into the stream of students,
the ripple of his deep-hearted laugh carried back.
And now, as we approach Stranraer,

we are swamped by a muddle-head mist.
Ailsa Craig, in all its certainty, has disappeared,
or has since been extracted. We pass by an empty
horizon, while our son's landscape keeps on reshaping.

THE POPE IN KILLINEER

Conor O'Callaghan

I was passing a layover in La Guardia airport, New York at the start of last April. I had just bought some fried noodles and found a free table when I overheard a newscaster on CNN say that the Pope had finally passed away. After the story's bones had been reported, they cut to the stock market report.

The morning Pope John Paul II kissed the tarmac in Dublin Airport was the only time I ever saw my father in tears. When His Holiness knelt and vanished into a sea of white robes, like a gannet catching a mackerel, our old man stood in the middle of the living room spluttering into a hanky. We thought he was choking. Before any of us could save him, our mother had given a curt headshake that said, 'Stay where you are.'

Two days after, our mother rented a car in which eight of us drove to Killineer, the parish north of Drogheda made momentarily famous by its famous visitor. Can 'eight' be true? It sounds too much like one of those preposterous exaggerations only memory washes ashore. Me and three of my four brothers (the oldest had recently grown his hair long, developed a taste for cider and declared his complete uninterest in, as he called him, 'that Polish fascist'); our mother; our Auntie Nancy and two of her three daughters (her eldest had fallen in love with the drummer of a heavy metal group and gone on the train). That makes eight, all sardined into a Triumph Toledo from Dundalk to our designated car park in Collon.

Our enclosure was at the very back. We had a picnic (no meat, out of respect) and waited. And waited ... The helicopter appeared on the horizon. We all cheered. It landed in a maelstrom of blades behind the stage. We cheered some more. Local dignitaries and religious leaders spoke. Then the tiny yellow speck got up. It was hard to work out what was being said. The PA was so echoey that he sounded as if he was addressing us from underwater. Something about peace and Northern Ireland. A man in the enclosure immediately in front of us started snoring. A wave of giggles rippled through our end of the crowd. His wife tried to wake him, explaining in stage whispers that he'd been working long hours lately. The yellow speck toured in the Popemobile, but never seemed to get any closer. After the helicopter vanished into the horizon, it was just a big field again and we all filed out through the one gate.

Me and my cousin Suki got separated from the rest of the family. We were holding hands, and realised that we were almost in Drogheda. I started blubbing and she, three weeks older, took charge. We went to the nearest house and pressed the bell. A family, clearly expecting visitors, appeared in tuxedoes. After a moment's silent confusion, the man of the house said, 'These are not the Gogartys. Who are you?'

'We're lost,' we said.

They brought us to a Garda and we told him our car park number. A Presbyterian vicar from Cookstown said he was going the same direction, and offered to shepherd us. He was very kind, but why was he there in the first place? It was, I've since supposed, like going to see Bob Dylan in Slane. You didn't have to be a true believer to recognise a good gig. Being reunited with the others was the highlight of the day.

The nineteen miles home took four and a half hours. The equation 'eight into one does not go' kept going through my head. My legs got very hot and Auntie Nancy, on whose knee I was sitting, suggested I take my corduroys off. I didn't want to in front of my brothers and female cousins, but Auntie Nancy wasn't taking no for an answer. My brother Brian got sick on his best pants. He said, 'I have to wear these to mass tomorrow.'

That it was only Saturday hadn't occurred to the rest of us. There was no special dispensation from tomorrow's mass for those attending today. I will never forget the long daisy-chain of brake lights disappearing into the mid-Louth darkness, and barely moving.

Next thing, the La Guardia tannoy was saying my name. I grabbed my things, left a bowl of cold noodles and headed for my connection.

THE SHOFAR

Judith Mok

Ten thousand candles would be lit in the Portuguese Synagogue in Amsterdam. I promised my little daughter a feast of light during our walk from home to the Synagogue. She wasn't exactly looking forward to sitting upstairs behind railings in the women's only section of that building. A religious ceremony was normally not part of our lives. But on this day of Yom Kippur, I thought it important for her to experience the spectacle of a Jewish feast day in one of the most beautiful syna-gogues in the world, as well as listening to the Kol Nidrei, the blowing of the shofar, the ram's horn, to soothe all evil spirits.

She met some of her girlfriends in the street just as I was pointing out the stone pelican above the side entrance. It was the symbol of Sephardic Jews during the seventeenth century. They had to get into this immense building through a side door, as Jews were not allowed to have a main entrance to their place of worship on a busy public road. The little girls shrugged and ran inside the courtyard through the now-open main entrance. I followed with the mummies, all dressed up and coiffed for the occasion. In the obscure light upstairs there was a lot of gold on display around wrists and necks. Some women were wearing perfumed furs and old-fashioned hats that made me wonder what people would have looked like back then.

The synagogue was built by Suasso and Pereira and Da Pinto with the money they had earned by financing both sides in the wars between the Dutch and Spanish armies. These Sephardic aristocrats became wealthy supplying both armies and were allowed to build their mansions on the outer canals of the city of Amsterdam. The inner circle of canals remained closed to Jews until the nineteenth century. But their money was good enough for the Spanish King Philip and the Dutch Prince, William of Orange. Across the road from the Ashkenazi Shul, the other synagogue, a new and magnificent building, was erected. To this day there is no electric light in the main hall.

Some of my ancestors came to Amsterdam when they fled the Spanish Inquisition. Now, while I was staring down at the orthodox men swaying back and forth in prayer and chant, I imagined my remote ancestors sitting up here with their daughters shifting impatiently in their seats. We were sitting so far away from the ceremony that there was plenty of opportunity for gossiping and sizing up each other's clothes.

I, who did not have the slightest notion of the religious aspects of this ceremony, was concentrating on my immediate surroundings. Now, a lot of the girls and women had curly fair hair, but back then there must have been a lot of luscious dark Spanish hair and eyes behind the bars we were allowed to look through. And the women would have pointed out future husbands to their daughters. I peered down intensely to see if there was some charming little boy hopping, or rather, swaying, around down there. But to no avail.

A bearded man came forward with the long ram's horn and blew the theme of Kol Nidrei. It was as if the sound haunted itself in between these ancient walls. Even my child grew quiet. For a moment, then, I had lost her again, in her red hat and coat, curls dancing on her back. She had disappeared down the rickety stairs. Probably to play hide and seek in the courtyard. I waved to my friends and left as well.

Down in the courtyard, a crowd had gathered. A group of older people dressed in their warm coats and hats, survivors of the camps or other atrocities, were chatting away and continuously turning this or that way to greet acquaintances and friends. Children and grandchildren were introduced and admired while I tried to get hold of my offspring.

And there he was; the wonderful, kind old man who recognised me and took my hands in his with tears in his eyes. And this is your daughter, he said, smiling at my pretty rascal, now hatless, who had appeared. He told her how he cherished the great books her grandfather had written. She seemed surprised and smiled at him, giggled when he told her a funny story about her grandmother. He stroked her hair gently, embraced me and walked away with the weight of centuries on his shoulders. I felt good. Just by remembering my parents, my own life had been lit up again. With at least ten thousand candles.

IN A GARDEN

Sinéad McCoole

Should you ever have met Catherine Kennedy, who died in 2000 in her eighty-seventh year, you might perhaps have glimpsed in her animated gestures the actions of her famous grandmother, Lady Gregory. Certainly there were those who insisted that they could see the similarity in the tilt of the head, as captured in Epstein's bust of Lady Gregory. It was not merely an obscure ancestral link that Catherine shared with her grandmother. Her earliest years were spent in her care, living at Coole.

Catherine Kennedy's ashes were scattered on Coole Lake. One of her last wishes was to return to the place which once upon a time she had called home. But with that last act, her presence did not completely disappear from Coole — if you know where to look, you will find her garden, a garden within a garden.

Her grandmother had laid out three tiny gardens for her grandchildren, 'her chicks', as she called them. They had all been born at Coole — Richard in 1909, Anne in 1911 and Catherine in 1913. By encouraging them to tend their own gardens, Lady Gregory wished to instil in her grandchildren the love she had for nature, for her native Galway, for Coole.

Richard, Anne and Catherine were the children of Lady Gregory's only child, Robert, and his wife, Margaret Graham Parry, whom Robert had met when she was a fellow art student at The Slade in London. The couple had no interest in living in Coole, and even after the birth of their son they departed from Galway, leaving the infant Richard in his grandmother's care.

Richard was sent off to boarding school at a very early age, but Anne and Catherine were always at Coole. It was in Coole they heard of their father's death. Robert, aged thirty-seven, had been killed in 1918, shot down over northern Italy, another casualty of the First World War.

Shortly after that, the girls were taken away from Coole for the first time, brought to England by their mother. Knowing that the girls were desperately unhappy away from Coole, their grandmother sent them great parcels of moss and little red toadstools on twigs from the Nut Wood, which the girls made into great flat dishes, and sniffed and sniffed the lovely wet mossy smell and imagined that they were back at their beloved Coole. It was not long before their mother, aware of their loneliness, sent them back to Ireland, to Coole.

Something of the time, that golden childhood, is captured in Anne's memoir, the enchanting *Me and Nu*. The voice of the child, who called her little sister Nu, brings characters of the literary renaissance to life. Stories of a grandmother, a very different lady to the one imagined as one studies images of a stern-faced woman in widow's weeds. George Bernard Shaw had played with *and* cheated them at 'hunt the timble'. So indignant were these young girls at his antics that despite their grandmother's urging would not address him as their 'kind playmate', even when he wrote a poem in their honour, addressing them grandly as 'two ladies of Galway.'

Yeats 'always seemed to be there' and they could remember him 'humming' away for hours while he wrote his verse. They also remembered his bad manners; he never said please and thank you. The girls met Sean O'Casey and witnessed him carving his name on the autograph tree at Coole. The tree is still there in the garden, standing proud.

Two years after Robert's death, Margaret told Lady Gregory that she wanted to sell Coole. She finally agreed to keep the house, the garden and 350 acres. But this was only a short-term respite. In 1927, Lady Gregory acted as a witness to Margaret's signature on the deed for the sale of Coole to the Department of Agriculture and Lands. The new owners formally took possession of the estate, but they did permit Lady Gregory to lease the house. It was some consolation to her, an old lady who was dying. She had already undergone two operations for her breast cancer.

Lady Gregory lived to see Richard's coming of age in 1930, but it was not what she had imagined. Shortly before her death in 1932, Lady Gregory had written of Coole: 'I have lived there and loved it these forty years and through the guests who have stayed there it counts for much in the awakening of the spiritual and intellectual side of our country. If there is trouble now, and it is dismantled and left to ruin, that will be the whole country's loss.'

The house has been gone for a long time now. Ironically, the property, that great historic house, had belonged to the Irish people, but a local official felt that it was better to be without the encumbrance of the house and sent in local men to undermine the roof. In time it was knocked because it was an unsafe structure. The lands of Coole had been saved because of the rare trees that had been planted by a Gregory centuries before.

The magic of the place still lingers in the garden and woods. If you have never been, I urge you to go. I am sure that you will find your way to look at the autograph tree and view the initials of the famous who visited Coole. Lady Gregory's grandchildren never carved their names on that tree – they were not famous – but if you look really carefully, you will find three tiny hedges that surround three areas of earth – and just imagine the children digging there a long time ago in a garden.

OCTOBER

MARY MACKER'S BLACKERS

Anthony Glavin

We saved our glass jars long before it paid to recycle, storing them in the garden shed beside the large circular pan for boiling jam. That outsized pan is what passes for an heirloom in my wife's family, on loan from her mother, whose four other daughters are equally serious about picking and preserving the fruits of summer.

We don't always scrape the original labels off the jars, nor manage always to label each season's preserve – raspberry, 2003 – as some jam-makers do. But there's no mistaking what we spread on our bread year-round, be it gooseberry, damson or rhubarb, for anything other than the real thing.

The rhubarb we get from our ninety-two-year-old neighbour Patricia, two doors down. The gooseberries and damsons we harvest from our own northside Dublin garden, although the damson tree failed to produce a single plum until we fed it some potash two winters ago. However, we've never had much luck growing strawberries, and our few raspberry canes provide only enough berries for the breakfast muesli, so we have to look elsewhere for these fruits.

Raspberries you can pay to pick, which we happily do at a Donabate fruit farm, where up until a few years ago you could pick strawberries too. However, the fruit farm, which once also sold fresh produce, is turning slowly into yet another Celtic Tiger garden centre, and the dwindling number of raspberry canes under cultivation each year suggests we may soon have to forage even farther afield for this delectable berry.

Of course, mileage matters not to serious jam-makers, and so most years we combine visits to friends in Roscommon and to yet another sister-in-law in Wales with the opportunity to pick blackberries on both sides of the Irish Sea. Indeed, blackberries can be got for nothing, provided you note where they grow, and we used to happily pick quarts of them at the secondary school abutting our back garden, until the school sadly padlocked off access to that corner of their grounds last year.

I bring to the enterprise my own berry-picking past, I suppose, fond memories of gathering Massachusetts huckleberries which my mother put into pies of a Proustian flavour. And, come to think of it, other memories are inextricably linked to other berries: like the huge logging truck I half-heartedly waved my thumb at in Oregon back in 1966, and the unbelievable bounty of blackberries I had to leave behind on that mountain road as the truck downshifted through a dozen gears to stop and offer me a lift. There are also those first Irish blackberries I gathered up in Donegal in 1975, or those I picked near Dingle in 1979, with English friends who subsequently served me my first blackberry fool. Or the state of Maine blackberries I picked the summer of 1983, feeding them over my shoulder to our year-old daughter, who, slung papoose style on my back, screeched her delight like a crow. Or, for that matter, the bright red deadly nightshade berries we pointed out the following Maine summer to her toddler self, accompanied by dire warnings.

All of our three children adored the mulberries we stripped from a tree beside our western Massachusetts swimming hole in the early 1990s, but I came to that particular fruit too late in life to truly love it. I also feel the same way about blackcurrants, which suddenly appeared in vast quantities on our kitchen counter just this past summer.

'Where did we get *them?*' I inquired, only to be told, 'They're from Mary Macker's garden!' Mary Macker is our young niece's affectionate nickname for our northside neighbour with the big house off the North Circular Road, where that niece's mother, yet another of my berry-mad sisters-in-law, working as an apprentice gardener, noted the blackcurrants falling off Mary Macker's bushes, and sought permission to harvest them.

I'll admit some of us in the family worry we maybe give away as gifts too much of our jam. However, I keep telling my wife, Adrienne, that she should take a jar of that same blackcurrant preserve up to Áras An Uachtaráin.

'You must be joking!' Adrienne says, but I assure her I'm entirely serious.

'It'll be like Bertie giving Bush the shamrock, only better!' I explain. 'You simply say, "President: your berries, my jam!"'

SWIMMING LESSONS

Leo Cullen

We had moved to Dublin, my father, brothers and sisters and I, in 1967.
He had bought an enormous old house in decline near the sea at
Monkstown and his idea was that he would convert it into flats. We
would live in one of them and he would let out the others for an
income. There was one flat in the basement with sitting tenants. That
was a part of the house that could not be converted. The Sullivans
would not budge, but I was not aware of that. I had become friendly
with them that summer. In their kitchen I ate Maltana, a juicy loaf
soaked with sultanas – the staple diet of Dubliners, as far as I could tell
– and I sang with them from their radio the songs of Englebert
Humperdinck – the staple songs, as far as I could tell. My father
employed a man named Oliver, a Longford man who claimed he could
put his hands to anything, and that included ridding a house of dry rot,
of rising damp and of unwanted tenants. I was supposed to be Oliver's
helper and henchman.

Then came a day when, baked by the heat and feeling suddenly hot
right into the very core of my being, an idea flew into my mind. It came
slap in the middle of a Maltana afternoon with the Sullivans. It was not
just the heat that had got to me. It was more; maybe the long days of
dry rot and rising damp had got to me at last. Maybe I'd had enough of
Maltana and inactivity and the criticisms of Oliver, who right at that
moment I was supposed to be helping with the knocking of a wall.
Maybe I resented the Sullivans making implications about my father and

about his designs for the house. Maybe I'd had just enough of my own disloyalty to him. I don't know what it was. But the moment the words came out of me, I knew I had made a mistake: 'Let's go for a swim,' I said, even as I remembered I could not swim a stroke.

'Good idea,' said the Sullivan boys. 'Let's go.' The Sullivans could swim. And the Sullivans' friend Luggy, who went everywhere with them and who was my mortal enemy since I'd come to live in Dublin at summer's beginning, could also swim. Luggy, whose name came from the lugworm bait he dug out of the sand. Down we descended with skimpy togs and towels, down on a tide way out on the flat beach of Seapoint, out, it seemed, as far as Howth. A cold breeze ripped in, skinning my white legs. After the sticky heat of the Sullivans' flat, I felt the sudden chill. I walked out until the water was halfway up my thighs. Stringy lengths of floating seaweed kept getting in my way. It was a slow business. I wasn't sure of my footing and the waves splashed up at me, making me draw my breath while I tried to keep my balance. Then I ducked down, and after a wave swooshed into my mouth, I thought I'd had enough and might return to the shore. But Luggy was behind me. The sawn-off trousers he wore for togs were now wet and hung from him, making him look like a salty, partially dressed scarecrow.

'You're not swimmin',' he said. And he was right. I had been crawling, hands and feet pegging along the muddy sand at the sea bottom.

Maybe it was because of the new element of salt water all about me, but I did not think of it as surrender when I capitulated to Luggy. 'No, I'm not able,' I said. 'Will you teach me?'

It was an admission, yes, but a clever one. By asking for his help, I was defending myself against his jibes.

Luggy taught me how to swim. He was just as vicious in the sea as out of it, but in there I was somehow buffeted from him. In the gulpy cold water and with the cries of the strand only a faint rumble in my ears each time I went under, the lungs took over from the thinking parts of the body. Every day for the remainder of a week in September that my father called an 'Indian summer', we went swimming and I had lessons. Luggy's face went black with cold and his arms around my waist holding me up in the water went hard as wire ropes. 'Kick, kick, you culchie,' he said. 'I'm not leaving the sea until you swim because you are only a culchie.' He was punishing me. By the end of that month, when only elderly people came down to bathe, in what I heard them say was the iodine, I had learned to swim and also to dive. It was no good just swimming with the Sullivans. Diving on the full tide was the business.

Luggy still hated me. Given half a chance he would still have had a crack at me. He was one of the world's great haters, and nothing much could be done about it. But I had learned to swim and learned to dive. The sea was my element. The sea was the place where all ... what was it ... all responsibility washed away. Learning to swim, after all, had not been a mistake. Oliver from Longford looked at me each day on my return as though I were a strange animal with fins and a tail. 'Swimming,' he said. 'Getting into that sea. I don't know what this world is coming to. And all the work here waiting to be done for your father.'

Swimming. That was only the start of it. All through one's life one is bullied, or one bullies oneself, into the learning of diversions that become essential to survival.

ONCE, ON LONG ISLAND ...

Gerard Smyth

... we wept and talked about leaving
and never left. — Kapka Kassabova

Once on Long Island, on a day of leaf-smoke
rising at the end of an ocean drive,
I came to a house that was like the home
of Jimmy Stewart in *It's a Wonderful Life.*

I was among three generations assembled
for an afternoon tea ceremony.
The octogenarian who sat beside me
took me through a long family narrative

that started on the fertile plain
and ancient roads of Slane and Tara.
From the year of her departure

she unlocked a big portmanteau of recollections
that started with a rooming house in America,
along avenues with their sidewalks of destiny.

GAVOTTE

Enda Coyle-Greene

She was thirty-two — at least that was the age the record company admitted to on her behalf. But we were so much younger than that. I was twenty-two and my best friend, both of whose names began with A and was therefore first in everyone's address book, was the same. We imagined her as ancient, not quite in the same league as our mothers, but getting there.

Despite this, we thought that she was wonderful, with her yellow hair that looked as if it had been chopped instead of cut, her blue eyes that seemed to have seen everything worth seeing, her high cheekbones that could have sliced cheese and, above all else, her very strange dress sense. Everything she wore appeared to have been made just for her. In the first photograph I ever saw of her, she posed in a pool of white light in a plain black knee-length dress that might have come from Coco Chanel but probably hadn't. She wore high, black, round-toed Minnie Mouse court shoes and had twisted one foot around in front of the other in a way that was graceful and gangling all at once. In moody, atmospheric black and white, her artfully unbrushed hair stood out straight around her head in a shock of straw-like static.

And that was one of her more sober outfits. Once, she appeared on television in a dress that looked as if had been fashioned from a black plastic bin-bag. With it, she wore a rough leather belt, chucked in around the middle to accentuate her waist. Another get-up was a butter-coloured mini-dress that might have been made from those chamois leather cloths our dads used to polish the car. It had a huge cowled collar. She wore over-the-knee pirate boots that matched. Her hair clashed beautifully.

The rest of us were still floating around town in outfits that were part medieval serving wench, part nun. Our long skirts swept the dust from the streets; we carried it home with us in our hems. We had our hair cut on a regular basis, only an inch off, though, just enough to deal with the split ends we worried about constantly. I remember ironing mine. Cheesecloth was our chosen fabric. Ironing it was a useless exercise but we did it anyway. Nobody ever wore anything that was warm.

But why did we need to be warm when we could dance? How we danced, my best friend and I. It was our way of getting through the week's tediousness, a glorious existence in itself with its own set of rules, its own language.

Not that we danced to just anything. Not for us, the yodels of those factory-made groups who jerked around on *Top of the Pops* like puppets. They were commercial. They had no rhythm, no soul, no passion. We had that in abundance and we were always, always in love. In my case, anyway, usually with someone who barely knew that I existed. At the weekends, the city glittered with all the glamour of promised romance, fizzed with the prospect of the truest of true love. And so did we.

Music, sweet, sweet music, was the great aural backdrop to everything.

When Debbie, who, later, much later, would prefer to be referred to as Deborah, sang, 'Oh Denis, I'm in love with you, Denis' to a heart-pounding beat, I was right there with her. Not with anyone she knew, or she might have stolen him from under my nose. Her beauty was not one that I could have competed with. No, for the first, and possibly, hopefully, the last time, I was in love with someone who might even love me back.

That night, my two A'd best friend and I danced on the steps that lead onto the dance floor in McGonagle's. Up and down and up and down we danced. We were happy in our innocence. We were happy.

Out on the floor, everyone else was dancing too, drenched by the glamour of the glitter-ball light, a relic of another, much calmer age. But it seemed as if it was for us alone that Debbie, beautiful Debbie, declared her love for Denis: over and over to our shake, our shimmy, our gavotte.

MEMORIES OF
DAVID THOMSON

Máiréad Ní Chonceanainn

Sorting through cluttered shelves, I have come upon the fraying fawn-coloured pages of a BBC radio documentary which has taken me back in time over fifty years. The frontispiece reads:

> The Enchanted Islands
> Compiled and produced by David Thomson
> Wednesday 6ᵗʰ September 1950 8.00-9.00pm Third Programme

Among the many autographs there on its pages by David Thomson and other BBC personnel, stands in Irish that of my late husband, who took the part of the Aran man in the programme.

We both met David Thomson earlier that year when he accompanied his BBC colleague and co-producer Bertie Rogers to the Aran Islands. Their visit then was for the making of Roger's documentary, *The Bare Stones of Aran*, in which later broadcast we both participated.

At that time I knew very little about those poets and writers employed by the BBC, but very soon I became aware of their dedication to research on the traditions, legends and lore of island dwellers and fishermen. David proved his skill in capturing all this in his documentary *The Enchanted Islands*, with its poetic and dramatic narrative backed by haunting folk music.

When David Thomson came to Aran in 1950, the name Kilronan evoked from him a reference to another Kilronan, which he said featured in his early life during the ten years when he was tutor to a family in County Roscommon.

It was a very long time after 1950 before the significance struck me. It happened when I read his very moving memoir, *Woodbrook*, in which he set out the story of his life there as tutor to the children of the Big House, with memories of his attachment to the family and servants, and sadly, of his doomed love for his young pupil.

Part-time work on the Woodbrook farm and tending animals was not daunting to the young tutor, since as a child he had lived on his grandparents' farm at Nairn in Scotland. His experiences there are splendidly detailed in his prize-winning book, *Nairn in Darkness and Light*.

David Thomson was born to Scottish parents in 1914 in India during his father's service in the Indian Army. When duty there ended and he returned to Britain, his wife, with her two small daughters and son, David, went to live in her mother's country house at Nairn on the Moray Firth. It was there, in the local schoolhouse, that the children's education began. Later on, when the family moved to London, David attended a college there, but his schooling was interrupted by a football accident which caused him serious eye injury. To aid his recovery, he was sent back to his grandmother in Nairn, and there he was taught in her house by private tutors. When he had sufficiently recovered, he returned to school in London, was a brilliant student and went on to Lincoln College at Oxford, where he read Modern History. It was customary for students and graduates at that time to take tutoring jobs with wealthy families. Thus, the opportunity in David's life arose when he became employed as tutor in the London townhouse of the County Roscommon Anglo-Irish family with whom he moved to Ireland and stayed for ten years with at Woodbrook House.

Back in London after that in 1943, Thomson joined the BBC, writing and producing radio documentaries. He was particularly interested in Irish folklore and visited Ireland many times to meet the people of the countryside to hear stories of land and sea, farming and fishing. He brought these tales to life in a radio series called 'The Irish Storyteller', in another programme on the famine and in his documentary *The Enchanted Islands*, with his stories of stout sea men and fair sea maidens.

His much-acclaimed book *The People of the Sea* calls to mind a personal experience with a pair of Kilronan porpoises (or *muca-mara*, as we call them) that once escorted me in a small lobster boat on a lonely crossing to the mainland. To distract me, the pair kept up their frolics, plunging and splashing all the way, fore and aft. The book is a fascinating collection of stories about Atlantic seals, a near-human species in their interaction with man and woman in music and song answering calls.

Nor did Thomson stop there. The fantasy extended to his writing of Danny Fox's adventures, the much-loved children's stories. *Danny Fox, Danny Fox at the Palace* and *Danny Fox Meets a Stranger* are no longer in print, but his other classics are still around and widely read. This is a lasting tribute to the brilliance and vision of this great writer, who died back in 1988.

MISCHIEF NIGHT

Chuck Kruger

At ten, eleven, even the ripe old age of twelve, while growing up in New
York I vaguely enjoyed Halloween, but robustly relished the night before
it, Mischief Night. On Halloween, groups of us would dress up in wild,
scary costumes, especially as witches and evil wizards, or as pirates or
skeletons, and go trick or treating around the neighbourhood. We'd hear
rumours that this night used to be a festival for the dead, but didn't
know that the celebration had a Druidic ancestry. Most houses had a
hollowed-out pumpkin on the front porch with a flickering candle
inside it revealing crooked teeth, mean eyes, an odd nose. Again and
again after ringing the doorbell, we'd laughingly say when the door
opened, 'Trick or treat?', sing a song and thrust out large paper bags.
Almost invariably the adult in the doorway would drop Toll House
cookies or tangerines, a piece of fudge or a brownie, some chocolate bits
or sometimes a few pennies or even a nickel into our bags. And off we'd
parade to the next house.

But on Mischief Night we revelled in high jinx. We'd pull pranks on
our neighbours – soap windows, blow our pea shooters from behind
trees toward front doors or lit upstairs windows. The night both scared
me stiff and thrilled me to the bone. Occasionally we'd ring a doorbell,
run for the nearest tree, usually between the sidewalk and the street, and
then see how our victim handled our rudeness. Other times we'd notch
the spindle that sewing thread came on, insert a small stick through the
central hole, wrap around the spindle and hold it against a door or

window pane as we pulled. What a rat-tat-tat. We'd scamper a few front yards away, hunker down behind a hedge and watch the consternation of the neighbour when he or she came outside to try to collar the culprit. Somehow, we never got caught.

One Mischief Night – I'm not certain whether I was sick or simply grounded – I was not to leave the small upstairs apartment where we lived. In my pyjamas, I snuck into my parents' closet and opened a window. Since we were situated near the top of a hill with a cemetery on three sides of us, and our house right smack across the literally dead end of a cul-de-sac, I had a fine view of all the houses running down the hill. I reached for my pea shooter and ammunition, took a steady aim at Mrs Messenger's house, three houses down the south side of the hill, and opened fire. Mrs Messenger was one of my mother's best friends, but someone my father wouldn't allow into our house as she touted gossip and Dad thought her a bad influence. Although Mrs M and her family lived in the far half of Number 70, to my delight I was still just able to bombard her upstairs front bedroom window. When she came out to see what was happening, from my secret perch I kept on firing the hard little pellets of dried peas at her porch roof. She hadn't a clue where they were coming from, but she could hear them pinging against the cedar shingles. Finally, she threw her arms into the air, slammed the door and shut off all the lights in the front of the house.

Yes, I thrived on Mischief Night. It was as if on that one special pre-Halloween night we could rid ourselves of our rascality, and if we were lucky, not get caught.

TRICK OR TREAT

Orla Donoghue

Growing up, I rated Halloween up there with Christmas and birthdays. From the age of six, I remember dressing up as a witch in a long black dress made of net. The dress was so scratchy that I had insisted on wearing a thick woolly jumper and trousers underneath it. I topped the dress off with a cardboard hat I'd made in school. By the time I was nine, I was bulging out of the dress like a miniature Incredible Hulk.

My best friend and I would start doing the rounds of the houses at six o'clock. Ready since about three in the afternoon, we were eager to unleash ourselves on the street. The best you could hope for was the odd Club Milk, but we were generally laden down with nuts and fruit. There was one woman who always gave us pick 'n' mix sweets. This was the ultimate prize in our plastic bag collection and we'd make a beeline for her house first. The chant at that time was 'help the Halloween party'. Of course, it wasn't an open invitation to join us, but there was always one wag who'd ask anyway.

When we went collecting, we never scrutinised what people put in our bags. We'd wait until we returned to my house and then we'd empty the contents on the floor. There was always a bit of scrambling about, especially if you were lucky enough to have bagged some money.

Many years later, when I'd put my witch's hat to rest, I vowed to always have a stash of goodies for kids calling on Halloween night. Last year was no exception. I left work early to make sure I was at home in time. A little after six, the doorbell rang. Peering up at me were two faces, painted like red devils, and yelling 'trick or treat.'

Not a plastic bag in sight. Both callers carried designer Halloween bags, emblazoned with ghouls and monsters. A third child ran behind them up our steep drive. They asked me to guess who I thought their friend had dressed up as. This was one of those moments when I knew the wrong answer was sure to cause offence. To me, he looked like an angel, but I knew that wouldn't go down well so I said I couldn't possibly guess.

'He's *Jesus*,' they both chorused.

I told them that deserved more chocolate.

Jesus smiled shyly while his two friends protested because they said everyone was giving Jesus more chocolate than them. Conceding that it was indeed unfair, I replenished all their bags.

The next caller was a boy dressed up like an old woman. Maybe he, too, was aiming to look like a witch, but I decided to keep this reflection to myself. He reached inside his bag and offered *me* a couple of old apples that looked like they had been run over by a car. I refused politely. Pulling himself up to his full height, he told me he was allergic to fruit at Halloween.

At the end of last year's Halloween night, with one bar of chocolate left, I hoped there would be only one more caller. When I answered the door, before me was a young Jedi knight, waving a light sabre. As the Jedi knight departed, I envied him his chance to be Luke Skywalker for a night.

I knew then that even with a new chant and designer costumes and bags, Halloween remains unchanged because its spirit, like that of young callers everywhere, is unquenchable. And do you know, I often wonder what happened to my black dress.

NOVEMBER

GLOVE STORY

Liz Nugent

Many years ago, while working in a ridiculously underpaid-but-worthy arts job, my journey to work took me past an exclusive design shop which sold all kinds of exotic goods, from unique couture to antique what-nots.

It was the kind of shop where one had to ring the bell to gain entry. At that time, I would never have been confident enough to ring the bell, and even if I had, it would have been pointless, as everything they sold was well beyond my budget.

Every day that winter, I stopped and looked through the window at a pair of gloves displayed on a shelf. They were exquisite – made of the richest, warmest black velvet. The cuffs were long and pleated, and each panel of these pleats was woven with a different design in golden embroidered threads. I dreamed of the day when I could wander into this emporium and charge such items to my account. But each day I would dig my freezing hands further into my pockets and walk on.

One day at the end of that bitter winter when the cold had lost its teeth and the weather had softened, I passed the shop again on the way to the bank to cash my paltry paycheck and stopped short. The gloves were no longer there. Somebody had had the audacity to buy *my* gloves. How dare they?

A handsome chap stood in the doorway. It was clear that he belonged to the shop, with his Riviera tan and his casual-but-smart cashmere sweater. I summoned up the courage to ask this gentleman the crucial question.

'Excuse me,' I said, 'the gloves that were in the win—'

I didn't even have to finish my sentence.

He knew exactly what I was talking about.

'Ah yes, we've changed the window display, moved all of the winter stock out of the window. Would you like to come in and see them?'

Oh dear. I had crossed the line. Somehow this man thought that I was like him – that I was used to such finery, that I would be blasé about such things.

'No thanks,' I replied. 'They were lovely. I was only wondering if someone had bought them,' I mumbled.

He urged me to come in and examine the gloves close up. I told him I was on my way to the bank before it shut – I'd be back in a minute.

I ran to the bank and queued to cash my cheque. I thought about the possibilities. If I didn't eat and walked to work for the next two weeks, I could maybe afford to spend £30 on the gloves, but that was the absolute most.

I nervously walked back towards the shop. Adonis was still standing in the doorway. He beckoned me inside. I went.

I was dazzled. Beautiful treasure of all shapes, sizes, colours, fabrics, textures; golden, shining *things!*

A lady I took to be Adonis's mother swooped down with the gloves in her carefully manicured hand. She was as elegantly suited, booted and coiffed as her handsome boy.

'Ah yes,' she said, 'you like the gloves? You must try them on.' Her voice was luxuriant, accented. Cultured Italian, I thought.

I took them into my hands. I knew even before I put them on that they would fit like the proverbial, but I hadn't understood how a fabric could feel like an extension of my skin. I held my well-dressed hands out in front of me, savouring the feeling. A label was attached to the wrist by a length of golden tassle. I turned it over. £92.

Suddenly, I was myself again.

'Thank you so much for showing them to me. You are most kind.' I peeled them off and it was as painful to me as removing a layer of my own skin.

The Contessa stopped me.

'No,' she said. 'You keep.'

I protested. 'I'm sorry, I can't ... ' I faltered.

'No – they are gift for you. You keep, you keep.'

I was quite overcome. I even tried to give the Contessa my £30, but she point blank refused and insisted I take them free, gratis and for nothing.

The next day I rang the bell and delivered flowers and chocolates, but I could never thank them enough. This was to them maybe just a generous gesture, but to me it meant so much more.

Afterwards, relating the story to my friends, we concocted several versions of the background to my tale. Maybe the Contessa was my real mother, forced to give me away at birth by her cruel father. She had me adopted in Ireland and moved here as soon as she could to track me down. She opened her shop of curious curios and waited for me to come to her, as she knew inevitably that I would. She put the gloves in the window to attract my attention, knowing that, just like the glass slipper, whomsoever the gloves fit ...

I wore the gloves until they frayed to threads, and to this day I keep their remains as a reminder of my own true glove story.

So thank you, kind lady, for such a magnificent gift. Your generosity touched my heart. And when I eventually make my fortune, I shall invite you to tea in my mansion and we shall sit on the terrace and chat about poetry, eating cucumber sandwiches, and even though the sun is shining, I shall be wearing very old gloves.

THANKSGIVING

Harry Browne

'We have meat and some have none – God bless the rrre-vo-lu-zi-on!'

When my dad said grace, with a flourish in a dodgy mock Italian-Spanish accent, it wasn't going to gladden the hearts of any capitalists who might have found their way to our 1970s New Jersey table, or any vegetarians, for that matter.

My father didn't bring radical rhetoric into everything; dirty jokes were sacrosanct, for example. But Thanksgiving? Sitting down for a word with God while the table groaned with turkey and trimmings, to celebrate a feast of dubious historicity and genocidal consequence, he was bound to have something political to say.

Not that he was cheeky or ungrateful to his Maker. Having spent more than twenty-five years as a Catholic priest, then having managed a dignified escape into domesticity, all the time fighting in the wider world for peace and social justice, my dad knew he had reason to give thanks and then some.

He just seemed to feel God needed to give a little more encouragement to the world's struggling, meatless majority. Anyway, God was only his secondary audience. Like the stories of his own hungry Hell's Kitchen childhood, the blessing was meant mostly for us kids, so we'd know there was nothing normal or natural about our meaty privileges.

For us, just risen from Thanksgiving movies and football on the television, it was a thoroughly good-natured reminder. He would end the prayer saying, 'We ask this through Christ, our brother. Amen.' Then we'd all join hands and shout three times '*Felicita!*' – Italian for happiness

— and we meant it, because my Italian-American mother was, and is, a fantastic cook. The ceremonials over, Dad might make a smutty allusion to Pocahontas, then he'd pass the mashed potatoes and creamed onion and corn on the cob.

He died on a Thanksgiving weekend. Leukaemia — or, more precisely, the attendant chemotherapy — took him. But I'll always believe it was the election of Karol Wojtyla as pope that made him sick, and the election of Ronald Reagan as president that finished my father off. As if to hammer home the awful, reactionary emptiness of the world without him, John Lennon was violently removed from it the following week.

That year, 1980, is pretty much the last Thanksgiving I can remember, and we couldn't think of many thanks to give. I moved away to college less than a year later. I lived in the US for a few years after that, and I'm sure I mostly went home to my mother for Thanksgiving — it's what Americans do. I'm also sure we had a spirited table, perhaps a few friends as well as family, but I don't remember thanking anyone other than Mom, or asking anyone to bless the rrre-vo-lu-zi-on.

It was something of a mercy to move away from America in the mid-1980s. From the distance of Ireland, Thanksgiving is just weird, peripatetic Yanks travelling hundreds and thousands of miles for a long weekend among unloved loved ones in the dark days of late autumn. I never marked the holiday at all, beyond answering a long-distance phone call, and feigned a quizzical look or a politically correct sneer when anyone here wished me a happy one.

Anyway, in Ireland in the mid-1980s, the rrre-vo-lu-zi-on seemed a little less remote than it did in Reagan's USA. I had no truck with God at all, thanks-giving or otherwise. Long gone were the days when the most real-life, grassroots global politics came through the door in the form of my father's subscriptions to the *National Catholic Reporter* and the magazine of the Maryknoll missionaries. Now politics were godless.

My resistance to Thanksgiving dropped last year when I accepted a dinner invitation from a Dublin group of ex-pat peaceniks and their Irish friends and families. They sensibly eschewed the fourth Thursday in November in favour of a Saturday — which meant I didn't quite have to feel my 'No Thanks' record was broken — and we ate delicious food and wondered aloud what America had given us to be thankful for.

I said something about jazz, but I was thinking of my Italian mom's cooking and my Irish dad's blessing.

DANCING WITH NUREYEV

Judith Mok

It can be amusing to tell somebody an outrageous story about yourself
and make them believe it is all true. But when you actually do tell the
truth about an extraordinary event in your life and people don't believe
you, you might feel slightly hurt. What should you do? Keep this
wonderful story to yourself and just cherish the memory, or go to great
lengths to prove that all the details in your story are actual, verifiable
facts? Well, here's one cherished memory I do love to tell the world
about. Imagine being ten years old and already filled with an ambition
to become the next Miss World Twinkletoes, or in other words, a top
ballet dancer. I stuck photographs of dancing men and women in tutus
and leotards on my walls, but soon had to take them down again because
our landlady screamed at me about damaging her plaster. We were living
on the Cote d'Azur, where my parents were renting an old-style English
villa situated in the middle of a lemon tree plantation. The view down
the valley was so spectacular that we did not need anything to look at on
the walls, but I had already seen the winter mimosa blooming, and the
sun hitting the Mediterranean Sea down below. I wanted to look at ballet
dancers and dance to the music of Chopin. In my bedroom I whispered
the name of Anna Pavlova and made her dying swan come back to life.

We lived very close to Monaco, where the famous Ballet Russes
founded by Diaghilev had been turned into the Monte Carlo Dance
Company. With the company came one of the most revered Russian
ballet teachers in the world: Marika Besobrasova. Three times a week I
joined twenty girls in immaculate pink leotards and ballet shoes with

satin ribbons tied around our minuscule ankles. Marika was Russian, rolled her Rs when she spoke French and held a big stick in her hands at all times. She did not use that stick to hit us, but to raise our legs painfully high or straighten our bodies. Everybody came in contact with that stick, even my classmate Caroline of Monaco. Sometimes her mummy, Grace Kelly, would bring her over, but most of the time it was her English governess, who soon became friendly with my mum. They would be chatting away in English in the dressing rooms while we were sweating on our way to ballet perfection.

No one escaped Marika's stick, not even the unique Rudolf Nureyev who came to work out regularly during the summer months. And so it happened a few years later: I was about fourteen years old and at an advanced stage in my ballet training, advanced enough to be allowed in the same warm-up classes as the great maestro, Nureyev. Once we had done our warming-up exercises it was time for the *Pas de Deux* exercise. Marika's stick pointed in my direction as well as Rudolf's. He stood at the other end of the studio and gracefully stretched out one of his famous hands. After a dazzling moment of hesitation, I flew. I flew across the room, entangled in *frappes* and balances and *pas de chats* until he lifted me up and it seemed the most natural thing in the world to be dancing with the greatest dancer on earth. Once we were finished he kissed me on the cheek and the earth started to turn again.

It never faded away, the memory of this legend lifting me up to his heights accompanied by the tinny sounds of the pianist banging away at a Chopin nocturne. Yes, I can still sing every note of it.

At first I did not tell anybody about my adventure. But when I was back home in Holland and started drifting away from ballet towards music, I did occasionally mention my moment of glory with Rudolf Nureyev to my fellow students. The reaction was always the same: disbelief, and amusement at my very vivid imagination. I eventually stashed the memory away in a brain cell labelled 'happy times', until I came to Ireland and ran into the writer Colm McCann. I had just read his novel about Nureyev, *Dancer*, and told him how much I admired it. I then added, as a shy little afterthought, that I had once danced with the maestro. He nodded and listened to my story. Yes, of course he knew all about Rudy's classes with the famous Marika in Monaco. He had done his research. So I was doing my training there as well? That did not seem at all unlikely to him. I produced a warm smile for Colm when he finally said, 'So you did a *Pas de Deux* with Rudy in class? Good for you, Judith.'

NICK DRAKE

Stephen MacDonogh

That a photograph of a scene from my schooldays should have survived nearly forty years is surprising. I was delighted to shake off the dust of school, and had no wish to hang onto pictorial representations of it. But I suppose the photo's survival owes most to vanity; that I kept it because I was in it.

The photograph is unremarkable, a standard team photo. Two lines of teenage boys stand on steps leading to a church. They are wearing white shorts and white tops and they are holding hockey sticks. Some of their hairstyles suggest the late 1960s.

Looking at those rows of faces and figures recently, I can't say that it all came flooding back. But one face caused a kind of shock recognition, as I was suddenly struck by how little he changed in appearance from that date until his later incarnation as the singer-songwriter who produced three remarkable albums before his career was tragically cut short.

Nick Drake and I went to the same school, Marlborough College in Wiltshire in England, but were not exact contemporaries. He was a year older than I, and in the hierarchy of relationships, one's friends were usually drawn from the same year. But at some stage in his studies he changed subjects, and that set him back a year, and so we shared an English class and came to share interests in William Blake, Wilfred Owen and Byron. We also both bucked a school tradition which the poet John Betjeman had described as a split between athletes and aesthetes. You were supposed to be either a sportsman or an intellectual, but the two of us had a foot in both camps and played rugby and hockey on the same teams (he was better than me at rugby, I was better than him at hockey).

He got involved in song writing, learned to play the guitar and started playing in a band. I did some song writing, too, but was more drawn to poetry. I published a critical study of Bob Dylan's lyrics in the school magazine, which led to some debate about the relative merits of Dylan, Simon and Garfunkel, Donovan and others, which Nick got involved in. Not that we were close friends. We got on well when we met, and we shared interests, but he hung out with boys who were, like him, a year or two older than me. Also, we were pretty much wrapped up in ourselves, just trying to get through the boarding school experience. Marlborough was a rarefied, unnatural world. If you were at all sensitive, the circumstances could be brutal. Some suffered agonies which were visible, while most of the rest succeeded, at least most of the time, in putting on an apparently invulnerable shell. Each of us, I think, had our own way of getting by.

I was involved in a campaign for the abolition of the compulsory military training in the school, and also a campaign against the Vietnam War. I don't think Nick was involved in these campaigns; he was more likely to be off playing the guitar and reading the Romantic poets.

He was a tall, handsome, quiet, self-contained yet charismatic young man. He was probably introverted, but not in an apparently painful way; in fact, he radiated self-confidence.

We did meet again once after he left Marlborough. I was visiting London, where he was in a bed-sit. I think I stayed a day or two longer than I had expected, and I borrowed a shirt from him. I arranged to bring it back to him later, but somehow he had gone missing and we didn't meet up again.

After leaving Marlborough, he went on to Cambridge University and dropped out after releasing his first album, *Five Leaves Left*, in September 1969. This haunting collection of songs was not a commercial success, but he pitched into work on a second album, *Bryter Later*, which came out in 1970.

He was much admired by other musicians, including John Cale, but success eluded him in his lifetime, and his final album, *Pink Moon*, was a sparse, pared-down collection which again failed to sell. He suffered a mental breakdown, was prescribed anti-depressants, and thirty-five years ago, on 25 November 1974, Nick Drake died. He was just twenty-six.

AT THE PARMENTIER

Fred Johnston

In those days, we stayed regularly at a modest, excellent little hotel run by Algerian Christians in the south-east of Paris. They would smile to see us arrive. It was the kind of hotel which, though always busy, had not lost the family touch, the need to keep the ordinary, important things ticking over. Across the street, upstairs in a frantic little bar, there was some good African blues a couple of evenings a week. And there was a café outside which you could sip coffee late into the night and watch the entire *arrondissement* roll by. I was sure there were people in the neighbourhood who had never strolled far outside it, or would have scorned the idea of traipsing as far as the fashionable Place Vendome, home to, among others, the house of Charvet, for a shirt.

The *quartier* was always teeming with life, colourful life, and loud. And across the street, nosing its way into the junction of several streets, was Le Parmentier.

Le Parmentier was a restaurant and café which, by some wonderful architectural freak, formed the point of two streets running alongside one another, eventually colliding, let's say, at the café's front door. Beside the entrance was the gaping art-deco entrance to the Métro. This venerable eating establishment was well named – as was the area – after Antoine-Augustin Parmentier, the eighteenth-century biochemist who, against opposition, introduced the humble potato into the French diet. Before him, the delectable tuber was thrown to pigs.

Above the entrance to Le Parmentier, in large, scrawled letters, hung its noble name in vigorous neon. It ached for another, more elegant age, of men in long coats with tied belts and turned-up collars, of women in curled, bottle-blonde hair, of old black Citroen cars with their snarling long snouts, a sense of mystery mingling with the cigarette smoke. This was a café fit for an Inspector Maigret. This was, in essence, Paris as our unconscious knew her. You could sit at an outside table, served quickly and with dexterous efficiency by a waiter in an apron and watch – *spy* on – the mass of Paris which had chosen to emerge from the underworld of the Métro. You could buy a racing page and sit there all day, for that matter. Inside, a big Alsatian dog splayed itself out on the sawdust while local men smoked heavily and argued about the merits of this and that horse or team, and there were, as always, a dozen different types of lottery to become involved in. There was loud conversation and small drinks, some flicked into black coffee.

There was nothing fake here, no toy-sized Eiffel Towers, no tourist consciousness at all. You ate well here. The fried eggs were wonderful with coffee first thing in the morning as you planned your day. When you emerged into that great star-shaped junction of streets where business of all sorts went on before your eyes – Arab women haggled over carpets as a man with a couple of carpets on his shoulders passed them by – there was Le Parmentier, a piece of Paris as gaudy and lively and magical as its great neon scrawl. You could be sure of Le Parmentier; it would be there forever. I took a photograph of the place, had it blown up and framed and sent it to the proprietors. They sent back a gracious thank you card and a voucher for breakfast. I was glad I took that photograph. Perhaps it was one of the last times Le Parmentier could show itself to the world.

For Paris, inevitably, was changing. Le Parmentier was too old-fashioned, too *then* and too little *now*. I felt like an orphan looking at the ragged place where that great Charles Boyer neon had been, staring – hardly believing, to be honest – at the tiny square sign with the new name. Later I could peruse the new menu, too, and be served by a waiter, young and slick and without an apron, who gave me cold coffee.

The Alsatian dog is gone and there's new shiny metal here and there that wasn't there before. And the racing banter is gone too. What happened to that flirty neon? And I often wonder where my photograph ended up.

SONG OF THE RUSH HOUR

Elaine Sisson

The air is thinning. Breathing in the cold tightens the lungs. The leaves relinquish their hold en masse, the evenings darken earlier and earlier and soon it will be the middle of winter again. Most of us grumble and fumble our way through winter, grousing about the drizzle, the light that never rises above pale grey and the particular cruelty that is commuting on an early winter's morning.

I have to confess that I love being up and out early on these mornings. I welcome the quiet dark of a city street and the sense of the rest of the world being still asleep. The pleasure of starting out to work when the roads are still calm is enhanced by feeling the miles tick away under my wheels. I love making it into work at half the time and double the speed than I would later in the morning.

Sitting in my car at a traffic light on an early morning, there is a strange unspoken communion between the drivers. Sometimes we find ourselves tapping out a tune on our steering wheels as we listen to the same radio programme. I don't look at my fellow commuters and think of us as mice on a treadmill or rats in a race. I see us as citizens, as workers, joined in the community of service. I am thankful for those who are out early setting the cogs in motion – the bus drivers, the bin men, the nurses, the cleaners – and even though I am sequestered in my car, I feel connected to a web-like, vibrant lifeforce.

Maybe it's because I'm a city girl. I love the city, with its energy, dirt, variety and particular beauty. Being married to a country boy has made me realise just how much I'm at home in a city. I remember once, driving through the wild splendour of north Mayo, we both saw a cottage high up on a mountainside. Looking up we gasped simultaneously. The house was whitewashed, low-roofed and set snugly into the mountain. There were no other buildings for miles around. My husband sighed wistfully, thinking aloud of firesides and singsongs, while my immediate thoughts had been of isolation and loneliness. Both of us were rather taken aback by the limits of the other's imagination. I confess that I'm not cut out for a country life where everybody knows your name and your business. For me, such a life would be one great invasion of privacy. I like the anonymity of city life, the friendships made through random and often unlikely links, the great sprawl of interconnectedness, the sense of possibility that living amongst millions of people offers.

I have a friend who moved to the country feeling that it would offer a better quality of life for her family. Now, two years later, they are all back in the city again. She says that at night when she's woken by sirens blaring up and down the North Circular Road, she offers up a silent prayer of thanks that she is back at the heart of city life. I find this to be a refreshing honesty as all around me people talk about getting out of the rat race. I once read a cynical commentator who maintained that city folk who sell up and move to the country are merely showing off that they are now wealthy enough not to work. I'm tired of reading smug articles on people swapping their urban lives for rural pleasures. I want the truth: I want to hear from those people who couldn't hack the quiet and the dark and the psychopathic cows. City folk are the only people who are not astonished that half the civil service doesn't want to sell up their overpriced homes and move to better lives elsewhere. For city lovers, there is no better life.

In his long poem *Leaves of Grass*, Walt Whitman, the nineteenth-century American poet, wrote an exuberant celebration of the world of work. In the section of the poem called 'A Song for Occupations', he praises the rhythm and energies of the working life, from the factory to the railroad to the city. He sings of jobs and work, listing trades and skills and professions, echoing the language and tempo of the Book of Psalms. There is something reverent, biblical, even joyful in his salutation to stevedores, carpenters, sail-makers, shopkeepers, milliners, all cogs in the wheels of city living.

'Happiness,' he says, is found 'not in another place, but this place …
not for another hour, but this hour.'

Every day I hear moans about the city – its traffic, gridlock, dirt and
expense – but cities are wonderful places to live in. I think of Whitman
and his ability to embrace the ordinary and the mundane and to make
poetry out of drudgery. Wouldn't he celebrate the sight of the Luas
snaking around silver corners? I think he'd like the experience of a
modern city chugging to life in the early morning – the breathy, fogged-
up windscreens, the swish of wheels on rainy tarmac, medleys of light
on street corners, all harmonies in the Song of the Rush Hour.

KAVANAGH'S HOLY DOOR

Una Agnew

During the year that is coming to a close, we have celebrated the life and works of Patrick Kavanagh in honour of his hundredth birthday. The longed-for holy door of acceptance and recognition has, in Ireland at least, been finally opened for him. One could say that his poetic life evolved in a space between two holy doors – his initial doorway to life on a farm in Inniskeen, and the ultimate holy door he dreamed of when he would at last claim his inheritance as a poet.

Love's doorway to life first opened for him on his small farm at Shancoduff in Monaghan when he fell in love with a field:

> They laughed at one I loved –
> The triangular hill that hung
> Under the Big Forth.

The Rocksavage fields were his patrimony – an eldest son's inheritance – economically speaking, a poor investment. Instead, they became his poetic territory, a landscape of the soul, a platform from which to experience the rhythms and moods of life as they pulsated for him through each month and season.

His life of love evolved, with the unhurried pace of a ploughman, from Mucker in Inniskeen, to the Merrion Nursing Home in Dublin where he breathed his last in November 1967. His poetry moved in harmony with an attendant liturgy, attuned to the moods and farming activities of each calendar month. He learned from Melville at the outset of *Moby Dick* that Ishmael, the narrator, was experiencing 'a damp and drizzly November in his soul'; so, too, did he discover that each month was not only a unit of time, but a state of mind, a season of the soul.

Christmas was his Eden time, a time which summoned up 'the luxury of a child's soul', culminating in 'a prayer like a white rose pinned on the Virgin Mary's blouse'. Each month in turn drew on the contents of his rag-and-bone shop-of-the-heart, comprised of bits and pieces from school books, the *Messenger*, *Ireland's Own* and T.S. Eliot. The months provided him with metaphors for the various moods and vagaries of his poetic soul.

In January, the intrepid coltsfoot breaks a hole in 'winter's wall' to announce its presence to the earth. This budding metaphor, later in his writing, becomes the mystical revelatory moment when 'Christ comes with a January flower'. As apprentice-poet he moved symbolically out of winter, through the harrow pins of non-acceptance into a Genesis of poetry and earth.

Meanwhile, in 'March':

> *The trees were in suspense*
> *Listening with an intense*
> *Anxiety for the Word*
> *That in the Beginning stirred.*

The poet is on his way. Soon March is a silversmith, advancing with glistening wand, brightening the poet's outlook and surrounding. Mystery broods over the harrowed fields, where:

> *. . . in the green meadows*
> *the maiden Spring is with child*
> *by the Holy Ghost.*

Then ecstasy erupts when April dances in a wild celebration of life:

> *O give faith*
> *That I may be alive*
> *When April's ecstasy*
> *Dances in every whitethorn tree.*

Although 'clouds over fields of May' remind the poet, sadly, of unrequited love, May can still fill him with a frisson of enchantment and romance:

> *There will be bluebells growing under the big trees*
> *And you will be there and I will be there in May . . .*

And so Kavanagh moves in and out of hope and disillusionment, claiming as his own the mixed moods of his soul as he pursues his illusive ideal of love across the months and seasons:

> *I followed you . . .*
> *Through April, May and June into September*
> *Now I woo the footprints that you make across November*

His 'Great Hunger' forlornly chides each passing month for its missed opportunities, lost dreams and wasted life. Time passes, and on New Year's Eve 1954, he bitterly remonstrates with a whole year that had almost cost him his lamp of contemplation – a lost lawsuit, a failed venture, the end of romance and worst of all, lung cancer.

> *O Nineteen Fifty-Four you leave and will not listen,*
> *And do not care whether I curse or weep.*

Then almost miraculously, and 'at the end of a tortuous road', the poet is healed in soul and body, on Dublin's Grand Canal, in the tremendous silence of mid-July. This mid-July moment is a time to let go of grief and regret and contemplate the healing sacramentality of earth. A new springtime of life awaits! Though now in the late summer of his life, a new April ecstasy pours over him its colourful catharsis.

> *Green, blue, yellow and red –*
> *God is down in the swamps and marshes,*
> *Sensational as April and almost incredible*
> *the flowering of our catharsis.*

This late summer, with its outburst of gratitude, released onto the world his Canal-bank poems, which speak of heightened sense-awareness and retuned to the cadence of flowing water, warm sunshine and the heady joy of being alive. It is fitting that his poem 'October' hints at the completion of a life perennially dedicated to sowing, reaping and eventually bringing home his harvest.

> O leafy yellowness you create for me
> A world that was and now is poised above time,
> I do not need to puzzle out Eternity
> As I walk this arboreal street on the edge of a town.
> The breeze, too, even the temperature
> And pattern of movement, is precisely the same
> As broke my heart for youth passing. Now I am sure
> Of something. Something will be mine wherever I am.
> I want to throw myself on the public street without caring
> For anything but the prayering that the earth offers.
> It is October over all my life . . .

And so, Patrick Kavanagh, you've experienced all the seasons and months of your star-crossed life. And this year, 2004, we have lived them with you all over again, and, at least posthumously, have wholeheartedly endorsed the opening of your holy door. It is truly October over all your life – you're 100 years old and your harvest is home. We rejoice as we listen once more to your prophetic words as you say 'Thank you! Thank you!' for the acceptance of a 'holy hearing audience'. You might speak these words now, perhaps with more conviction, than when you first uttered them to an audience of students at University College, Dublin almost fifty years ago:

> . . . How glad
> I am to have lived to feel the radiance
> Of a holy hearing audience
> And delivered God's commands
> Into those caressing hands.
> . . . I thank you and I say how proud
> That I have been by fate allowed
> To stand here having the joyful chance
> To claim my inheritance,
> For most have died the day before
> The opening of that holy door.

KILLING ME FATHER

Peter Woods

I was in a hostelry one night, a place with literary pretensions. There was a big dictionary on the bar. Mebbe it attracted a better class of customer, though I doubt it, since there was a chain coming from its binding locking it to the Guinness tap. Anyhow, I was with a friend of mine from Galway, a great man for silence, and when you've nothing to say, there's nothing wrong with silence. Corky, on the other hand, saw silence as a challenge. He came lurching across the bar at me.

'You have to kill your father, boy,' he says.

'I what?'

'Kill your father, it's the only way you'll ever be a writer.'

'But my father is dead, I said.'

'I don't mean you have to kill your father literally – though you do have to kill him literally, if you know what I mean. What I mean is you have to kill your literal father.'

I was nonplussed, but he continued. 'In your case that's Kavanagh – seeing you're from Monaghan. You'll have to kill Patrick Kavanagh if you want to write a word. It's like *Hamlet*,' he said.

I was going to say that Kavanagh was dead and what had Hamlet to do with it, but mebbe that was a bit obvious.

'And you're lucky,' he went on. 'All you have to do is kill Kavanagh. I mean, I had to kill O'Connor and O'Faolain, to say nothing of that Dorgan fella, an' he still alive.'

After that, every time I'd see Corky he'd shout at me, 'O stony grey soil of Monaghan – you have to kill Kavanagh, boy.'

Needless to say, it wasn't Kavanagh I was thinking of killing – not then, at any rate. I tell that story because Corky was the first Leaving Cert genius I met. You see, one time, if you were from Monaghan and people wanted to get a handle on you, and not being one of them counties with a rake of All-Irelands and the Lakes of Killarney to boot, the only thing they'd know about was Big Tom or mebbe Barry McGuigan. So they'd say Big Tom or Barry McGuigan and you'd nod. It was boring and predictable and it would do your head in, but it was nothing compared to that poem. You see, that was when the national curriculum thing kicked in and the 'stony grey soil' thing started happening. And – believe me – everyone who has ever said those words has said them like they'd written them themselves.

Oh yeah. There have been others, men and women who travelled, as they say, up there and were astonished. The land was good. To someone from Monaghan, this is like discovering they sell sangria in Spain. And what they ask about those Black Hills that had never seen the sun rise – well, neither has the north face of the Eiger. I mean, I often think that Allingham was from Donegal – OK, he was no Kavanagh – but do they believe that that county's full of 'Wee folk, good folk,/Trooping all together;/Green jacket, red cap/And white owl's feather'? I'm owning up to something now, and owning up to it for the first time – there's many the day I wanted to kill Kavanagh. And I'd wish they'd put *The Butcher Boy* on the curriculum so they'd know what we're really like 'up there' in Monaghan.

After a while, though, I calm down. There's plenty I admire about Kavanagh – his use of place names, Shancoduff, Glasdrummond and Rocksavage; the sound of Monaghan in his writing; his use of the vernacular. That he knew the value of silence, that what wasn't said was more important than what was. That border county ambiguity, where you can be both smuggler and revenue man. Like the man who asked me, what are you at now?

'Radio,' I said.

'Couldn't be at that,' he said, 'there's talking involved.'

So on balance, when the Corkys of the world come barrelling out of the shadows with the words of that poem on their lips, it's not Kavanagh I want to kill. He was only a poet, after all, and poets can only do the one thing. No, it wasn't Kavanagh's fault.

No, in the end I blame free education. In fact, I blame Donagh O'Malley, who introduced free education – but that's another story.

You see, it's important to keep perspective. When a youth standing on a street corner in Carrickmacross was asked recently what centenary the area was celebrating this year, he replied, 'A hundred years since the arrival of Budweiser – a hundred years of Budweiser.'

ON THE BUS WITH ROSA PARKS

John O'Donnell

Next time you take your seat on a public bus, spare a thought for Rosa Parks, the forty-two-year-old seamstress who on Thursday, 1 December 1955 in Montgomery, Alabama stepped onto a bus, and into history. Why? Because Rosa Parks was black, and while blacks were tolerated on public buses back then in Alabama, they were obliged to sit only at the back and to give up their seat if a white person needed it. Well, not long into her journey, the inevitable happened. A new – white – man arrived onto the crowded bus. Imagine the scene: the seats and aisle full; the new passenger, impatient, standing expectantly beside the seat that was, after all, his entitlement by law.

But Rosa Parks sat still. She did not argue, but she did not move. So the bus was stopped, the police were called and Rosa Parks was arrested.

Rosa Parks was not the first black person to be arrested for committing this 'crime'. But she was well known among the black community in Montgomery. She had once been secretary to the president of the NAACP, the National Association for the Advancement of Colored People. And when the NAACP and other similar organisations heard of Rosa Parks's arrest, they decided that some form of protest was called for. One of the people who organised the protest was the local pastor of the Dexter Avenue Baptist Church in Montgomery, a man called Dr Martin Luther King. He arranged a meeting at his church. Huge numbers attended. To an overflowing crowd, Dr King announced that the only way to peacefully fight back was to boycott the bus company. Over the weekend, the movement known as the Montgomery Bus Boycott came into existence. Thousands of handbills were printed and handed out. Meetings were held. On 5 December 1955, the black community in Montgomery refused to board the city's buses. Most of them walked. The very few that owned cars arranged carpools. Some even travelled by mule. But not by bus.

The bus company didn't like it. Nor did City Hall. Certain elements of the white community (including members of the police force) tried to intimidate protestors. Carpool drivers were arrested for picking up hitchhikers. Black people waiting for a lift were arrested for loitering. The mood in Montgomery was tense, and sometimes ugly. Dr King's house was bombed in January 1956, his wife and baby daughter narrowly escaping injury. An angry crowd of his supporters gathered outside his house, thirsting for revenge. But King sent them away. 'We must learn to meet hate with love,' he said.

Eventually, after over a year, the boycott ended. Not by agreement or peaceful negotiation, but by court order. In November 1956, the United States Supreme Court declared that Alabama's laws providing for racial segregation on buses were unconstitutional. Orders were served on the city's bus officials compelling them to comply with the Supreme Court ruling. And on 21 December 1956, Dr Martin Luther King and a white minister, the Reverend Glenn Smiley, shared the front seat of a bus in Montgomery, Alabama. So think of Rosa Parks the next time you board a bus and wonder where to sit.

DECEMBER

MAYO MANTRA

Gerald Dawe

Lawrence Durrell tells the following story in *Prospero's Cell*, his fascinating little book about Corfu: 'in the dazzle of the bay [he writes] stands Mouse Island … this petrified rock is the boat, they say, turned to stone as a punishment for taking Ulysses home.' To which Durrell adds the poetic 'get-out' clause, 'It might have been here.' Corfu is quite an island and one can well imagine Ulysses setting sail from any one of its small bays and inlets before taking the seaward journey home to Ithaca.

Stuck in the lee of one of our own stunning rivers and bays, the Moy in County Mayo, there is a time-locked ruin of a concrete boat. I have looked upon this boat very many times over the past thirty years, staying with family in Ballina, watching the shoreline, heading up past Belleek Castle towards Bartra Island and beyond, until the Atlantic opens in all its splendour and power.

The concrete boat on the Moy has become a kind of proverbial story in my mind, an installation from the past. Why it got there, why it is still there, doesn't really matter. The retelling of a childhood spent on the river points to a very different way of life to the one I knew, and one that may have itself remained the same in its essentials for hundreds of years.

I suppose my poem 'Mayo Mantra' tries to bring that sense of timelessness to the tale of what once was, while keeping in mind the classical resonance of what might have been as Ulysses took sail for home and his Penelope:

Many's the time and oft' —
as we skirt the Moy,

at that particular turn in the road,
the river can be low,

the ridge pool sunken, unmoving,
the concrete boat

upright where it was left
unmasted, broken down,

graffiti sprayed on its hulk,
a monument of the sea,

not that far out from the estuary,
the woods and castle,

and, without a second thought,
I think of you

in the arms of your father's boat
the salmon jump so high

it takes your breath away,
Crossing the bar,

between land and sea
and the incomparable sky.

IN MEMORY OF TIM KENNELLY

Cyril Kelly

Plough and spade and seine boat shaped them for the deeds they were to do,
Street and school and mountains heard their victory cry,
Now their memories arch like rainbows o'er the meadows of the mind,
The Alive who'll live forever and the Dead who'll never die.

With days descending fast into December, with darkness cockily cock-stepping earlier every afternoon to a man's windowsill, he could do with being spellbound by a few arching rainbows of memory. With songbirds silent in stark winter hedges, with mallards below on the Royal Canal, their blue and bottle-green heads already tucked under the quilt of their wings, a man sitting by the light of a table lamp, a man gazing out at his reflection in the glass, listening to wars and rumours of wars from the radio on the shelf beside him, such a man could do with memories arching like rainbows o'er the meadows of his mind.

And then Brian Carthy, GAA correspondent, comes on to relay the tragic news. Tim Kennelly, renowned Kerry footballer, famed centre half back during the golden Kingdom years, has died suddenly. So if the listening ear just so happens to be listening within a fifty-yard free of Croke Park, it is easy to hear the hoarse roar of the crowd swelling, rising, tumbling through the tunnel of thirty years. Here they come, those memories, and never was their colour more needed, their sparkling showers more welcome, arching like rainbows o'er the meadows of my smitten mind.

Ague of age falling from my shoulders, I am standing on the Canal End. Waiting for the two teams to sprint onto the hallowed turf, excitement is arcing like bolts of electricity through the crowd. It is 1975 and it's twenty years since Kerry and Dublin have met in an All-Ireland final. During the preceding weeks, there has been saturation coverage. Were The Blues going to do what the sky blues, Heffo, Freaney and Co., had failed to do in 1955, namely, shut The Green and Gold Kingdom up?

Suddenly, the Kerry team, the youngest ever sent out, raced onto the pitch. The crowds, like the swash and backwash of the tide, swayed ominously down the terracing towards the pitch, paused precariously, righted itself again, heaved back towards the Royal Canal once more. I had heard about this team's redoubtable march to the final. Cork dispatched in Munster, Sligo in the semi-final, but this was my first time seeing them in the flesh. My friend Pat was with me. He could name them all. In a true display of jingoistic fervour, the only one I knew was fellow Listowel man, Tim Kennelly. What delight and vicarious pride I got from watching the exploits of that prodigious horse of a man.

That day was the first of his heroic tussles with Tony Hannahoe. Like two warriors of old, like Cúchulann and Ferdia, prey and predator, at times so tigerishly brawn to brawn the terraces trembled. At times almost balletic, almost slow motion; brain throwing down gauntlet to brain; athlete to athlete, instinct covering instinct; a feint, a counter; a shimmy, a shoulder; a fetch dispossessed by a block.

Watching Tim, his stamina, his strength, his resolve – to paraphrase Hannahoe's famous admonition – I never lost the faith. 'Cos I knew they made them tough out in Coolaclarig, where he was born and reared. Out there, a few miles outside Listowel, you can be sure that you won't get things easy from the Cloonmacon lads, or the lads from Cloontubrid and Kylebwee. And any young lad who played in the Listowel town league, as Tim did for the Boro, knows what it's like to be forged in the intimate, white, defining heat of adversity.

And I see Tim now, his fleet-footed shape on a solo run this misty morning, solo runs he often did in the Cork Athletic Grounds or bursting up along the wing below the Hogan Stand, only this time he's thundering over stretches of bog in Bedford or Curraghatoosane. And there he is, borne shoulder high once more, a cavalcade over Gale Bridge. It is 1979 and, captain of that legendary Kerry team, he is holding the Sam Maguire aloft in triumph.

Memories arch like rainbows o'er the meadows of the mind,
The Alive who'll live forever and the Dead who'll never die.

DOUGLAS 'WRONG WAY' CORRIGAN

Sheelagh Mooney

Douglas Corrigan, an Irish-American, developed an early passion for planes when in his teens he took a ten-minute sightseeing trip. From that moment on, he was hooked. In 1927, at the age of twenty, he met the young Charles Lindbergh when he was involved in the construction of his plane, the *Spirit of St. Louis*. When Lindbergh made his historical flight from New York to Paris, he inspired Corrigan to aim for a non-stop transatlantic flight from New York to Dublin.

He spent years renovating an old Curtiss Robin, purchased for the princely sum of $325, but hit a wall of bureaucracy trying to get the necessary permission for his flight. He was forced to obtain a radio operator's licence although the plane had no radio. When he reapplied for permission in 1937, Amelia Earhart had just disappeared over the Pacific and nobody in Washington wanted to take responsibility for another solo flight. Even worse, the government refused to renew his licence. Undeterred, he flew regardless. When the authorities finally caught up with him, the now-named *Sunshine* was detained in a hangar in California for six months.

Finally, he succeeded in getting an experimental licence to fly non-stop from New York to California. On the way to New York the plane's main fuel tank developed a leak. On landing, there was a mere four gallons of fuel left. A cursory check revealed that it would take a week to repair the plane and he decided against it. So at 4.00 a.m. on a foggy 17 July, he took off from Brooklyn's Floyd Bennett Field, New York carrying two chocolate bars, two boxes of figs and a bottle of water with only a US map, the route from New York to California marked out.

Because of the recent leakage problem, the plane was so laden down with fuel it could barely lift off the runway and was only fifty feet above the ground when it disappeared into the fog at the eastern edge of the airfield.

Ten hours into the flight over the Atlantic, his feet began to feel cold. To his horror, he realised that the floor of the cockpit was covered with fuel. The plane was losing fuel by the minute and time was not on his side. Of more immediate concern was the danger of leakage near the exhaust pipe, which would have instant and fatal consequences. He used the only tool he had, a screwdriver, to bore into the floor opposite the exhaust pipe. The fuel slowly trickled out. He now faced the obvious predicament of losing fuel faster than he was travelling. At this rate he was unlikely to make the distance. He boosted the engine to run as fast and straight as possible. When eventually he sighted a small fishing boat, he knew he was near land, but when green hills loomed he knew he had made it and he landed in Baldonnel Airport on 18 July 1938, twenty-eight hours after take-off.

He had achieved his dream, but at what price? He had neither permission nor passport.

The repercussions of this could affect him for many years to come. But Corrigan was nothing if not resourceful, and in his first meetings with army officers he simply said, 'I left New York yesterday morning heading for California, got mixed up in the fog and flew the wrong way.'

By the following morning, when Corrigan met the Taoiseach, Éamonn De Valera, congratulatory telegrams were pouring in from all over the States and Ireland. His feat carried the day and his lack of permit or passport were conveniently forgotten. Corrigan and *Sunshine* were returned to the US on the liner *Manhattan* as heroes.

In the end, he faced nothing worse than the suspension of his pilot's licence until 4 August, the day the ship arrived back in New York. Corrigan always maintained that he had initially intended to fly east for a while to burn off excess fuel, but that due to fog and a mysteriously broken main compass, he had flown the wrong direction. Even in his autobiography, 'Wrong Way' Corrigan stuck to his story. While there were reports before he died at the age of eighty-eight on 9 December 1995 that he had finally admitted his famous mistake was intentional, there is no official record that he ever did.

ABOVE US ONLY SKY

John O'Donnell

I am standing, tousle-haired, in the doorway of my bedroom, hungover after another night of too much college beer. My father is above me, on the stairs. 'Bad news,' he calls down. 'John Lennon has been shot.' There was the slim hope, early on, that Lennon had been only wounded. Shot, but not killed. Not dead. But soon the voices on the radio confirmed the worst, playing all those songs and replaying his life as they speculated on why anyone would want to kill a Beatle. Assassinated, some said. But this was surely wrong. Politicians were assassinated. Kennedy. Bobby Kennedy. Martin Luther King. But not pop stars. Pop stars died (if they died at all) as glamorously as they had seemed to live. They disappeared in planes that vanished over oceans. They succumbed to orgies of drink and drugs and sex in heaving hotel rooms. They blew their minds out in a car, the twisted metal of the latest racy sports model a lurid reminder of everything our parents had warned us about: live fast, die young.

But John Lennon was forty by the time Mark Chapman approached him as he entered the Gothic archway of the Dakota building where he lived, overlooking New York's Central Park. Chapman, a twenty-five-year-old Texan security guard, claimed he'd heard voices in his head telling him to kill Lennon. He'd spent the weekend camped outside the Dakota, apparently no different from the many other fans who'd often waited there for a glimpse of their idol. In the afternoon he'd even spoken to Lennon, requesting that he autograph the first album Lennon had recorded in five years, the album *Double Fantasy*, and Lennon had obliged. The cover is a photo of John and Yoko Ono in a passionate kiss. There on Yoko's neck is the signature: 'John Lennon, 1980'. A few hours later, Chapman was back, still carrying the album and also a .38 calibre revolver. 'Hey, John!' he called as John and Yoko walked through the entrance of the apartment building. Then he fired four shots into Lennon and sat motionless on the steps, waiting for the police to arrive.

The police were not alone. Soon the entrance arch and street outside the building were thronged with tearful fans. They brought cards with little messages. Mountains of flowers filled the doorway. In the days that followed there were candlelit vigils in New York and in Liverpool, the city John had not lived in for some time but had never really left. Lifelong fans wept as one in these huge gatherings. But there were tears also in the small clusters who gathered in record shops and bars; tears even among people who'd missed out on the full impact of Beatlemania and the delirium of the 1960s. Yes, they were crying for the music, but the Fab Four had gone their separate ways a long, long time ago. As America in particular was all too painfully aware, public figures had been killed before for political motives. So maybe what was most shocking of all was the realisation that the world was even crazier than anyone had thought up to now; that now, a pop star could be gunned down and killed for no reason at all.

Famously, Chapman carried a copy of J.D. Salinger's *The Catcher in the Rye* with him on the night of the murder. But maybe it's a later novel, an iconic coming-of-age work of fiction of the 1960s, that provides a more apposite coda. 'Shoot all the bluejays you want,' Atticus Finch tells his son and daughter in Harper Lee's novel of the Deep South, 'but remember it's a sin to kill a mockingbird.' 'Your father's right,' neighbour Miss Maudie explains. 'Mocking birds don't do one thing but make music for us to enjoy. They don't eat up people's gardens, don't nest in corncribs, they don't do one thing but sing their hearts out for us. That's why it's a sin to kill a mockingbird.' A sin as well to kill John Lennon, the mocking Liver bird who'd teased us that the Beatles were more popular than Jesus; who during the Royal Variety Performance urged the people in the cheaper seats to clap their hands and the rest of you just to rattle your jewellery. On that December morning, the birds seemed quieter than usual, as if honouring the passing of one of the most tuneful, original and distinctive voices that ever wrote or sang a song. Suddenly the world felt different as we mourned what we had lost; our landscape empty, above us only sky.

DARKNESS AND LIGHT

Gavin Corbett

Oh, he scoffed at Pol Pot. The same with Idi Amin and Nicolai Ceausescu. No, the manager of our local shopping centre set his sights much lower. Why get the most evil men on earth to usher in the festive season when you could have the most evil man in the universe? Why stop at mere genocidal loons when you could get someone who destroyed not only whole peoples but their home planets as well? Yes – one year, Darth Vadar dropped by to switch on our Christmas lights.

Darth Vadar, for anyone who's never heard of him before, was the chief of staff of the imperial forces in the *Star Wars* films, Mr Numero Uno McNasty. How the shopping centre managed to swing his appointment, I don't know. We were amazed when word first went round. Could it be true – the real Darth Vadar? Did they have George Lucas's phone number? Or were they in communion with darker powers?

The posters went up. They were black and white and grainy, like poor exercises in pointillist art. It all seemed like a fudge.

'No, no, if you stand back far enough, you can definitely make out that it's the real Darth Vadar,' somebody shouted from the other side of the street.

'Yeah, but it could be just a film still,' somebody else shouted back. 'Anyone could photocopy a film still. It doesn't mean anything.'

The rest of us nodded in agreement. We would just have to wait and see who turned up on the night.

In the meantime, we went through the usual annual rigmarole of Santa Claus arriving by helicopter in the shopping centre car park. To be fair to the management, they really did pull out all the stops at Christmas. How many other shopping centres had their Santas make such a grand entrance? For years we believed that because Santa came by helicopter, then he must have been ferried from the North Pole. So this year, as we took our places at the side of the car park, and heard the watery wah-wah of the chopper blades from way off, and the excitement spread through the crowd like a nice panic, we agreed that if they could lay it on this well, then maybe there was a possibility they had secured the visit of the Dark Lord.

But then the helicopter touched down on its skids. We watched Santa step out of the cabin. We observed his red and white garb rippling in the down-draught over skin and bone instead of pressing tight on flabby, jolly flesh. And a realisation dawned on us. We were being hood-winked. And if we were being hoodwinked about who was being flown in to sit in a plywood grotto for a month, then it was most likely that the man they would try to pass off as Darth Vadar would be just some other Joe Soap, kitted out in a bin-liner and a crash helmet.

Still, it didn't stop me dreaming. For the next while, my thoughts were occupied by the notion of the wickedest man in space descending to be amongst us. If you have no concept of Darth Vadar, I'll tell you this: a more mean-looking dictatorial sort you never saw.

I had visions of him parting the crowds as he took those huge mechanical strides of his towards the stage in front of the shopping centre.

I saw his cape fluttering magisterially behind him.

The submarine sonar sound of his breathing apparatus would slither and swirl its way around people's necks.

And we'd look up into those deadest of dead-shark eyes fixed straight ahead and see not a man but a simple, cold, relentless impulse.

And then suddenly, everything was for real, and the stage was built, and the bunting went up, and the night came. The manager ran up a flight of wooden steps.

'Ladies and gentlemen, boys and girdles,' he said through a sustained note of feedback. 'We are very proud to welcome here tonight, for the annual switching on of the Christmas lights, the Dark Lord of Sith himself, the most evil man in the universe … Darth Vadar!'

Over the loudspeakers came a baleful drum roll. For a good half-minute, hot breaths ceased to condense in front of faces. Then the drum roll segued into Darth Vadar's signature tune from the *Star Wars* movies, a couple of spotlights jittered about the stage, and from behind a plastic tarpaulin, a massive, menacing figure emerged.

We scanned the figure from toe to top, checking off the details.

Jackboots. Yes.

Ribbed PVC body suit. Ditto.

Computer breastplate. Okay.

Dracula cape. All right.

Helmet modelled on Wehrmacht head gear. Present.

And just as he towered above his imperial retinue in the films, this man seemed too huge to be anyone other than you know who.

Yes. No doubt about it. It was him all right. Imagine, we thought. Imagine! And some provincial supermarket having to settle for Ted Bunny, or Lieutenant General Videla, the head of the Argentine military junta of the late 1970s.

Truly, it was an awful start to Christmas, in the best possible way.

THE ROASTMASTER

Michael James Ford

My father was a man who took Christmas seriously. A dedicated doctor, he would usually visit his patients on Christmas morning, and as children, my brothers and I would be dressed up and brought around the hospital where the nurses would indulge us with presents and sweets. At the final ward on the route we'd watch him carve the turkey with surgical finesse before heading home to our own eagerly awaited feast.

My father's last Christmas dinner was an unforgettable affair. In the intervening years, and with a second family to raise, he'd established a considerable reputation as a master of the roast and expectations were high for the annual gastronomic showcase.

He'd always regarded himself as a good plain cook and could turn his hand to most things. He'd taught me the simple mystery of the perfect omelette when I was only eight, all vigorous whisking, sizzling butter and careful folding of the foaming eggs. He could make a formidable plum duff and had never lost his enthusiasm for the manufacture of marmalade and damson jam. But as time passed, his skills became more specialised and he concentrated on just the one menu, the traditional Sunday roast.

His beef was exquisite. Always a well-hung joint set aside by the local butcher and purchased after much inspection and analysis. It would emerge from the oven dark and glistening on the outside and a tender pink within, and was accompanied by the crispest Yorkshire pudding and a rich, thick gravy, the remains of which he would gleefully eat cold during one of his insomnious grazing sessions. His pork crackling was legendary, his lamb all sweetness and succulence, and his turkey always escaped the dreaded curse of the dry breast.

But that year, the bird of choice was goose, and we arrived from Dublin on Christmas Eve to the rich aroma of fried goose liver and simmering stock and the comforting sounds of Radio Four's *Festival of Nine Lessons and Carols*. This broadcast, from King's College, Cambridge, was one of my father's sacred rituals and invariably accompanied the preparation of the stuffing. It often seemed that the soloist in 'Once in Royal David's City' would bring a tear to his eye, but it was difficult to be certain since he was usually chopping onions as he listened.

That evening he was tired and turned in early from the inevitable night of festive merriment. But next morning he set about his task with quiet determination, padding around the kitchen, peeling vegetables, steaming the pudding, planning his timetable with meticulous care. When the family had gathered, he popped open the champagne and presided over the present-giving ceremony. He assumed the paternal role of distributor, chuckling over gift tag witticisms and the appropriateness or otherwise of particular choices. A Christmas like any other, all bonhomie and warmth, and only rarely did his now-gaunt face show hints of sadness or regret.

While we guests teased our appetites with a walk on Epsom Downs, my father resumed in the kitchen, for once allowing his wife, my step-mother, to act as commis chef. She sliced runner beans, peeled sprouts, quaffed white wine and chatted happily of family and friends, yet remained watchful as he masked his fatigue with his steady pottering around the oven.

The dinner was a triumph. No starter, no faffing around – just an aperitif of chilled bubbly, then straight to the main event. In pride of place was a large bowl of golden potatoes, lightly parboiled, the edges scuffed for maximum crispness, then dusted with seasoned flour and roasted in goose fat. A cardiologist's nightmare. Equally irresistible were the crunchy roast parsnips and the tantalisingly al dente runner beans, sprouts and broccoli. On the side was his beloved bread sauce: a thick concoction of milk, onions and bread, suffused with cloves to provide a subtle complement to the highly flavoured meat. And the goose was magnificent: firm, succulent, utterly satisfying and carved with noncha-lant skill. It was served with gooey chipolata sausages, brittle spirals of smoked bacon and a stuffing of apple, apricot, goose liver, ginger and coriander — my father's one nod to the gastronomic new wave.

The gravy was reassuringly traditional, a liquid essence of goose derived from the long-simmered giblets.

Glugging a powerful Rioja, we tucked in, and for the first ten minutes or so nothing was heard but sighs and murmurs of utter contentment. My father sat back, acknowledging the plaudits, beaming with satisfaction, his mission accomplished. The Roastmaster had delivered.

Second helpings were served. The goose carcass was stripped bare. Every last potato, parsnip and sprout was devoured. And then the plates were cleared, some practically licked clean, others with debris of bones and gravy. But my father's portion seemed untouched, with two big slices of goose breast at the centre. He handed up his plate with a look that said 'don't ask, don't comment'. Nobody did. And nobody volunteered to plunder the leavings.

The moment passed and the dinner moved on to plum pudding and coffee. Over a large brandy, he lit up a modest Havana — a small pleasure he'd only recently returned to. 'If I'd known I'd get sick, I'd never have given these up,' he remarked. Then he shut his eyes and inhaled deeply, reflecting perhaps on the struggle that lay ahead.

It was his last Christmas, his last goose, his last loving gift as the Roastmaster.

SAME OLD CROWD

Gerard Smyth

Once a year we gather to reminisce
on things that happened, things that didn't.
Together we are a reunion of shadows

huddled around a table of drinks;
the occasion on which again we are part
of the same old crowd.

Each is his own biographer,
each the maker of his own folklore and myth.
There is one who remembers

and one whose memories have been eclipsed
by disillusionment and the passage
of years since our initiations

in fellowship, high-spiritedness,
the antics of youth; since first we heard
Into the Mystic, slow-danced to *Hey Jude*.

THE BOUNCING BALL OF THE SUN

Cyril Kelly

The window is south facing. Sitting here, looking out at the back garden, my mind is indolent, idling. Thoughts coasting along in neutral, kinetic energy powered by an association of ideas, January, last month of winter, first month of the year. Janus is the month of god, from the Latin, *Janua*, meaning gate. Hence, the god of gates and doors, of exists and entrances, of endings and beginnings. Always, it is depicted with two faces, one bi-focal face gazing down the already darkening vista of the past, the other peering into the opaque possibilities of an impending future.

It occurs to me that that small garden at the back of the house is a perfect metaphor for this moment of mutation. That scrawny clematis, grasping in desperation to the back of the wall, has to be a symbol of the past. Where once it had clustered flowers, now it is cursed with the brown claws of a hag. Its tendrils, all suppleness sapped, are perished ligaments, clinging to scented, starry-eyed memories of May. And what of the future? Those snowdrop and narcissus shoots are surely semaphores of hope, anticipating time yet to come. All during the dark days of winter, with the mercury plummeting into the bulb of the thermometer, those tubers had been biding their time underground, storing up reserves, waiting to unleash perpetual powers of regeneration.

That deciduous broom in the corner, the implement of the witch, saturated with superstitions at this superstitious time of New Year. Stalking through the language of superstition is the baleful spirit of prohibition. Don't sweep ashes from the hearth. Don't sweep the floor or you'll sweep away a friend. And, of course, tomorrow is Hansel Monday. So, don't forget, in order to avoid penury, don't pay your debts and don't, in the name of Janus, give anything away.

For more than a week now, I've been watching the slow morning bounce of the sun ball across the southern sky. Its trajectory, rising above the serrated ridge tiles of the roofs across the way, nudges a daily cock step higher. At this time of year, those horizontal rays of the early sun are wondrous. Their light has none of the opulence of summer. It is a clinical, frugal clarity, eschewing blather and blarney. It is, as Yeats described, 'cold and passionate'. Its rays define the tactile trunk of trees; glassy bark of the cherry, vertical ribs of oak and chestnut. Rays up-light bare winter branches, highlight the lazy lofty gulls, the snowy whiteness of their breasts as they hover above the morning.

Now that we are on the cusp of the New Year, a man I think of this morning is my friend Paddy. I call him friend but really he is but a familiar stranger. Paddy bestrides the roads of the north inner city like a colossus. Receding red hair, weathered wildly into ringlets. His blue eyes are ablaze with conviction. He never wears shirt or coat. His *geansaí* is in *giobals*. All his earthly possessions are contained in a black sack which he totes on his broad back like a tiny *tòisín* – unless, of course, he is dining. When the sack is opened on the ground before him, the culinary contents – unrolled from plastic pouches with the precision of a silver service waiter. For me Paddy is a latter day Neolithic man. His favourite topic of conversation is the sun, followed closely by classical music. It wouldn't surprise me but he is having breakfast at this very moment on some high knoll where he can observe the pale early bounce of the solar ball, his battered two-in-one balanced in some bush behind his head, throbbing to the strains of shrill *Winter* from Vivaldi's *The Four Seasons*.

Suddenly, a red admiral is fluttering against the glass in front of me, trying to get out. His wings are a symmetrical melange of chocolate browns, white and orange. I presume he has been hoodwinked from hibernation by the heat of the room. Maybe, like the line from Brendan

Kennelly's poem, 'Begin', he has been summoned 'to the sight of the light at the window'. Maybe he has been nestling behind that pile of books during the dark months which brought this year to a close. Maybe his impulse to waken is inspired by the final lines of that same Kennelly poem:

> *Though we live in a world that dreams of ending*
> *that always seems about to give in*
> *something that will not acknowledge conclusion*
> *insists that we forever begin.*

CONTRIBUTOR BIOGRAPHIES

UNA AGNEW: Born in Courtbane, Co. Louth. A St Louis Sister, educated at St Louis Convent, Carrickmacross, Co. Monaghan. Read English and Irish at UCD. Studied Spirituality at Duquesne University, Pittsburgh, USA. Published *The Mystical Imagination of Patrick Kavanagh: A Buttonhole in Heaven*, her doctorate thesis on Patrick Kavanagh. Head of the Spirituality Department at Milltown Institute, Dublin.

DENISE BLAKE: Lives in Donegal. Her first collection of poetry, *Take a Deep Breath*, was published by Summer Palace Press. Translates Cathal Ó Searcaigh's Irish poetry into English. Their work has been published by Arc Publications, England.

PAT BORAN: Born in 1963 in Portlaois. Lives in Dublin, where he is the publisher of the Dedalus Press. Has written ten books of poetry, fiction and non-fiction, including *The Portable Creative Writing Workshop*.

CATHLEEN BRINDLEY: Born in India and educated in Ireland, where she received a degree in Modern Languages. Enjoys travel and has written extensively on the subject.

CATHERINE BROPHY: Born, reared and educated in Dublin. Has written novels, short stories and screen plays and facilitates writing workshops.

HARRY BROWNE: A lecturer in Dublin Institute of Technology, he writes for *Village* magazine.

PAT BUTLER: A broadcaster, documentary maker, writer and journalist with RTÉ. Has won many awards, including for *Ballyseedy* and *Kilmichael*. Regular columnist with *Foinse*, *Lá* and *Beo*. *Cois Life* will publish his first book, Saol Craoltóra, in 2007.

TIM CAREY: An author and historian, he is currently Heritage Officer with Dún Laoghaire–Rathdown County Council.

ELIZABETH CARTY: A native of Loch Gowna, Co. Cavan. Married to Noel, with two daughters, Niamh and Aisling. Lives in Meath. Works as a writing tutor for Meath VEC. Contributes to RTÉ Radio's *A Living Word, Quiet Quarter* and *Sunday Miscellany*. Short-listed three times for the Francis McManus RTÉ Short Story Award and published in a number of writing anthologies.

PATRICK CHAPMAN: Born in 1968. Poetry collections are *Jazztown* (Raven), *The New Pornography* (Salmon) and *Breaking Hearts and Traffic Lights* (Salmon). His book of stories, *The Wow Signal* (Bluechrome), is to be published in 2007. Wrote the multi-award-winning film, *Burning the Bed.* He won first prize in the story category of the 2003 *Cinescape* Genre Literary Contest. With Philip Casey, he founded the Irish Literary Revival website.

MARY COLL: A freelance writer and broadcaster from Limerick, has published a collection of poetry, *All Things Considered*, contributes regularly to programmes on RTÉ Radio and reviews for various magazines and journals.

WILLIAM J. COOK: A native of Maine, USA. A freelance writer, artist and sampler of diverse careers, currently anchored in Roscommon.

GAVIN CORBETT: Born in Dublin, a journalist and author of the novel *Innocence*, published by Town House. His writing for children and adults has featured on RTÉ Radio.

JAMES COTTER: Living in Co. Wicklow, a film script writer. His writing for adults and children has featured on RTÉ Radio.

ENDA COYLE-GREENE: Has published her work in numerous magazines and is a regular contributor to RTÉ Radio's *Sunday Miscellany, Living Word* and *Quiet Quarter.*

BRYNN CRAFFEY: Now years further on along the road to self-acceptance, he plies the streets on his mountain bike, pleased to reside in the land of his grandparents. He is ever vigilant of roadway rail tracks.

CATHERINE ANN CULLEN: Writer of children's books, including the award-winning *The Magical, Mystical, Marvellous Coat*, and poetry. A freelance radio producer.

LEO CULLEN: Author of *Clocking 90 on the Road to Cloughjordan* and *Let's Twist Again*, published by Blackstaff Press. A frequent broadcaster on RTÉ Radio I, Lyric FM and BBC. Hails from Co. Tipperary and lives in Monkstown, Co. Dublin with his wife and sons.

GERALD DAWE: Born in Belfast. Lectures in English at Trinity College, Dublin, where he is director of the Oscar Wilde Centre for Irish Writing and co-director of the Graduate Creative Writing Programme. Elected Fellow of TCD in 2004 and was Burns Visiting Professor at Boston College in 2005. Poetry collections include *Sunday School*, *Heart of Hearts*, *The Morning Train* and *Lake Geneva*, published by The Gallery Press. Has published three essay collections and edited anthologies of poetry and criticism. Lives in Dún Laoghaire.

JOHN F. DEANE: Born on Achill Island, Co. Mayo. Writes poetry full time. A founder of Poetry Ireland and a member of Aosdána. His latest book is *The Instrument of Art*.

EAMON DELANEY: A writer and novelist. Author of *An Accidental Diplomat* and editor of *Magill* magazine, Ireland's cultural and political monthly.

ORLA DONOGHUE: Has a doctorate in Chemistry. Works as a communications officer in a research centre at University College, Dublin. Contributes articles to a number of publications. Writes poetry and short stories.

THEO DORGAN: Born in Cork. Poetry collections are *The Ordinary House of Love*, *Rosa Mundi* and *Sappho's Daughter*. Edited *The Great Book of Ireland* (with Gene Lambert); *Revising the Rising* (with Máirín Ní Dhonnachadha); *Irish Poetry Since Kavanagh*; *Watching the River Flow* (with Noel Duffy); and *The Great Book of Gaelic* (with Malcolm Maclean). A former Director of Poetry Ireland. A member of Aosdána. Appointed to The Arts Council in 2003. A broadcaster with RTÉ.

MYLES DUNGAN: An RTÉ broadcaster, with radio programmes including *5-7 Live* and *Rattlebag*, and the author of two books on World War I as well as a stage adaptation of Jane Austen's *Mansfield Park*. His most recently published book is *How the Irish Won the West*.

MARY FOLAN: From Galway, she works as a freelance publicist. Lives in Stoneybatter in Dublin.

CATHERINE FOLEY: Born in Waterford City. Moved with her family to the Irish-speaking area of Ring in west Co. Waterford when she was still at primary school. An *Irish Times* staff journalist. Her novellas are *Sorcha sa Ghailearaí* and *An Cailín Rua*, both of which won Oireachtas Literary Awards. Lives in Dublin.

KATE E. FOLEY: Lives in Dublin. Her keen interest in travel and culture feature in her writing.

MICHAEL JAMES FORD: An actor, writer and director based in Dublin. As a performer he is particularly associated with the Gate Theatre, and for several years ran the lunchtime programme at Bewley's Café Theatre.

ANTHONY GLAVIN: Born in Boston, is a short story writer, novelist, editor and freelance journalist. His fiction titles include *One For Sorrow*, *Night Hawk Alley* and *The Draughtsman and the Unicorn*.

VONA GROARKE: Born in Edgeworthstown, Co. Longford in 1964. Grew up on a farm outside Athlone. Poetry collections are *Shale, Other People's Houses, Flight* and *Juniper Street*, all published by The Gallery Press. Currently teaches poetry at Wake Forest University in America.

MARGARET HACKETT: Born and educated in France, came to live in Ireland when she met her Irish husband in Paris. Now lives in Ireland's mid-west region and lectures in the Limerick Institute of Technology.

MICHAEL HARDING: Has written two books of fiction and numerous plays for the Abbey Theatre and other Irish theatre companies.

MARGARET HAWKINS: A freelance journalist, originally from Tinehely, Co. Wicklow, now living in Broadway, Co. Wexford. Writes articles, short stories and plays. Her novel *Restless Spirit – The Story of Rose Quinn* was published this year.

JUDITH HILL: An architectural historian and writer. Her books include *The Buildings of Limerick, Irish Public Sculpture: A History* and *Lady Gregory: An Irish Life.* Has taught Irish cultural history and written on the subject for journals, including the *Irish Arts Review*, the *Irish University Review* and *The Times Literary Supplement.*

SHARON HOGAN: A Canadian-born actor, she is a frequent contributor to RTÉ Radio as a performer and as a reader of her own writing.

ARNOLD HORNER: Has an interest in local studies, maps and the environment. He lectures in Geography at University College, Dublin.

HENRY HUDSON: A novelist and playwright. Worked in Dublin power stations and led efforts to save Pigeon House as a national science centre. A French translation of his novel, based on a fictional Dublin power station, will be published in Paris in 2007.

VIVIEN IGOE: A graduate of University College, Dublin. Has a deep interest in all aspects of Ireland's heritage. Has worked on archaeological excavations; as a Publicity Officer for Bord Fáilte; as a researcher in the Department of the Taoiseach, and as Research and Heritage Manager at the Royal Hospital Kilmainham. A Joycean, her books include *James Joyce's Dublin Houses and Nora Barnacle's Galway, City of Dublin, A Literary Guide to Dublin* and *Dublin's Burial Grounds and Graveyards.*

PETER JANKOVSKY: Born in Berlin in 1939. Worked for ten years as an actor in Germany. Has lived in Dublin since 1971, where he has been teaching, acting and writing. His translation, together with Brian Lynch, of Paul Celan's *65 Poems* was published in 1985. More work with Lynch resulted in *Easter Snow/Osterschnee*, a book of photographs, poems and translations. His memoir, *Myself Passing By*, was published in 2000.

FRED JOHNSTON: Born in Belfast in 1951. A founder of Galway's Cúirt literature festival and of The Western Writers' Centre. A novelist, short story writer, poet and critic.

MARK JOYCE: Artist and lecturer at the Dun Laoghaire Institute of Art, Design and Technology. Lives in Dublin.

JOE KANE: Born in Dublin. Studied ceramics and glass and opened a studio in Donegal in 1976. Won the Arvon Foundation International Poetry Competition for 'The Boy Who Nearly Won the Texaco Art Competition'. Has been published in *The Shop*, *The New Writer*, *The Irish Times*, *The Times*, the *New York Review of Books* and *Fortnight*.

JOE KEARNEY: Born in Kilkenny in 1951. Worked in the oil industry for over thirty years before becoming a full-time writer. Has had prize-winning short stories and poems published and currently working on his first novel.

CYRIL KELLY: From Listowel, Co. Kerry. Was a primary school teacher in Dublin for many years and a regular contributor to RTÉ Radio.

NIAMH ANN KELLY: Born in Galway. Lives and works in Dublin as an art writer and critic. Lectures in critical theory at the Dublin Institute of Technology.

PAT KINEVANE: A native of Cobh, Co. Cork. Has worked as an actor in theatre, radio, television and film for the past seventeen years. His own plays include *The Nun's Wood*, *The Plains of Enna*, *The Death of Herod*, *La Feria*, *The Basin* and *Forgotten*.

CHUCK KRUGER: Grew up in New York's Finger Lakes. In protest against the Vietnam War, moved to Switzerland. Twenty-six years later he moved to Cape Clear Island. A regular contributor to RTÉ Radio's *Sunday Miscellany*, *Quiet Quarter* and *Seascapes* and NPR's *Weather Notebook* (USA).

MAE LEONARD: From Limerick, now lives in Kildare. A broadcaster, award-winning writer and poet. Publications include *My Home is There*, *This is Tarzan Clancy* and *Six for Gold*.

NICOLA LINDSAY: Published works include a children's book and a collection of poetry. She is the author of five novels. Her work has been broadcast and anthologised in Ireland and Britain.

BRIAN LYNCH: Award-winning poet, playwright, screenwriter, art critic and novelist. His book, *The Winner of Sorrows*, about the poet William Cowper (1731–1800), was published in 2005 by New Island, Dublin.

STEPHEN MACDONOGH: A publisher with Brandon/Mount Eagle. His books as author include *Open Book: One Publisher's War*, *The Dingle Peninsula, Green and Gold: The Wrenboys of Dingle* and *Dingle in Pictures* as photographer.

CATHERINE MARSHALL: An art historian and Head of Collection at the Irish Museum of Modern Art. Has curated many exhibitions from the IMMA collection and has written widely about Irish art.

JOSEPHINE MCARDLE: A teacher from the Midlands, inspired by Derek Mahon's poem 'Antarctica' to embark on a journey of discovery. A member of the Ireland Beyond Endurance 2006 Expedition following the trail blazed by Shackleton and Crean in their epic voyage around Antarctica.

SAM MCAUGHTRY: Author, broadcaster, journalist and trade unionist. Has published nine books. Columnist of the Year with *The Irish Times* in 1986, a member of Seanad Éireann from 1996–99. Received an Honorary Doctorate from NUI Maynooth in 1998.

NUALA MCCANN: A freelance writer and journalist. Lives with her husband, Roger Patterson, and their son, Ruairi, in Belfast.

DERMOD MCCARTHY: A priest and broadcaster. For many years he produced documentaries for the ground-breaking *Radharc* film unit. During the 1980s was administrator of St Mary's Pro-Cathedral in Dublin. Since 1991 has been editor of religious programmes on RTÉ television.

SINÉAD McCOOLE: A historian and author of a number of books, including *Hazel: A Life of Lady Lavery* and *No Ordinary Women*. Keeper/curator of the Jackie Clarke Library, Ballina, Co. Mayo.

PÁDRAIG McGINN: A retired school principal, living in Carrick-on-Shannon, Co. Leitrim. His stories have been published in *The Leitrim Guardian* and *First Cut*. Has been shortlisted in a number of Irish writing competitions including The Bard of Armagh and the Strokestown Poetry Award.

BERNARD J. McGUCKIAN: A Jesuit priest. Spiritual Director of the Pioneer Association since the 1970s. The intersection of history and religion has always fascinated him.

JUDITH MOK: Born in the Netherlands, now lives in Dublin. An internationally renowned soprano, has also published many works of poetry and fiction. Her most recent novel, *Gael*, was published by Telegram Books this year.

SHEELAGH MOONEY: Orginally from Skryne, Co. Meath, now lives in Naas, Co. Kildare. Works as an Environmental Health Officer with the HSE South East. Contributes to *Sunday Miscellany* and the book *Kildare Ways*.

GERRY MORAN: From Kilkenny, was a primary school principal for many years. His writing has featured in many publications.

VAL MULKERNS: Born in Dublin in 1925. Moved to London after working in the civil service. Returned to Ireland in 1952 as associate editor of The Bell. Her novels include *A Time Outworn*, *A Peacock Cry*, *The Summerhouse* and *Very Like A Whale*. Her short stories are collected as *Antiquities*, *An Idle Woman* and *A Friend of Don Juan*. She jointly won the AIB Prize for Literature in 1984. She is a regular broadcaster.

DEIRDRE MULROONEY: A writer, specialising in dance. Lecturer in drama, and a stage director. Her radio series *Nice Moves*, out of which her recent book, *Irish Moves*, grew, was broadcast on RTÉ Radio I.

DYMPNA MURRAY FENNELL: Hails from Co. Westmeath. Lives in Lucan. Recently retired, she still identifies with that 'September feeling', having spent many years on the teaching circuit in places ranging from Nigeria to Newry to Naas.

MÁIRÉAD NÍ CHONCEANAINN: Born in east Galway. A civil servant for many years. Married to an islander, she lived for many years on Aran. A regular actor in An Taibhdhearc with a life-long interest in literature.

SUE NORTON: Grew up in America. Lectures in the Dublin Institute of Technology.

LIZ NUGENT: Has worked as a story editor on RTÉ's *Fair City* for over three years. Recently started to develop her own writing skills. Has written several pieces for radio and some children's stories. Shortlisted for the 2006 Francis McManus Award for her story, 'Alice'.

BETTY NUNAN: Born in Cork. Married and has six children. Moved to Baghdad with her husband in 1982. Has lived in many other countries since, including Saudi Arabia, Kenya and Zimbabwe. Has a Masters degree in Semitic languages from University College, Dublin.

FACHTNA Ó DRISCEOIL: Works as a television reporter and radio producer for RTÉ. Brought up in an Irish-speaking family in Dún Laoghaire.

TADHG Ó DÚSHLÁINE: A senior lecturer in Nua Ghaeilge at NUI Maynooth. Director of the Frank O'Connor Project. Writer in Residence with Cork Corporation and The Munster Literature Centre from 1999–2000. Has poetry collections and books of criticism published.

ÉAMONN Ó HUALLACHÁIN: Lives on the border between north Louth and south Armagh. Has long had an enthusiastic love of the culture, language and history of his native place. Often takes groups around this scenic and historically interesting area.

CONOR O'CALLAGHAN: Has published two collections of poetry and one book of non-fiction prose, *Red Mist: Roy Keane and the Football Civil War*.

JULIE O'CALLAGHAN: Writes poetry for adults and children. Her most recent book is *The Book of Whispers*. She received the Michael Hartnett Award for Poetry in 2001 and is a member of Aosdána.

SANDRA ANDREA O'CONNELL: A writer and editor. Born in Ulm, Germany, came to Ireland in 1993 to study Anglo-Irish literature at Trinity College, Dublin. Has written literary criticism for various anthologies. Currently working on a literary biography of the Irish-Russian poet, George Reavey (1907–1976). Editor of *Architecture Ireland*, the journal of the RIAI.

JENNIFER O'DEA: An actress, she comes from Dublin, where she lives with her partner, Peter, and their children, Molly and Luke.

JOHN O'DONNELL: A barrister and poet, born in 1960. His work has appeared in newspapers and journals in Ireland, Britain, the US and Australia, and has been broadcast on radio. Winner of the Hennessy/*Sunday Tribune* New Irish Writing Award for Poetry, The Ireland Fund's Listowel Writers' Week Prizes for Best Individual Poem and Best Short Collection and the SeaCat Irish National Poetry Prize. Poetry collections are *Some Other Country* and *Icarus Sees His Father Fly*.

MARY O'DONNELL: Her novels include *The Light-makers, Virgin and the Boy* and *The Elysium Testament*. Her *New and Selected Poems* has just been published. Other collections are *Spiderwoman's Third Avenue, Rhapsody, Unlegendary Heroes* and *September Elegies*. A regular broadcaster and member of Aosdána.

VAL O'DONNELL: Born in Dublin, a former civil servant. Has a long association with the theatre as an actor and director.

CLODAGH O'DONOGHUE: Studied at Trinity College Dublin. Has worked as an actor with many companies including the Abbey, the Project, Pan-Pan, Pigsback and Fishamble. Has written many short stories for children for RTÉ. Co-edited the book *Contemporary Irish Monologues* with Jim Culleton.

RONAN O'FLAHERTY: Works in the Forestry Service. Has a PhD in Archaeology from University College, Dublin. Lives in Co. Wexford with his wife, Niamh, and their children.

BAIRBRE O'HOGAN: Born in Dublin in 1958. Inherited her love of Ireland and its culture from her parents. Taught Irish and Celtic Studies in the Dominican College, Sion Hill, Dublin for fifteen years. Started writing to ensure that her sons Oisin and Eoin would have access to their family stories.

JOE O'TOOLE: Born in Dingle, Co. Kerry. Qualified as a teacher at St Patrick's College of Education, Dublin. An independent member of Seanad Éireann since 1987. Former General Secretary of the Irish National Teachers' Organisation (INTO) and former President of the Irish Congress of Trade Unions (ICTU). Published his autobiography, *Looking Under Stones*, in 2003.

FIONA POOLE: A retired primary school teacher. Has many interests, including reading, designing mosaics, gardening, cooking and education.

CATHY POWER HERNANDEZ: Lives in Kilkenny with her Salvadorean husband and two children. A producer with local radio KCLR 96FM and a loyal Kilkenny hurling supporter.

TONY QUINN: A barrister, educated by the Christian Brothers, and at Trinity College, Dublin and the King's Inns. A member of Irish PEN and a former chairman of the Irish Writers' Union. Author of the recently published book, *Wigs and Guns: Irish Barristers in the Great War*.

MICK RAINSFORD: Born in Athy, Co. Kildare. Has travelled extensively. Has just completed a collection of short stories and is currently looking for a publisher.

MARY RUSSELL: A journalist and writer with a particular interest in travel.

GAIL SEEKAMP: Lives in Dublin with her family. Enjoys travelling, writing and rearing her children.

TED SHEEHY: A freelance journalist and critic born in Limerick and living in Dublin. He first contributed to *Sunday Miscellany* in the early 1990s.

PETER SIRR: Born in Waterford in 1960 and now lives in Dublin. Former director of the Irish Writers' Centre, he works as a freelance writer, editor and translator and is currently editor of *Poetry Ireland Review*. The Gallery Press has published *Marginal Zones, Talk, Talk, Ways of Falling, The Ledger of Fruitful Exchange, Bring Everything, Nonetheless* and his *Selected Poems 1982–2004*.

ELAINE SISSON: A senior lecturer in Visual Communications at Dún Laoghaire Institute of Art, Design and Technology. The author of *Pearse's Patriots: St. Enda's and the Cult of Boyhood*.

AILBHE SMYTH: Has been a feminist activist since the 1970s, and is head of the Women's Education, Research and Resource Centre (WERRC) at UCD.

GERARD SMYTH: Has published poetry widely in Ireland and abroad since the late 1960s. His most recent collections are *Daytime Sleeper* and *A New Tenancy*, both published by Dedalus.

BRIAN THUNDER: From Galway, he is a graduate of University College, Galway. He has performed in numerous acting roles in film, theatre, radio and television.

DENIS TUOHY: Born in Belfast. A writer, broadcaster and actor. Spent many years as a television presenter and reporter with BBC and ITV news and current programmes such as *Panorama, This Week, Tonight* and *ITV News*. His memoir, *Wide-eyed in Medialand*, was published in 2005.

JOHN WAKEMAN: Author of two poetry collections. He founded *The Shop: A Magazine of Poetry* in 1999 and has edited major reference books on literature and film.

GRACE WELLS: Poet and author, lives in Co. Tipperary. Her first book, *Gyrfalcon*, won the Eilís Dillon Award and was an International White Raven.

JOSEPH WOODS: Born in Co. Louth in 1966 and trained as a scientist. Completed an MA in Creative Writing at the Poet's House, Co. Antrim. He is Director of Poetry Ireland. His first book won the Patrick Kavanagh Award for Best First Collection; his second collection, *Bearings*, was published in 2005.

PETER WOODS: Born in London and grew up in Monaghan. A novelist and radio producer. Series producer of the *Documentary on One* on RTÉ Radio. Wrote *Hard Shoulder.*

ENDA WYLEY: Born and lives in Dublin. Has published three collections of poetry: *Eating Baby Jesus, Socrates in the Garden* and *Poems for Breakfast.*

GRACE WYNNE-JONES: Her novel *Ready Or Not?* was called 'one of the best Irish novels this year (2003)' in *The Evening Herald. The Irish Times* described her novel, *The Truth Club*, as 'an entertaining, intelligent and genuinely funny story … a great read.'